Life and Letters of

General W. H. L. Wallace

Shawnee Classics
A Series of Classic Regional Reprints for the Midwest

W H L Wallace
Ottawa
Illinois.

Life and Letters of General W. H. L. Wallace

Isabel Wallace

With a New Foreword by

John Y. Simon

Southern Illinois University Press

Carbondale and Edwardsville

First edition published 1909 by R. R. Donnelley & Sons Company

Shawnee Classics edition published 2000 by Southern Illinois University Press

Printed in the United States of America

03 02 01 00 4 3 2 1

The publisher gratefully acknowledges the cooperation of Morris Library, Southern Illinois University Carbondale, in providing the text of *Life & Letters of W. H. L. Wallace* that was used for the present edition.

Library of Congress Cataloging-in-Publication Data

Wallace, Isabel, b. 1857.

Life and letters of General W. H. L. Wallace / by Isabel Wallace ; with a new foreword by John Y. Simon.— Shawnee classics ed.

p. cm. — (Shawnee classics)

Originally published: Chicago : R.R. Donnelley & Sons, 1909.

Includes bibliographical references and index.

1. Wallace, William Hervy Lamme, 1821–1862. 2. Generals—United States—Biography. 3. United States. Army—Biography. 4. United States—History—Civil War, 1861–1865—Campaigns. 5. United States. Army. Illinois Infanty Regiment, 11th (1861–1865). 6. Shiloh, Battle of, 1862. I. Wallace, William Hervy Lamme, 1821–1862. II. Title. III. Series.

E467.1.W3 W2 2000
973.7'473'092—dc21
[B] 00-038784
ISBN 0-8093-2347-8 (alk. paper)
ISBN 0-8093-2348-6 (pbk. : alk. paper)

The paper used in this publication meets the minimum requirements of American National Standard for Information Sciences—Permanence of Paper for Printed Library Materials, ANSI Z39.48-1992. ♾

FOREWORD

William Hervy Lamme Wallace, the highest-ranking Union officer who fell at Shiloh, is rarely commemorated. Many standard reference sources botch his two unfamiliar middle names, and his career, which lasted less than one year into the Civil War, is neglected even in his hometown. He deserves better, as his adopted daughter recognized when she wrote a biography first published in 1909 and now ripe for presentation to a new circle of readers. Wallace was, indeed, a hero of the Union cause.

Major General Ulysses S. Grant had divided his forces into six divisions at and near Pittsburg Landing, Tennessee, before Confederates launched a surprise attack at Shiloh Church on Sunday, April 6, 1862. Grant himself had spent the night at the Cherry mansion in Savannah some nine miles downriver, planning to meet General Don Carlos Buell to coordinate their two armies for an advance upon Corinth, Mississippi. The guns of Shiloh announced to Grant his army's peril.

Of Grant's six division commanders, only General William T. Sherman had professional military training, and of all the field commanders, he had been most scornful of ominous signs of attack. Confederates possessed every advantage of surprise. Yet even before Grant reached the battlefield, Union troops had rallied from initial panic to mount a stubborn defense. Confederate General Albert Sidney Johnston had promised to water his horses in the Tennessee River that evening, a boast that required the destruction of Grant's army. Even though Johnston died on the battlefield, his army came close to fulfilling his ambition. Wallace played a major role in saving the Union army.

Wallace held command by accident. Major General Charles F. Smith, one of the most admired officers of the old army, commandant of cadets when Grant attended West Point, had injured his leg on the way to Pittsburg Landing and was confined to bed in the Cherry mansion. Wallace commanded Smith's division, presumably on a temporary basis. Smith's minor scrape led to an infection that ended his life two weeks after the battle, a tragedy that might have given Wallace permanent command. But Wallace himself had already died.

Wallace was a citizen soldier and lawyer-politician of Ottawa, Illinois. Born in 1821 in Urbana, Ohio, he was the son of a carpenter with eleven children and little money who had moved to Illinois in 1834. William was educated at the Rock Springs Seminary in Mount Morris. On his way to study law with Abraham Lincoln in Springfield in 1844, he had been persuaded by T. Lyle Dickey to join him instead in Ottawa. Wallace developed a taste for military life during the Mexican War, then settled into a legal career in Ottawa, where he married Dickey's daughter. Eleven years younger than William, Martha Ann, who rarely used her first name, was only sixteen when they were engaged, eighteen in 1851 when they married. The biography written by their adopted daughter Isabel is a love story as well as a political and military biography.

Isabel Wallace, born January 14, 1858, was the daughter of Thomas Good and the former Eliza Parrott, residents of Ottawa, married in 1852, and parents of four children. At the age of thirty, Eliza died bearing Isabel, who, on May 3, 1858, formally became Wallace's ward. Thomas Good died two years later at the age of forty. Isabel, an only child, called Blossom by the Wallaces, remained a devoted daughter for seventy-five years.[1]

In addition to its worth as a biography of General Wallace, the book serves as a source of information about T. Lyle Dickey, more prominent in Illinois politics than his son-in-law. Born in Kentucky in 1811, Dickey was raised in Ohio, where he graduated from Miami University. In 1834 he settled in Illinois, where he practiced law, edited a newspaper, and speculated in real estate before moving to Ottawa in 1839; here law absorbed all his talents. He frequently practiced in informal partnership with Lincoln, a relationship maintained for a half dozen years. Dickey later served as judge of the Ninth Judicial Circuit (1848–52). Lincoln, who usually followed the adjoining Eighth Circuit, had enough legal association with Dickey to continue their close relationship.

Although unsuccessful in obtaining a Whig nomination for Congress in 1850, Wallace served as district attorney (1852–56) while retaining higher political ambitions. The political revolution that followed the Kansas-Nebraska Act in 1854 eventually created a rift between Wallace and Dickey. Both Lincoln and Dickey, ardent Whigs, were reluctant to join the emerging Republican party. Nonetheless, Lincoln became a candidate for a U.S. Senate seat. "*I love you* & want you to be a U.S. Senator," wrote Dickey, offering his own assistance and that of his father, "a genuine old fashioned–moderate Kentucky Abolitionist," then a Presbyterian minister in Springfield.[2] Lincoln failed to win that seat, and when he tried again four years later, Dickey deserted him.

In 1856 Lincoln delivered a stirring speech at a Republican convention in Bloomington, declaring that the nation could not exist half slave and half free. "What in God's name could induce you to promulgate such an opinion?" Dickey asked Lincoln. "I think it is true," Lincoln replied, but he eventually agreed to drop the argument as impolitic.[3] When abolitionist Owen Lovejoy received a Republican nomination for Congress in 1856, the more conservative Dickey ran as an opposition candidate. Lovejoy's nomination "turned me blind" wrote Lincoln, who nonetheless gave Lovejoy his support.[4] Elected in 1856, Lovejoy remained in Congress until his death in 1864; despite continuing political prominence, Dickey never won another election until 1875, when he was elected to the state supreme court. In the "House Divided" speech that opened the 1858 senatorial contest with Stephen A. Douglas, Lincoln repeated the argument that appalled Dickey. When Lincoln came to Ottawa to encounter Douglas in the first of seven debates, Wallace gave full support to Lincoln while Dickey endorsed Douglas. Lincoln "did not know of any of his friends he felt so badly about losing, as Dickey."[5] As a member of the local Republican committee, Wallace wrote a series of letters to Lincoln concerning his reception before the debate, adding, "perhaps it is proper, considering the relations between Dickey & myself, that I should assure you that his course will have no influence with me—I cannot support Douglas & shall do all I honorably can to secure your election."[6] Under such circumstances, a mutual friend made no mistake in May 1861 in identifying Wallace as "one of Mr Lincolns best friends." Judging by 1859 correspondence from Dickey to Lincoln, their legal association continued, although Dickey remained a Democrat. Wallace, who was building a handsome limestone house, proudly named The Oaks, on the bluff adjacent to that of his father-in-law, did not permit politics to erode their close relationship.

When the Civil War broke out, both Wallace and Dickey promptly volunteered for service. Dickey had served as captain during the Mexican War and Wallace as second lieutenant in the same company. Now both were colonels, Wallace commanding infantry, Dickey the Fourth Illinois Cavalry. As Grant later wrote, Wallace "was soon followed by three brothers, his father-in-law, and two brothers of his wife, all the brothers and brothers-in-law that he had that I know of. All of these relatives except one brother who had previously lost his life, were in the battle when the General fell. . . ."[7]

Assembled in Springfield, Illinois, the volunteers of the Eleventh Illinois elected Wallace as their colonel. A successful lawyer, a friend of President Lincoln, a generation older than most privates, an officer with Mexican War experience, Wallace was entirely fitted for command. The volunteers soon entrained to defend the tip of their state. The journey took two days; no food had been provided. Colonel Wallace declared that he would not eat until his men were fed.[8]

Stationed at Villa Ridge, a few miles above Cairo, the regiment drank spring water and encamped in nearby groves, thus avoiding the diseases that struck the crowded and unsanitary camps at Cairo, where physicians debated the relative healthfulness of water from the Mississippi and Ohio rivers. To turn farm boys into soldiers, Wallace embarked upon a strenuous program of discipline and drill. To punish two men who had slipped away from camp and insulted women in a nearby town, Wallace arranged an elaborate ceremony of public humiliation before they were drummed out of camp.[9] Some six weeks in this isolated setting bonded officers and men before they moved south to Bird's Point, Missouri, across the river from Cairo.

Their principal Confederate adversary in that region was Brigadier General M. Jeff Thompson of the Missouri State Guard, nicknamed "Swamp Fox of the Confederacy." Drawing on local support and flamboyant manners and using the flooded terrain to his advantage, Thompson commanded a force of unknown size and whereabouts that constantly kept Union troops off balance. Amid this uncertainty, the Illinois volunteers, originally enlisted for three months, were now asked to enlist for three years or return home. Only half of Wallace's men remained.

On September 1, 1861, Grant, who had arrived at Cape Girardeau, Missouri, to take command of the District of Southeast Missouri, issued his first orders to Wallace. Through the fall, Grant pursued the wily Thompson with no more success than his predecessors. On November 7, however, while Wallace commanded yet another expedition to ensnare the Swamp Fox, Grant landed three thousand men at Belmont, Missouri, across the Mississippi River from the Confederate stronghold at Columbus, Kentucky. Despite its inconclusive results, the fierce fighting established Grant as an aggressive general willing to take risks. If Wallace immediately saw greatness in Grant, he left no record, but shortly after Belmont, Grant wrote to his congressional patron, Elihu B. Washburne of Galena:

> We have here an Illinois man that I want to call your attention to. I mean Col. W. H. L. Wallace. He is not aware that I feel any personal interest in him but if I could be

> instrumental in calling the attention of the country to him sufficiently to secure him the appointment of a Brigadier Generalship I should feel that I had done the country a greater service than himself. Col. Wallace is evry inch a soldier. A gentleman by nature and a man of great modesty and great tallent. He served in Mexico and now since the first call for three months troops. But few such soldiers have been called to the higher positions in our Army.[10]

Had immediate action followed Grant's letter, Wallace would have won promotion before engaging the enemy. As it turned out, Wallace's appointment followed his first major battle.

On Grant's expedition to Fort Henry on the Tennessee River, Wallace, as senior colonel, commanded a brigade of about thirty-four hundred men. Wallace's brigade included the Fourth Illinois Cavalry, commanded by his father-in-law. Landing downriver to march to the fort, Wallace found that Confederate defenders had already surrendered to Union naval bombardment. Most of the garrison had already fled about one dozen miles to Fort Donelson on the Cumberland River. Wallace's brigade had missed the fighting, but he hoped for "better luck next time."

Fort Donelson brought enough fighting to satisfy anyone. Wallace's brigade left Fort Henry on February 12, 1862, and reached Fort Donelson the next day without major incident, then took position on the right of the Union siege line. The warm weather of the previous few days was followed that night by snow and bitter cold, with troops camped too close to the enemy to risk campfires. The next day brought minor skirmishing, while the army listened to the thunderous encounter between Union gunboats and Confederate batteries.

At daylight on February 15, the Confederates threw their full strength against Grant's right, occupied by the brigades of Colonel Richard J. Oglesby and Wallace. With some fifteen thousand Confederate troops already besieged in Fort Donelson and more Union troops on the way, General Gideon J. Pillow planned to open the road to evacuate the garrison to Nashville. Wallace's troops had to face the fury of the Confederate onslaught while panicked troops, already pushed back in disorder, rushed through the lines. Wallace behaved like a veteran, realigning his troops under fire and stabilizing the defense.

When the Confederates struck, Grant was away, visiting Commodore Andrew H. Foote, wounded during the gunboat attack. Grant returned in the afternoon to discover that the Confederates had packed their knapsacks with food before launching their assault and concluded that they intended to escape. Quickly ordering a counterattack on the other end of his line (weakened by the concentration on the right) and taking advantage of Pillow's hesitancy to exploit his breakthrough, Grant forced the unconditional surrender of some fifteen thousand prisoners the next day. Grant won promotion to major general for this first notable Union victory of the Civil War.

Wallace was appointed brigadier general. His troops had saved the day, although at fearful cost. Wallace's own regiment, the Eleventh Illinois, had lost nearly two-thirds of its men, either killed, wounded, or missing, suffering nearly 60 percent of all the casualties in the brigade.[11] Grant had cracked the entire Confederate defense line in Kentucky and Tennessee. Twelve days later, Wallace accompanied Grant to the occupied Tennessee state capital of Nashville, where he reclaimed eighty-five wounded men of the Eleventh Illinois. Wallace sent home its bullet-riddled and bloodstained regimental flag, thereafter proudly displayed at The Oaks. During his military service, Wallace had kept his hand in politics as well, writing to Lincoln to recommend David Davis for a federal judgeship; now friends back home wrote to Wallace about sending him to Congress, an attractive prospect as viewed from the bloody field of Fort Donelson.[12]

Instead, Wallace took his brigade up the Tennessee River to Savannah, Tennessee. Major General Henry W. Halleck, commanding the department from headquarters in St. Louis, aroused by jealousy of an aggressive and successful subordinate, had ordered Grant to remain at Fort Henry while Charles F. Smith commanded the Tennessee River expedition. On March 21, just as he received his appointment as brigadier general, Wallace learned that he might advance from brigade to division commander due to Smith's injury, an event that also restored Grant to command.

Within a few days, Wallace had moved his brigade about ten miles upriver to Pittsburg Landing, a point some twenty miles from the Confederate bastion at Corinth. Wallace had taken command of Smith's division. He corresponded with General Lew Wallace, stationed a few miles downriver at Crump's Landing, about mutual support in case of attack. The two had first met at Fort Donelson, where they commented on the confusion caused by two colonels named Wallace in Grant's army, one commanding the Eleventh Illinois, the other the Eleventh Indiana.[13] On the day before Johnston crashed through the woods at Shiloh Church to destroy the army at Pittsburg Landing, William Wallace had admired the blossoms of spring and had received assurances from his fellow division commander Sherman that encounters with rebel forces were mere skirmishes and no cause for concern.

Wallace knew nothing of Confederate movements and was equally ignorant of the whereabouts of his wife, who had succeeded in reaching Pittsburg Landing despite orders banning civilians from ascending the Tennessee River to visit the army. Nearly distraught with concern about her husband's health and using the rather considerable connections of the Wallace-Dickey clan, Ann Wallace had traveled with a somewhat dubious pass and an indomitable spirit. She arrived shortly before daylight on April 6, but before she could see her husband, who was encamped not far from the steamboat, the great battle had begun.

As gunfire roared, Wallace moved his division forward to support troops already engaged. He promptly filled a gap in the line between the divisions of Generals Benjamin M. Prentiss and John A. McClernand. Together with Prentiss, Wallace occupied a defensive position, later known as the "Hornet's Nest," that withstood repeated assaults until late in the afternoon and probably saved the entire army from disaster. Eventually, the Confederates massed enough artillery to drive the federals back, and Wallace began to withdraw his division. While doing so, he rose slightly from his saddle and was mortally wounded. His brother-in-law Cyrus Dickey tried to bring him back to the Union lines but came under heavy fire and, believing that Wallace could not survive, left him on the battlefield. Wallace was recovered the next day, when Grant, reinforced by Lew Wallace's tardy division and troops from Buell's command, launched a counterattack that routed the Confederates.

Wallace survived for only four days. He died in the Cherry mansion at Savannah, which also housed General Smith, who lived another fifteen days. "We meet in Heaven," Wallace told Ann as he died. Members of the family brought Wallace's body back to Ottawa for burial in a private cemetery near his house that eventually became the Wallace-Dickey cemetery. Wallace's horse, Prince, who accompanied the mourners, outlived his master by a quarter century and was buried nearby.

Colonel Dickey continued to serve under Grant, who thought highly enough of him to place him in command at Memphis, assign him a cavalry brigade, and make him his chief of cavalry. In the fall of 1862, Dickey led an "eminently successful" cavalry raid during Grant's Mississippi Central campaign.[14] In January 1863, Dickey resigned because his age made service in the field difficult, he had matters at home to look after, and he thought that he could better serve the government in Illinois politics.[15] That same year, looking for a suitable home for his wife, Julia, and his children, Grant considered "Ottoway," where Dickey and Ann Wallace lived.[16] In 1868, writing to urge an increase in Mrs. Wallace's pension, Grant praised her husband as "the equal of the best, if not the very best, of the Volunteer Generals with me at the date of his death."[17]

Following Wallace's death, his widow, not yet thirty, devoted herself to preserving his memory at The Oaks, which became a shrine to her beloved husband. Her father, who had been an unsuccessful

Democratic candidate for Congress in absentia in 1862, ran for congressman-at-large in 1866 against the formidable John A. Logan, who won the seat despite Dickey's active campaign. President Andrew Johnson rewarded Dickey in July 1868 with an appointment as U.S. assistant attorney general. While visiting her father in Washington and planning a trip to Europe, Ann received letters of introduction from both President Grant and General Sherman. In 1882 Ann left for two years in Hawaii with her brother and sister (who had married a brother of her husband). After reading an 1885 article by Grant on Shiloh, Ann sent him a copy of a letter received by her husband from his friend Lew Wallace that partially exonerated him of ineptitude during the first day's battle.[18] Ann lived until 1889, and her daughter, Isabel, who never married, continued to live at The Oaks until her death in June 1933.[19]

Only four when her father fell, Isabel based his biography on extensive family papers. She printed many of his letters in full and included enough of her mother's Civil War letters to provide a rounded view of an extraordinarily literate and loving couple. More a documentary compilation than an ordinary biography, her book remains both highly readable and of great scholarly value. While confined to a wheelchair for the last twenty years of her life, Isabel maintained her home as a shrine to General Wallace.

Through efforts of a local legislator, the house was donated to the Illinois State Historical Society in 1941 and opened to visitors.[20] In 1950 it was closed because "not enough persons were interested in it" and sold for $14,500.[21] The Oaks has since been remodeled into apartments.The adjacent Wallace-Dickey cemetery is unadvertised and screened by private homes. In the local Episcopal church, the stained-glass window that serves as a memorial to Ottawa's citizen soldier has fallen into disrepair.[22] Wallace is better remembered farther south. On the Shiloh battlefield stands a monument to mark the spot where this valiant soldier received his fatal wound.

John Y. Simon

Notes

1. Family information supplied by Ronald E. Slack, Ottawa, Ill. For valuable assistance, I am also indebted to other residents of Ottawa: Stan Gaul, Robert S. Jordan, and Leonard Lock.

2. T. Lyle Dickey to Abraham Lincoln, 19 November 1854, Lincoln Papers, Library of Congress.

3. Dickey to William H. Herndon, 8 December 1866, Douglas L. Wilson and Rodney O. Davis, eds., *Herndon's Informants: Letters, Interviews, and Statements about Abraham Lincoln* (Urbana: University of Illinois Press, 1998), 504–5.

4. Lincoln to David Davis, 7 July 1856, Roy P. Basler, ed., *The Collected Works of Abraham Lincoln: Supplement 1832–1865* (Westport, Conn.: Greenwood Press, 1974), 27; Lincoln to Henry C. Whitney, 9 July 1856, Basler *et al.*, eds., *The Collected Works of Abraham Lincoln* (New Brunswick: Rutgers University Press, 1953–55), 2: 347.

5. Henry C. Whitney, *Life on the Circuit with Lincoln* (Boston: Estes and Lauriat, 1892), 382–85. See also Willard L. King, *Lincoln's Manager David Davis* (Cambridge: Harvard University Press, 1960), 112–26; Edward Magdol, *Owen Lovejoy: Abolitionist in Congress* (New Brunswick: Rutgers University Press, 1967), 156–66, 190–207.

6. William H. L. Wallace to Lincoln, 18 August 1858, Lincoln Papers.

7. Ulysses S. Grant to Sidney Perham, 14 February 1868, John Y. Simon, ed., *The Papers of Ulysses S. Grant* (Carbondale: Southern Illinois University Press, 1967–), 18: 159–60. Wallace had another brother serving as a commissary clerk, and Dickey had another son employed as a telegrapher.

8. Jim Huffstodt, *Hard Dying Men: The Story of General W. H. L. Wallace, General T. E. G. Ransom, and their "Old Eleventh" Illinois Infantry . . .* (Bowie, Md.: Heritage Books, 1991), 12.

9. Ibid., 14–15.

10. Grant to Elihu B. Washburne, 20 November 1861, *Grant Papers*, 3: 205.

11. *The War of the Rebellion: A Compilation of the Official Records of the Union and Confederate Armies* (Washington: Government Printing Office, 1880–1901), Series I, 7: 168, 182.

12. Wallace to Lincoln, 28 January 1862, Lincoln Papers.

13. *Lew Wallace: An Autobiography* (New York: Harper & Brothers, 1906), 1: 403–5.

14. Grant to Col. John C. Kelton, 2 January 1863, *Grant Papers,* 7: 162.

15. Grant to Julia Dent Grant, 6 March 1863, ibid., 397.

16. Ibid.

17. Grant to Perham, 14 February 1868, ibid., 18: 159.

18. *Personal Memoirs of U. S. Grant* (New York: Charles L. Webster & Company, 1885–86), 1: 351–52.

19. *Ottawa Daily Republican Times*, 8, 10 June 1933.

20. Ibid., 26 April 1941; John Drury, *Old Illinois Houses* (Chicago: University of Chicago Press, 1948), 160–62.

21. *Journal of the Illinois State Historical Society* 44 (Winter 1951): 377.

22. *Daily Times*, Ottawa, Ill., 10 April 1995,16 April 1999.

THIS BOOK IS DEDICATED TO THE MEMORY OF

MRS. ANN DICKEY WALLACE

WHO RADIATED GOODNESS, SWEETNESS AND CHEER AROUND HER
BRAVE AND UNSELFISH IN A GREAT SORROW,
SHE MADE THE WORLD BETTER
BY HER PRESENCE.

"*True glory consists in doing what deserves to be written, in writing what deserves to be read, and in so living as to make the world better and happier for our living.*" —PLINY.

CONTENTS

CONTENTS—*Continued*

ILLUSTRATIONS

PREFACE

IN the days of chivalry men of action performed deeds which were heralded by tuneful bards, thus perpetuating noble lives to be admired and emulated by succeeding generations. All through the ages these heroic men appear on the pages of history as links in the great chain wrought by the eternal hand of God in His plans for the betterment and advancement of the human race.

General W. H. L. Wallace can be called the Chevalier Bayard of the North, as was General Kirby-Smith the Chevalier Bayard of the Southern Confederacy. The life of General Wallace, in the short space of forty-one years, touched on some of the great events of American history in the nineteenth century, and side-lights from private letters and papers are here thrown on these momentous times.

Some glimpses are also given of the bravery and suffering of the women at home during the Civil War with soldier husbands in the army, a phase not so often dwelt upon as the heroic deeds of the men at the front.

ISABEL WALLACE.

The Oaks, Ottawa, Illinois.
August, 1909.

Life and Letters of
General W. H. L. Wallace

LIFE AND LETTERS OF GENERAL W. H. L. WALLACE

CHAPTER I.

Parentage and Early Life.

WILLIAM WALLACE of Illinois resembled William Wallace of Scotland in more respects than the name. They were alike in devotion to their country, for which each gave his life—one dying in a most inhuman manner by the hands of a foreign foe outside his own country; the other by the hands of a foe, 'tis true, his own countrymen, but in battle honored and admired by the enemy surrounding him no less than by his own soldiers. The body of William Wallace of Illinois was laid to rest with honor and respect, not cut and placed on poles to be jeered at by his enemies, as was the sad fate of the great Sir William Wallace of Scotland five hundred years before.

In another point are they alike—in their devotion to home and the beloved wife sheltered there.

Even in appearance, if history tells true, they again meet; both tall, with sandy hair and gray eyes, which betokens the Scotch ancestry of William Wallace of Illinois. Both were Nature's noblemen, firm in duty, gentle and considerate to all who required their aid—two great souls, akin in name no less than in exalted motives.

In personal appearance William Wallace of Illinois was tall, erect, dignified almost to reserve, commanding by nature, but simple and unassuming, a gentleman in the highest sense of the term. Cowardice and meanness he abhorred and branded them as such in no uncertain words. Wrong was wrong and right was right; no glossing over for any temporary gain, ever standing firmly for the highest ideals.

There was something in his personality that begat the deepest devotion and intense loyalty from his friends, who acknowledged his superiority without envy or jealousy; wishing to see him advanced, they put him forward as their leader, and felt honored in giving him honors. In war his soldiers almost idolized him, for to him fear was unknown and his bravery inspired them to heroic deeds.

William Hervy Lamme Wallace was born in Urbana, Ohio, July 8, 1821. He was the fourth child and second son of John and Mary Lamme Wallace. His grandfather Wallace lived in Sussex County, Delaware, and removed to Rockingham County, Virginia, in 1782, where his father, John Wallace, was born. About 1817 John Wallace moved to Champaign County, Ohio, where he married Mary Lamme, daughter of James and Elizabeth Lamme, who were born in Augusta County, Virginia, and moved from there to Cynthianna, Kentucky, in 1791, and to Champaign County, Ohio, in 1808. James Lamme's father was born in Ireland and came to America in 1740, settling in Shenandoah Valley, Virginia.

William was but four years old when his mother, Mary Lamme Wallace, died. His father married Sarah Hitt for a second wife.

John Wallace was a carpenter and builder, but meeting with an accident that injured his back, gave up his business and moved to La Salle County, Illinois, taking up an original grant from the United States Government in Deer Park Township. In 1834 he, with his wife and eleven children, moved into this new country.

William, then a lad of twelve years, assisted a young relative to drive out a large flock of sheep from the old home to the new one. A log cabin was built and the family sojourned in this picturesque locality for some six years. It is now the beautiful park near the Deer Park cañon, so rich in material for the naturalist and pleasure-seeker.

Interspersed with the laborious battle with life that those pioneers waged was many a pleasant ramble in which the thoughtful, refined boy roamed through the neighboring cañons and over the far-famed Starved Rock, where he gathered arrows and beads left by the vanquished Illini.

With so large a family John Wallace desired better educational advantages for his children and moved in 1840 to Mount Morris, Ogle County, where was situated the Rock River Seminary, in the organization of which he was very active. The Wallace home here was a suburban farm and William manfully took an elder brother's share in its work, interspersed with his studies at the Rock River Seminary.

The martial spirit of young Wallace was early aroused, as when a mere lad in Ogle County he with the men of the community encountered and drove out a murderous band of horse thieves and robbers that infested that region.

In all newly settled countries these gangs of outlaws for a time seem to have full sway, unmolested by law or force. Although few districts were entirely free from these outlaws the counties of Ogle, Winnebago, Lee and DeKalb contained the most numerous and powerful bands. In Ogle County especially they overruled all law; any conviction for crime came to naught. The law-abiding citizens determined to take the law into their own hands, and organized into companies of Regulators to drive these desperadoes from the country. "One family, by the name of Driscoll," as Randall Parrish says, "determined not to leave and resolved to terrorize the Regulators by threatening death to the members of that organization, actually assassinating the captain before his wife and family. Indignation was intense and the father and sons were captured and given a day's trial and ordered to be shot, which was done by the three hundred Regulators present as one man, so no blame would be attached to any one individual."

A young student, by the name of J. H. Aylsworth, was wending his way to the Rock River Seminary for the first time, and passed the bodies of the three desperadoes. Many years afterwards he wrote of this scene: "On my way to Mount Morris I passed the spot where an enraged people had just dispatched three horse thieves by the name of Driscoll, and, upon reaching the Seminary, I found the question before the lyceum for debate as follows: 'Resolved, That the lynch law under certain circumstances is justifiable,' with W. H. L. Wallace leader in the affirmative.

"Everything in readiness, Mr. Wallace rose with dignified bearing, and looking around upon the audience a moment he announced with commanding emphasis the following telling words: 'The letter of the law cannot touch every case, but the spirit of the law will.' Another sentence of like sweeping force or profound import is scarcely to be found in the English language. The negatives were not able to rise above the conviction of this self evident declaration, and the more they labored to combat it the clearer it became that conviction is justifiable, and so said the judges."

About 1837, the Hitt brothers, Samuel, Martin, Thomas, and Daniel, settled in Ogle County, joined later by their sisters, Mrs. Wallace and Mrs. Reynolds. As there was no public school in this section at that time the citizens sent to Maryland for a teacher, who began his work in a log house about a mile from Mount Morris, which was called "The Pine Creek Grammar School." But something better was desired, and Rev. Thomas S. Hitt, a Methodist divine, visited the Illinois Conference in 1838, and urged them to establish a school in Ogle County, offering four hundred and eighty acres of land with eight thousand dollars in money, a most munificent offer in those early times in a new country and the settlers few.

The Conference was at the time looking for a suitable place to establish a school and gladly accepted the liberal offer. On the Fourth of July, 1839, the corner stone was laid amid the rejoicings of the community who gathered from far and near to do honor to the occasion to the number of some five hundred, the families nearby providing entertainment for those from a distance.

Then arose the great difficulty of procuring suitable material and workmen. But these almost insurmountable obstacles in the way of its immediate erection were overcome through the indefatigable and energetic exertion of the trustees and the contractor.

The Institution was opened for students December 1, 1840. The building was situated in a high and beautiful prairie, the view almost boundless. The town of Rockford, twenty miles distant could be distinctly seen from the top of the building, as well as many other small towns on the Rock River. The town of Mount Morris grew up around the school.

The men who planned and built this seminary were enthusiastic in their views of the good effect of a high grade school upon the community. "They builded better than they knew." In its earlier history when seminaries and colleges were few and far apart it wielded a very great influence in the western country, especially in Illinois.

The Hon. R. R. Hitt, in an address at a reunion of the old students in 1888, said: "The course of instruction pursued in this institution was admirable and was just the kind to produce well-rounded minds—men, the kind needed for that active and exacting period in the history of the country. The classical and mathematical training was thorough and the attention to general literature, begetting a taste for reading the best work, and the knowledge of the things best worth knowing, facility in composition and facility in speech, fitted men for any occupation in life, fortifying them at all points. Much stress was laid upon the moral instruction of youth. It gave them elevated character, sound principles, and produced men and women who have vindicated in useful and excellent lives the lessons of a healthful moral training.

"Fifty years ago, when this country was filling up with the laborious pioneer population and with slender provision for primary education, there was need of young men of strong natural abilities, and with that equipment for the world which comes from a general training of the faculties which was given here, and the result of which is seen in the shining names that star the old catalogues of the Seminary—two governors of this state, ten judges, renowned generals, eminent preachers, and educators, merchants, merchant princes, senators and members of Congress."

Some of the men who claimed the Rock River Seminary for their Alma Mater and afterwards rose to distinction, were John L. Beveridge, Shelby M. Cullom, Robert R. Hitt, S. M. Fellows, J. V. Farwell, John A. Rawlins, M. R. M. Wallace, W. H. L. Wallace.

There were three literary societies connected with the

school with debates on immense subjects—by the students who here gained the practice that gave them eminence in their country's legislative halls.

At a reunion of the Rock River Seminary in 1886, H. O. McDaid had the topic of the "Amphictyons," one of the strongest of these literary societies.

"The Amphictyons of the 'Old Sandstone' meet again—not in solemn debates—not to decide problems relating to the happiness and prosperity of their country—but, after the test of battle—after the crucial struggle in life with most of us—we come with shattered and depleted ranks to renew old associations and recall old memories. One of the objects of the Amphictyons of old was to secure the happiness and prosperity of their country, and to this end, says Æschines, they bound themselves with an oath.

"The Amphictyons of 'Old Sandstone' can point to an honorable record, testifying their devotion to the happiness and prosperity of their country. What debates were held! What subjects discussed! From the northeastern boundary to the constitutionality of the Fugitive Slave Law. Questions of political economy and the policy of internal improvements, and the great questions relating to the preservation and integrity of the national government. All these questions were discussed and decided. No vacillating policy was adopted, no hesitation as to remedies—Who will deny that in this society, the foundations were laid to shape, in a measure, the destinies of war, to sway listening senates; to direct the course of justice; to spread the peaceful sway of Christianity.

"From out these weather-stained halls have gone heroic souls; some to the battle-field; some to the halls of legislation; some to humbler walks of life; but all, I believe, with as sincere purpose as ever Amphictyons assembled at *Delphi* or *Anthela*.

"Some have fallen in the freshness of the morning, ere the sun had reached the meridian. Some of them, like the Amphictyons at Thermopylæ, lie in honored graves at their country's command. If we call their names they answer not.

"Sanford, Rawlins, Wallace. Sanford! Alas, he, who with heroic calmness, sacrificed his life for country, sleeps in the soil of his own loved Byron, almost within sound of the murmuring river that flows with the same majesty and music as in years gone by.

"Rawlins! Whose place in the history of this Republic will be recognized more and more as time goes by. Rawlins! the friend of the 'Old Commander'—a friendship prized by him as Cicero prized the friendship of the illustrious Scipio. And when Rawlins was laid to rest on the banks of the Potomac, no eyes were moist with sincerer tears than those of Ulysses S. Grant.

"Rawlins! the military companion of the Silent Soldier on every battle field from Belmont to The Wilderness. If the world knew the truth, perhaps Stanton did not more to strengthen and cheer the sometimes drooping spirits of Lincoln; . . . . . than did Rawlins to round out, into complete symmetry, the character and military genius of U. S. Grant. No storied urn or stately monument yet marks his resting place. The Amphictyons—his brothers, would, if they could, place above his dust a monument that would meet the sun in his coming, and whose last departing rays would linger and play upon its summit. Illinois is proud of her son. Time alone will reveal to her the debt of gratitude which she owes to the intellectual, the brave, the devoted John A. Rawlins.

"Wallace! At the mention of thy name a flood of old associations and memories come thronging to the hearts of many who knew thee in young manhood at Mount Morris.

"He fell on Shiloh's field while facing fearful odds. He met his fate, amid the thunder roar of red-mouthed cannon 'where sabres were clashing and death shot were pouring':

> "For how can man die better
> Than in facing fearful odds,
> For the ashes of his fathers,
> And the temples of his Gods."

After the Northwestern University at Evanston was established, the old Seminary did not have its former patronage and did not pay expenses, and was finally sold on a mortgage. Robert R. Hitt bought it in, at the earnest desire of his mother, and afterwards sold it to the Dunkard denomination, and it is now called the Mount Morris College.

CHAPTER II.

Goes to Ottawa, Illinois. Studies Law.

PROFESSOR D. J. PINCKNEY, the principal of the Rock River Seminary for many years, was a "truly great man as a teacher and seemed to possess preëminent power to interest young men and attach them to him." As one of his students in after years said of him, "His life was a poem in itself." When young Wallace left school and home to make his own way in the world this friend and teacher gave him the following letter of introduction, which is both complimentary and prophetic:

"Rock River Seminary, December 7, 1844.

"This may certify that the bearer, Wm H. L. Wallace, has been for more than three years a student and instructor in the R. R. Sem'y, more than two years of which time I have had the pleasure of being personally and intimately acquainted with him. From an intimate and, as I think, thorough knowledge of his talents, attainments, character and habits, I am fully prepared, and embrace with great satisfaction the opportunity now offered, to recommend him to the friendship and kind attention of those with whom his lot may hereafter be cast.

I have no hesitancy in predicting that his *success in life*, if at all comparable to his *merits* will be preëminent; and, hoping that his course may be as much onward and upward, his reputation as unsullied, his friends as firm and faithful, as they have hitherto been, I remain ever

"His quandom instructor and faithful friend as also the humble servant of all

"Who may befriend him.

"Danl J. Pinckney,

"Principal of the Seminary."

But Professor Pinckney, desiring his pupil's best welfare, could be also Mentor as well as earnest friend, as is shown in an extract from a letter written by him to Wallace the 26th of the same month—"If you do not look to your grammar, as the schoolmaster would say when you write letters, you'll be scolded hard. Carelessness in little things is productive of much evil to public men. This is impertinent, Will, I know, but you must excuse it because of the *Intention.* In writing, a man must be careful to *form* correct habits, or, when crowded with business, he will mourn the *want* of *habitual correctness.* For three or four years be most scrupulously exact in all your business, incidental—off-hand writing after that you may go on swimmingly and carelessly because *habitual.* Neither scowl nor fret at this homily as needless or inapropos in a friendly letter. You know these things, I acknowledge; but you will be prone to neglect them in common writing, and soon all your writing will be common. But here I resign the office of *Mentor,* which ill suits me, and talk to you as I was wont to talk in days of yore. Oh! 'tis ever so, the past, the past!—how much of the mind it fills, how much of our joy and sorrow it engrosses! What a kind of vacuum is mind without it."

In the winter of 1844, after some preliminary legal study, Mr. Wallace went with his stepmother's brother, the Hon. Samuel Hitt, a member of the Legislature, to Springfield, intending to study law with Logan and Lincoln. In the long stage journey they fell in with the Hon. T. Lyle Dickey, of Ottawa.

Arrived at Springfield, Mr. Dickey and Mr. Wallace took a suite of rooms together and Wallace assisted Mr. Dickey in preparing his cases for the Supreme Court then in session there. The result of this intimacy was that young Wallace arranged to go to Ottawa—his home henceforth, and entered the law office of T. Lyle Dickey instead of that of Logan and Lincoln.

Mr. Dickey was especially proud of his eldest little girl, Ann, and when in Springfield had received a letter from her, then a little girl of twelve years, which he read out loud to a little circle of friends. Among the number was the grave young man of twenty-three, Mr. Wallace. The thought flashed through his brain—"What if that bright, winning little girl should some day be my wife—time will show."

Mr. Wallace studied for a year when he was admitted to

the bar, being duly examined by John Dean Caton and Samuel H. Treat, Justices of the Supreme Court; the 2d of December, 1845, he took the oath—"I, William H. L. Wallace, do solemnly swear that I will support the Constitution of the United States and of said State, and that I will well and truly and faithfully perform the duties of an attorney at law according to the best of my knowledge, understanding and ability." Which promise he faithfully kept even to the giving of his life's blood.

His friend, James C. Parks, writes to him in May, 1845, from Buffalo, where he was studying for the ministry:

"You speak of our professions differing. They do, but responsibility in one runs parallel with the other. There was a time when the administration of justice, pleadings for the oppressed and for precepts of law and the preaching of righteousness were all blended in the same man, or performed by the same individual, and that, too, in accordance with the instructions of the Divine Law-giver. From this to infer that he who takes a license to indulge in all kinds of trickery of which he is capable merely because he is a lawyer misunderstands the obligations of his profession and the origin of the precepts he pretends to advocate. I must say when I first heard you say you were intending to pursue the study of law I felt gratified. I looked forward to a time when you might aid at least in making the law profession what it should be and in driving loafers and demagogues from the bar."

Mr. Wallace stepped into the pleasant social circles of Ottawa—where were many bright men whose names went far beyond their own town borders. Ottawa was settled largely by educated and cultivated people from New York State, with a sprinkling from Pennsylvania, and Kentucky, Being a county seat and having the Supreme Court and other courts meet there, the legal profession held a leading position, giving the town an atmosphere of culture almost from the beginning.

The town is beautifully situated, at the mouth of the Fox as it enters the tranquil and beautiful Illinois River. High bluffs to the north and south, the town itself in a valley. Rich prairie farm lands lying in all directions. Varied scenery down the banks of the picturesque Illinois River, of cañons, and the far-famed Starved Rock seven miles below the town, with its historic interests, both from the early French explorers and the no less picturesque, but ill fated tribe of Illini Indians. A few miles distant is the Deer Park Glen, where in old Indian days the guileless deer were driven in and captured. Nature with a lavish hand endowed Ottawa with her beauties, it remained for man to mar or improve the opportunities given him.

Mr. Wallace was steadily rising in his chosen profession, working earnestly and industriously, gaining friends both near and far. But his old friends of his Alma Mater did not lose sight of him, as in March, 1846, came a letter from there, saying they intended having a public debate at the close of the term and desired a large attendance of all old members of the Amphictyon Society. Three of the number were especially requested to prepare each an address to deliver on that occasion. They were S. M. Fellows, J. H. Beveridge and W. H. L. Wallace.

When the time came for the debate to occur, Mr. Wallace was on sterner work intent than addressing a college debating society. He with his company was speeding down the Mississippi to take part in the Mexican War then in progress.

One of the other students chosen with Mr. Wallace to address the society, S. M. Fellows, afterwards a college president, wrote him a letter about this time. It could not be seen at that date what an important acquisition was to be ours in annexing Oregon, California and Texas to the territory of the United States. "May 1848. I suppose you intend to be here at the close of the term if not before. I am afraid but few of the old students will find it convenient to be here, though I hope they will come up and help to enliven the occasion. If all the Amphictyons could meet they would present a pretty strong phalanx of talent and ability. Enough at any rate to give the world a pretty good stirring wherever they may be. By the way, what subject have you selected for your address for the close of the term? I have not determined what I shall write about. * * * *

"The warlike spirit of your letter considerably alarmed

me. What! you become a soldier? Why if you wish to do that you should enlist in the royal guards of Prussia, where you could be surrounded by your peers. Perhaps though your disposition would lead you to prefer a situation where your *eminence* would be conspicuous. But really, Wallace, are you in earnest about military glory? Do you think you could face the cannon's mouth and rush upon the glittering steel of an enemy? Not that I would wish to intimate a want of true courage in your composition, but I should almost hope you were deficient in this kind of brutal courage. I have not been able to bring myself to believe that we should be involved in a war with England on the Oregon question. I do not think that two such nations as the United States and Great Britain will resort to this ultimatum. Neither power could conquer the other, and after a ten years' war, the matter must be settled by negotiation as entirely as it would be without war.

"And even if we should succeed in obtaining the whole of the territory, which is quite improbable, it would be a miserable compensation for the loss of millions of money and thousands of lives.

"Of the war in Mexico, or rather with Mexico, late accounts seem to make it quite certain that hostilities have really commenced. Whether it will be prosecuted with much vigor by Mexico is very doubtful. I do not exactly understand this question of national interference, but I can see no reason why England or France should have anything to do with the Mexican affair. Even if the United States should conquer and annex Mexico, which I hope they will not do—it would be only acting upon the principle of the British in Asia. There they conquer and subject whole countries without scruple as to its righteousness.

"For my own part I have not much desire for the honor and glory of a military hero, and shall not probably start for the seat of war immediately."

CHAPTER III.

MEXICAN WAR. JOURNEY TO MEXICO.

THE war with Mexico was now actually a fact. Ever since Texas had gained her independence from Mexico and joined the United States as an integral part of the Union there had been friction over boundary lines. When the Mexican soldiery actually shed the blood of Americans on American soil, the war spirit was aroused. Congress on the 11th of May, 1846, acknowledged that war already existed by the act of the Mexican government and placed ten million dollars at the disposal of the President to prosecute the war.

War meetings were held in all parts of the country and within a few weeks three hundred thousand men rushed forward to join the ranks. Six regiments went from Illinois. In La Salle County the war spirit also found its way. T. Lyle Dickey gave up his fine law practice and organized one of the first companies, of which he was chosen Captain. W. H. L. Wallace naturally followed. He enlisted as private, but was soon elected Second Lieutenant. This company from Ottawa and vicinity consisted of seventy-five men.

The company was organized in May, going direct to Alton, where they were attached to the First Regiment, of which John J. Hardin was Colonel. The other regiments were here also. The Second, under Colonel William H. Bissel. The Third, under Colonel I. H. Farman, and the Fourth under Colonel Ned Baker. All four were organized and mustered into the service of the United States for one year. In July these four regiments were sent to New Orleans and there divided, the First and Second going to San Antonio; the Third and Fourth to Vera Cruz.

The American forces were organized in three divisions for the invasion of Mexico, as planned by General Scott: The *Army of the West,* under General Kearney, was to cross the Rocky Mountains and conquer the Northern Mexican provinces: The *Army of the Centre,* under General

Scott as commander-in-chief, was to march from the gulf into the heart of the enemy's country. The *Army of Occupation,* commanded by General Taylor, was to subdue and hold the districts on the Rio Grande.

The work of mustering the American troops was entrusted to General Wool. By the middle of the summer he succeeded in dispatching to General Taylor a force of nine thousand men. He established his camp at San Antonio, Texas, and from that point prepared the gathering recruits for the field. Meanwhile General Taylor resumed active operations on the Rio Grande, pushing on toward the fortified town of Monterey.

The company and regiment in which W. H. L. Wallace was serving joined the *Army of Occupation* under General Taylor. From letters and a journal written by Mr. Wallace and here given, a pretty full account is received of this part of the year's campaign in Mexico of the First Regiment's movements. Mr. Wallace's first letter is from Alton on July 3d:

"On the ground in our immediate vicinity are encamped some fifteen hundred troops, some of the companies well trained, and the whole presenting a scene to me novel and highly enchanting. I just begin to enjoy the life of a soldier—for my duties have been so arduous up to this time that I had not time to enjoy anything but my mess and my sleep."

On July 19th, he writes in his journal: "Six companies of the First Regiment embarked on the Steamer Hanibal at an early hour. Before we could get on board our men had to stand for an hour on the bank, and those who were drunkenly inclined slipped out of the ranks and filled their canteens with "Old Red Eye," and by noon we had a fine set of fellows to manage. One of our privates, Frank —, was particularly savage and I was charged by Major Warren with the unpleasant duty of choking him into submission. His rum and rage threw him into a fit from which he came near dying. But as soon as he was held up and received fresh air he seemed to acquire fresh madness and he kept the whole company in disorder until twelve o'clock. Something must be done with the fellow."

As they passed down the river they stopped but an hour at St. Louis, where he says: "We anchored in the stream between the foot of 'Bloody Island' and St. Louis. I wonder that ever a duel was fought on 'Bloody Island.' One would imagine that in crossing the dark and angry current of the river, some thought of the impassable gulf over which one or both combatants were likely to pass would stay their murderous hands. I looked upon the sandy banks and willow shade of this 'dark and bloody ground' with emotion. Desolate and dreary as it is in itself, it appears yet more so when we see it surrounded and cut off on all sides by this boiling Mississippi. I have been studying this strange river all day. As we left Alton I saw we were sailing on a clear and beautiful stream. My attention was called to business in the cabin and when I looked again, the river was as muddy as a frog pond. My first impression was we were running in shoal water, but in looking around, it was all the same, the river seemed to have undergone some necromantic change—that some demon was stirring the 'Father of Waters.' It is indeed a mysterious and terrible stream. Nothing of romance about it, and nothing to render it an object of admiration but its immensity. It was Sunday when we went ashore at St. Louis, and the quiet narrow streets appeared to me like some deserted town of the old world. The mighty business heart of the city had ceased its pulsation and the quiet wharfs and streets presented a vivid contrast to the hurrying stream that pelted along at their foot. * * * * Our quarters are comfortable, much more so than I had anticipated. The officers have the whole of both cabins and the men are conveniently quartered in different parts of the boat. We are making a fine run. We have on board Brigadier General Shields, who has orders to join General Taylor with two regiments, the Third and Fourth. The First and Second will land at La Baca in Metagorda Bay and join General Wool at San Antonio de Bexar, who will then march upon Chihuahua" and, as he writes to a friend: "I shall have the opportunity of gratifying my wish, but whether you will 'crown me with laurel' depends much upon circumstances."

He again writes in his journal in journeying further

down the Mississippi: "Memphis is a most lovely place. A bold but not very high bank rises from the water's edge, and slopes back as far as the eye can reach, and everywhere one sees clean streets and whole blocks of new brick buildings not crowded together, but placed at a comfortable distance from each other, as though they dreaded close contact might cause sickness in this southern climate. It is the most beautiful place I've met anywhere on the route, and when I return I've a great mind to settle there. Just before reaching Memphis our company was ordered forward with their knapsacks and accoutrements, but without their arms. They were all on the qui-vive to know what this might mean. Some said we were to go ashore for drill and some that we were to land and join the Tennessee cavalry, a regiment which were encamped opposite the town; some thought one thing, some another, but all agreed that we were to go ashore. As the boat rounded up the Lieutenant Colonel (Weatherford), with the Sergeant-Major, came on deck and the latter proceeded to read a general order addressed to Captain Dickey ordering him to call up Frank (the private who behaved so badly on Sunday), take from him his uniform and all the public property in his possession and drum him out of the company, which was accordingly done with all due form. Frank braved it out until the yawl touched the shore, swearing that 'he would rather a hundred times be drummed out of that regiment than stay in it and be deprived of the liberty of speech by choking.' But as he stepped on shore the band played the 'Rogues' March,' the other companies hissing and hooting him and hallooing to the people on shore 'not to stop that man but let him go, that he was drummed out,' etc., the sense of his disgrace seemed to force itself upon him, and he walked up the bank with tears in his eyes. Our company, I am happy to say, added nothing to wound his feelings, though many of them had been sadly abused by him. The scene left an impression on the minds of all that will produce a good effect."

He writes further in his journey: "July 22d, passed some most splendid plantations. The negro quarters generally appeared comfortable—even more, there is an appearance of neatness and order about them—their white-washed walls and thick green shade present an appearance of more comfort than the residence of nine-tenths of their fanatical friends at the North. The country to-day has looked more like living than any thing since leaving St. Louis. Broad fields covered with heavy crops of corn and cotton—fine residences buried in rich foliage of the China tree, which is peculiar to this climate, tall forests of cypress from whose branches hang long pendants of Spanish moss—extensive orchards of peaches, the rich fruit glistening in the sun as we ran near the shore and looking as tempting in our eyes as did the forbidden fruit to Mother Eve." * * * * In passing these fine old plantations, he further says: "I like the state of these old planters, each being in his own castle on his own domain, with his own retainers about him—there is a charm of chivalry about it that delights me. * * *

"Yesterday some of the high-blooded lieutenants of the regiment saw fit to amuse themselves with the genteel game of poker. This morning General Shields called a meeting of the officers in the after cabin and read to them the army regulation respecting gaming. He also proposed to close the bar against all, both officers and men, which proposition met with general opposition. * * * * July 24th. Through a scene that throws the Arabian Nights into the shade. * * * * We are gliding on toward the Crescent City. On either bank is a street of planter's houses, negro quarters and sugar houses, all in the most tasteful style and the greatest order and neatness. * * * * About nine o'clock we began to reach the city of New Orleans and my first feeling was one of disappointment. There is a dingy appearance about the town as seen from the river that does not comport with our ideas of a magnificent city, but as we passed on the Crescent City in all its grand extent gradually presented itself, as the tall spire of the upper Cathedral and the lofty dome of the St. Charles hotel shot up their fine proportions and we passed the foot of long streets running far back with tall buildings almost overshadowing them on either side; as we glided past the forest of masts at the upper ship landing and entered the world of steamboats at their landing and saw the wharfs covered with active business men, bales of goods and negroes attached to them and heard the indescribable hum of a great business city, I began to have some idea of the immensity of the place. And when after landing the troops at the battle grounds, I returned to the city on business and walked through the narrow crowded streets, with millions of wealth obtruding itself upon the public gaze, when I approached the St. Charles Hotel, the pride and glory of the traveling world, with its massive proportions, Corinthian columns and majestic dimensions covering an entire square and ascended through its six lofty stories to the splendid dome that surmounts it, and gazed upon the broad extent of the city unrolled at my feet like a living map with its thousand narrow streets overhung, and almost shaded by the old French houses, the windings of the Mississippi and the blue glistening of Lake Pontchartrain far into the southwest, with the long line of the new 'Shell road' leading off towards it, with the hum of the streets below, the old French buildings rusty with age and the dampness of the climate, my wonder and admiration was roused to a degree I never felt before. I had never seen a place of more than five thousand inhabitants. I took advantage of the business I had to do to see as much of the place as possible. I spent four dollars for cab hire in visiting different parts of the town besides running myself down afoot. * * * * I dined at the St. Charles for the gratification of seeing a good dinner eaten according to the rules of etiquette. I relied on Colonel C., with whom I went in, to act as chaperon, but I found him about as green as myself. We sat during the hour mincing over some cold ham and tomatoes while the fashionable bloods around us were cracking the champagne bottles.

"July 25th. Slept upon the ground where Jackson achieved his glory (8th of January, 1815), but felt none of Byron's enthusiasm upon the plains of Marathon, perhaps because I was very tired, probably because I am not Byron. * * * * At dark we embarked on board the Brig Albertina, a small craft of two hundred tons that had been employed by the Quartermaster to carry us out to La Baca. I find we will be considerably crowded tho' we have only our own and Captain Morgan's companies and the Quincy Riflemen, the most quiet, gentlemanly set of fellows in the regiment, and I hope we shall have a pleasant trip. I am glad we are going by sailing vessel; it adds a variety to our journey, but whether it will be a pleasant variety remains to be seen. The vessel is small, but well built, with a small cabin on deck with eight berths. In this seven by nine affair slept six commissioned officers, a surgeon, captain of the brig, a would-be gentleman soldier named I. S. T., and two or three sick privates of the two companies. On deck the men were equally crowded. There was but one fire place, on which about four camp kettles could boil, and here the whole one hundred and eighty men had to do their cooking, and none but the best natured fellows could have got along without quarreling at least, if not fighting. On board the brig we found provisions for thirty days. Colonel Hardin appointed me commissary for the trip."

On the 31st of July they sighted land, but did not enter Metagorda Bay until late, and the companies did not land until the third of August. On the eleventh they set out on the march to San Antonio, the journal continues: * * * "After crossing the creek we struck a wet prairie with water from three inches to two feet deep for eighteen miles. We reached Victoria about dark, weary, wet and hungry, and without cooking utensils or tents, lay on the wet ground beside a frog pond in our dripping clothes, but I slept well."

They were about two weeks on the march and reached San Antonio on the 25th of August, first camping at Mission de Conception ruins, and from there they moved to Camp Crockett. The command remained in San Antonio about six weeks. General Wool organized the army here to proceed to the conquest of Chihuahua. "This army consisted of the two Illinois regiments, First and Second, an Arkansas regiment of infantry, two companies of Kentucky cavalry under Major Williams, a body of six hundred regular cavalry under Colonel Harney, and a battalion under Major Bourneville, a splendid battery of artillery under Captain Washington, of the Fourth United States Artillery, and an Engineer Corps in charge of Robert E. Lee. These batteries, with others under W. T. Sherman and the brave Mississippian, Bragg, who afterwards commanded the Confederate forces at Chickamauga, with two other volunteer batteries, were what gave the Battle of Buena Vista to the American side with less than five thousand men against twenty thousand Mexicans."*

Although the climate of San Antonio seemed both healthful and delightful, there was much sickness among the men. Captain Dickey found it necessary to resign on account of ill health and returned home on September 28th. B. M. Prentiss was made Captain in his place, and W. H. L. Wallace took his place as First Lieutenant and Adjutant of the regiment. In writing to some friends from Camp Crockett, on September 23d, Wallace says:

"I have been so busy latterly that I fear the news is all written. M— and some of the rest of the boys spend most of their time in writing letters, journals and so on, but it has been my peculiar fortune in this campaign to be placed constantly in new positions, and before I have fairly learned the duties of one place I find myself in another, so that I am compelled to steal time from these new duties to write letters. I suppose you have heard of my promotion to the position of Adjutant of the regiment. I say it not in the spirit of boasting, but looking back upon my course for the last three or four months I can but be thankful for my good fortune. First a Sergeant of the line, then a Lieutenant and now Adjutant of the First Regiment, truly I have taken a rise!

"But these new places successfully presented new and arduous duties, and in my anxiety to learn to fill my place I have sometimes, perhaps, appeared neglectful of my friends. You will receive this by the hand of Captain Dickey. The cause of his going home is ill health, and no circumstance that has occurred since we left home has caused me more regret than to be deprived of his company. But this climate would kill him in short time. He stuck to it bravely, but it would not do, the only safety for him was in returning as rapidly as possible.

"Our company is now commanded by Captain Prentiss, the late Adjutant, and the best officer in the two regiments."

*William Osman.

CHAPTER IV.

Marching into Mexico.

ON October 2d the First Regiment left San Antonio and crossed the Rio Grande at Presidio. There on the 13th Wallace writes in his journal of meeting General Shields and G. T. M. Davis, and hearing of the hard fighting at Monterey. They continued their march and on the 16th reached San Juan de Navo after twenty-five miles of hard marching with no water. They still continued, and on the 17th and 18th encamped near the mountains for the first time. On the 19th they encamped on a plain near water, but an arid stony country with no wood. From this point an interesting letter is written from Wallace to his father:

"Camp 80 miles west of the Rio Grande,
October 19, 1846.

"As an express starts in the morning for San Antonio, and as this is our only mode of communication with the civilized world, I snatch a moment from other duties to write you. * * * * We have gotten so far into the 'bowels of the land,' that all certain conveyance is cut off. We left San Antonio on the second instant; the last detachment of the division leaves there in a day or two from this time; they may bring some letters; if so, they will be the last from that way; for they will bring along all the public stores, and the route will be abandoned and we enter Mexico, like Cortez, cutting off all possible retreat.

"We passed the Rio Grande on the thirteenth, after a march of twelve days from San Antonio, a distance of one hundred and eighty miles. Six miles distant from the river we passed through a Mexican town of fifteen hundred inhabitants called Presidio. It is a long, straggling street, with mud huts scattered along its sides for near a mile. Three miles out from Presidio we encamped with the advance corps, which had preceeded us five days. We were here joined by General Shields and G. T. M. Davis of Illinois.

General Shields took command of all the infantry, and on the morning of the sixteenth we took up the line of march for Manclova."

While on the march Wallace received a letter from his old friend and mentor, Professor Pickney, who gives his quandom pupil sage advice as to his actions, even in warfare: "Ah! war is a sorry game, which, were people wise, kings would never play at; query, would Presidents? But I said there was a kind of glory in it, good and true, earned as in every state of life, by discharging duty: and that is not to see how often we can kill, how near he can get to the front and thickest of the fight: but to wisely, carefully, humanly consider how, with the least suffering to his friends and foes, he can effect the greatest good to his country? Yes, and to the enemy's, too. Don't lose sight of that, Will. There are men, some good, true, useful,—you are not personally opposed to them nor they to you. You and every man and all the boys in our army are bound to act for their good. The spirit of party raging in the ranks will have a powerful tendency to make you forget that you are anything else but a soldier of the Union: Think of Goldsmith's very just satire on Ed. Burke—

"'Who, born for the Universe, narrowed his mind
And to party gave up what was meant for mankind.'"

On the 20th the army continued their march and reached Los Alamas, a deep and rapid mountain stream which they cross on the 21st. The Santa Rosa Mountains were like a dark cloud in the distant west. On the 24th they passed through the pretty little town of Santa Rosa, and reached Hot Springs on the 28th. On the 30th they encamped three miles from Monclova and on November 2d they marched through the town and camped near there until the 24th of the month. Monclova was the capital of Coahuila and a city of eight thousand inhabitants. From this camping place Wallace writes his father:

"Camp near Monclova, Mexico,
"November 6, 1846.

"I believe I wrote you while on the march from San Antonio, but in the hurry and bustle of new events I have no distinct recollection of what I wrote and from what precise point. These letters seem to me like firing at the moon, the distance is so great and the means of communication so uncertain. Yet I cannot resist the inclination to write whenever I have any time or any thing like an opportunity of sending.

"We are now lying in camp on the edge of the town of Monclova, a place of some eight thousand inhabitants, situated at the foot of a lofty and barren chain of mountain range. In whatever direction you look from the camp the bold or indistinct outlines of these mountains, as they are near or remote, rise like mighty barriers to oppose our progress or our retreat. A stream comes down from the mountain, rushes past the town, supplying innumerable ducts and hydrants watering every part of the town. A broad valley of fine land borders this stream and is dotted here and there with ranches and haciendas (cattle and plain farms), some of them in a fine state of cultivation, covered with luxuriant crops, corn, cotton and sugar cane. All the cultivated lands here require to be irrigated, and for this purpose their fields and farms are intersected with numerous ditches running in every direction. The farms or ranches are generally miserable affairs, with little or no fencing and mud huts, though occasionally we passed one of a superior order. Two days before we reached here we encamped at the Hot Springs, where was the finest hacienda I have seen. The main buildings and out houses, including a sugar house and store, were enclosed by a heavy stone wall twelve feet high, the whole covering a space of seven acres. The place is owned by two brothers, Sanchez, one of whom lives in Saltillo, and the other in the City of Mexico. They own all the county from San Fernando to this place and on to near Saltillo, a scope of country some two hundred and fifty miles in extent. The hacienda is now occupied by Señor Miguel Blanco, a nephew of Sanchez. He works one hundred and sixty servants. I visited every part of the establishment in company with a Texan who speaks Spanish. The quarters of the working people were far inferior to those of the slaves on the Mississippi, but appeared neat and clean as far as could be. A system of slavery exists here which is not an improvement on the slavery in our Southern States. Whenever a man is in debt, his creditor sues him, gets a judgment, and if the debtor has not the means to satisfy it, the creditor may take him as his servant and compel him to work out the debt at the rate of three dollars per month, finding his own clothes. I am told that hundreds of men here enter this kind of service to avoid being drafted into the army.

"Before he can discharge the original debt, they have necessarily contracted others, and thus they continue for years in slavery until old age and hard labor have made them unfit for further service and then they are released to the wretched liberty of a penniless old age. The difference in the classes is as distinctly marked here as in the slave states. The *peons,* or servants, are generally a dark, swarthy, shaggy-haired race, evidently a mixture of Indian and negro, with occasionally a touch of the Spanish blood. The leading men and men of wealth are much whiter and more intelligent in appearance, and some of the women of the upper classes are decidedly beautiful.

"It is difficult to tell their true feelings toward us—some of them confess to be greatly dissatisfied with the rapacity and imbecility of the Central Government, and are very willing to sell us corn and other commodities at about three prices. On the other hand, I have concluded from what I have seen in Monclova that there is a deep feeling of hostility toward us; and I know that Señor Blanco, at the Hot Springs, had assembled a considerable force at his hacienda to oppose our progress, and only disbanded it a few days before our arrival.

"I am informed by a young Spaniard, a resident of Monclova, who speaks English, that the priests exerted their utmost influence to raise the people against us, representing us as a plundering band with whom their property and families would be ruined. Thus far, they have nothing to complain of, and indeed, they say themselves that we are not half so great a terror to them as their own armies. From the policy that General Wool has adopted, I think we will not give them any reason to complain. We pay them their own price for every thing we get from them, and the war thus far is more injury to us than to Mexico.

"General Shields thinks all these northern provinces are ripe for revolution. He came up from Metemoras to Presidio and was very kindly received by the authoritives of all the frontier towns, and the feeling he found there is what he bases his presumption upon. But I've no doubt he overestimates the extent of this feeling; if we should meet with any reverses these very fellows who are now so kind and so full of professions of friendship, would be the first to cut our throats. Treachery is a characteristic of the race, and after getting all our money I've no doubt they would shoot us for the sake of our clothes. I don't think they will ever fight us with anything like equal numbers. Taylor's victory at Monterey over a superior force, and that force entrenched, has frightened them. It is said that Santa Ana is now fortifying San Luis Potosi, and if peace is not concluded before the expiration of the armistice General Taylor will push on to that point; and our greatest hope is to join him. Wool is very unpopular with the command; he has quarreled with every field officer in it. His orders are positive and peremptory to go to Chihuahua and take the place. There are two places on the Rio Grande named Presidio and another town in the province of Chihuahua named Monclova. Wool, mistaking his orders, now finds himself after a march of four hundred miles over mountains and rapids and deep rivers as far and some farther from Chihuahua than when at San Antonio, and the route from this place is almost impracticable, and as I said before, our only hope is to be detached from this column and sent to General Taylor, to meet him at Saltillo after the termination of the armistice. General Wool is very old and a very vain man: I do not blame, tho' I pity him. The management of an army in the field is 'above his head,' and the Government and the department is culpably and criminally foolish for putting him in command of a division."

Orders here came to General Wool to turn his column southward and give up the march to Chihuahua. The army left Monclova on the 24th of November, after marching thirty miles one day without water over exceedingly rough roads in narrow passes of the mountains, they reached Parras on December 5th, where Wallace again writes to his father:

"Camp near Parras, Mexico,
"December 8, 1846.

"We reached this place on the fifth inst. after a march of twelve days from Monclova. We left the latter place on the 24th of November, leaving Major Warren with two companies of the First Regiment (Captain Morgan's and Captain Prentiss', formerly Dickey's) and two from the Second Regiment and three companies Arkansas cavalry.

"He had liberal instructions and will no doubt quit himself with honor should anything turn up that requires prompt and vigorous action, for the Major is not the man to back out an inch from any position he assumes. Cool, calm, and determined in everything, he is my beau ideal of an officer. * * * *

"The country between here and Monclova is the most perfect desert. On all sides the rugged and barren heights of the mountains frown upon us and the valley we traveled through is almost as barren, save when a stream is reached which afforded facilities for irrigation.

"Some of the route we marched thirty miles without water. This, with the thermometer at eighty-five at noon, was very hard upon the men, but they stool it like soldiers. On the whole route we saw evidences of the imbecility of the government, ruined ranches, laid waste by the Comanches, and wooden crosses stuck upon the side of the road to mark the place where murder had been committed by Indian or robber, told fearfully what was the state of things in the country. Occasionally we passed a fine rancho where all the evidences of wealth and comfort were found, in one spot, and all around were the most squalid poverty and wretchedness.

"Six miles from this place we passed the most splendid hacienda we have yet seen. It is owned by Don Manuel de Ebarba, a Spanish gentleman educated at the Catholic school in Bardstown, Ky. He is an American in feeling, and when Santa Ana sent to him to collect a contribution the other day, he armed his peasants or slaves and resisted the collectors. We encamped one night within a mile of his house, and in the evening I went with the band of our regiment and gave him a serenade. He invited us in and treated us in the most hospitable manner. He speaks English very well, and I had quite a conversation with him. He says the Comanches trouble him very much, that the government cannot protect the citizens, nor would allow them to protect themselves, that they had taken his arms from him several times, but he had supplied himself again. He expressed himself greatly pleased at the occupation of the country by an American force, and hoped this part of Mexico would be annexed to the United States, at the close of the war.

"His place is the most magnificent affair I ever saw. He has an extensive vineyard and manufactures large quantities of wine and brandy.

"He was very profuse of his liquors which were very fine, as several of our officers can testify. Even the Commanding General was not proof against their seductive influence and returned to camp from his visit to Don Manuel in a decidedly *glorious* state. It is astonishing what an amount of labor has been expended in the improvement of this hacienda. The whole grounds, including about a section and a half, are enclosed by a wall of unburnt brick some twelve to fifteen feet high as a protection against the Indians.

"The house is built in the old Spanish style, with a front of about two hundred feet and a paved court yard inside surrounded by tasteful buildings and filled with flowers and trees and everything in the most substantial style.

"The town of Parras is a better place than any town we have heretofore seen. The houses are of a more tasteful and substantial style, and the inhabitants more like white folks. Many of the 'upper ten thousand' have been in to see us in camp. The ladies ride in heavy carriages drawn by a pair of mules that look like mice hitched to those ponderous vehicles. These carriages are rich in finish and the mules are loaded down with plated trappings, and then a great

Mexican postillion in jack-boots seated astride of the near mule and two footmen mounted behind complete the strange show which every day rolls through our camp.

"We take a few Mexican prisoners, but can learn but little of the movements of the Mexican army. One thing is certain, Santa Ana is lying at San Luis Potosi with a force of thirty or forty thousand men. General Worth is in Saltillo with three or four thousand Americans, and General Taylor is moving on toward San Luis. We will act in conjunction with General Taylor, but will not actually join him before we reach San Luis. We will probably take the route by Durango and Zacaticas to San Luis. From present appearances we will not leave here for a month or six weeks. All the forces left on the road between here and San Antonio and at San Antonio will join us before we move again. I doubt whether we have any more fighting. The Mexican Congress met on the 6th inst. and no doubt they will give the question of peace a speedy consideration. Santa Ana finds great difficulty in subsisting his army, as we are now in the heart of the bread country of Mexico.

"General Wool is as popular as ever. He makes a great display of his feathers, greatly to the amusement of these hidalgos."

The command remained in Parras from December fifth until the seventeenth, when they left for Saltillo, reaching Aqua Nueva, eighteen miles from Saltillo, on the twenty-first, having marched one hundred and twenty miles in four days. From this point Wallace writes to his father:

"Camp at Aqua Nueva,
"December 23, 1846.

"I last wrote you from Parras, where we arrived on the fifth, and where we expected to remain all winter. On the 17th we were lying in camp at that place—all was quiet—the Colonel had gone off with General Wool to look for winter quarters for some of the troops. We had a day or two previous received command from General Taylor to occupy that position—that he had received advices from the department to hold on to what he had acquired in Northern Mexico, but to push no further. All were expecting to spend an inactive month or two there. I had that morning acted as Adjutant of the Day and had returned from guard-mounting and was sitting in my tent writing letters when an express on a foaming horse rode up to the General's quarters and alighted. Soon after the Colonel rode up in haste, dismounted and went straight to the General's marque—but he had scarcely got there before he turned round and came back on a run and before he was half way back halloed to me, 'Adjutant, call up the Sergeants! Give notice to prepare for march immediately!' In two minutes the roar and bustle of preparation was heard in every part of the camp. Tents were struck, wagons loaded, sick men sent off to the hospital in town, and in an hour we were ready to move.

"Then there was 'mounting in hot haste' and we were off on the road to Saltillo. As I rode beside the Colonel at the head of our column I had time to inquire the cause of this movement. Dispatches had been received from General Worth at Saltillo, stating that a large Mexican force had left San Luis Potosi and were within three days' march of Saltillo, and it was supposed that Santa Ana, with the main force was marching upon that place.

"We made a forced march, starting each morning at three o'clock and moving eleven to fourteen hours each day. We accomplished the whole distance (about one hundred and twenty miles) in four days with a train of artillery and baggage wagons amounting to some five hundred, over one of the roughest roads imaginable.

"You can form no idea of the disappointment and chagrin we felt, when arriving here within eighteen miles of Saltillo we learned it was a false alarm, that a body of Mexicans *had been* within three days' march of this place, but nothing further could be learned from them. We are now lying in camp opposite a pass in the mountains through which the San Luis road passes, and commands the only water there is for fifty miles in that direction. The position is said to be a very strong one, but I confess I can not see its strength. The pass in the narrowest part is five hundred yards wide, with sloping hills on either side, and the plain in which we are, and which can be reached without coming within range of our guns, is a most splendid place for cavalry to act; and the Mexican force consists principally of that arm.

"General Wool will not go to Saltillo because Major General Butler is there, and he is fearful of losing his command. If General Butler leaves within a day or two, Wool will go in, for he ranks General Worth, who is stationed there.

"We had quite an excitement on the march about this matter of rank. General Wool preceded us some six to ten miles with the Dragoon and Artillery and we were left to bring up the train and so encamped separately from the General. Colonel Churchill was with us and wanted to assume the command. There is a question that has produced difficulty in the regular army as to the right of staff officers to command unless assigned by the President. On this occasion Colonel Hardin, as the senior officer in the line of the army, took command, and he and Churchill had quite a quarrel—*officially* of course—which ended by Churchill ordering Hardin under arrest, and Hardin laughing at him. The question is still unsettled, and whenever Wool is out of camp Hardin assumes command and all the officers of the line, both regulars and volunteers, recognize him as commander. This annoys Churchill horribly to be ranked and commanded by a volunteer colonel."

"December 24th.

"We have news to-day from Parras that two or three thousand Mexican troops are close to that place. Captain Hoffman, of the Sixth Infantry, has been ordered up, and has left the place. He is now at Potos, thirty-five miles from here.

"Before he left the Comanches had made an attack on the hacienda of Don Manuel Ebarba that I spoke of. Captain Hoffman sent out a detachment of Arkansas men to protect the place. One of them was returning to town and a Mexican attempted to 'lasso' him as they do wild horses. He failed in the first attempt, and before he could repeat it the Arkansite drew up his carbine and killed him.

"We know not what will be our next place of destination. There are rumors of twenty or thirty thousand Mexicans moving upon us in three columns—one to Parras—one here —and another to Victoria. On the other hand it is rumored that the Mexican Congress has passed a resolution proposing to receive a commission to adjust the difficulties between the two countries."

CHAPTER V.

ON THE MARCH TO BUENA VISTA.

CHRISTMAS day the regiment camped at La Encantado and William Osman, a member of the Ottawa company, writes: "After tents were up and in order, the impulse was to take a rest. Our mess had a few gallons of wine left, and having come in possession of a couple of jack rabbits, and our cook having in addition to roasting them concocted a delicious corn pone and a plum pudding out of Mexican figs and raisins, we celebrated Christmas with a state dinner, which Colonel Hardin, Adjutant Wallace and Secretary Goodell honored with their presence." Mr. Wallace writes from this new camp to his father:

"Camp La Encantado, Mexico,
"January 9, 1847.

"Our column is fast breaking up; everybody seems pleased with it. * * * * Major Bourneville's battalion, Sixth Infantry and the Squadron Second Dragoons, were ordered to join General Worth's division and are now on their march to Camargo. * * * * The knowing ones say that all the regular force that can be spared is to be concentrated at some point on the coast for a descent on Vera Cruz. General Scott is in the field, and the 17th inst. is fixed upon for a conference between him and General Taylor at Camargo. There is little doubt but Scott will be governed in a great measure by Taylor. * * * * All the regular troops have left Saltillo except one company of the First Artillery with two howitzers. All we have remaining is Washington's battery, Fourth Artillery, and a squadron First Dragoons. Vera Cruz is the only assailable point in this country. Tampico is of no value, as there is no practicable route for artillery into the interior, the only means of conveyance being by mules.

"The route from here to San Luis Potosi is almost destitute of water and is entirely impracticable at this season of the year. After passing the range of the Bolson Malpini that now rise before us on the south, there is no water for ninety miles. The only season of the year when it can be traversed by an American army is in the summer during or shortly after the rainy season. Mexicans can probably cross it at any time, as they eat nothing and their horses require but little water. And if their animals should all fail, the next drove of mustangs would supply their places. * * * We have no definite rumors of peace. The Mexican people and government seem determined to have another brush at us. I wish we could get a chance to give them a sound thrashing and go home."

On January eleventh Wallace, with his friends, Dr. Herrick and R. E. Goodell, went to Patos, and on their return on the 12th found the camp had moved to Buena Vista, five miles south of Saltillo, and from here Wallace writes to his father:

"Camp San Juan de Buena Vista,
"January 19, 1847.

"Our little camp has been in commotion for several days past in consequence of a rumor that gained credence in camp that a large Mexican force, variously reported from seven to nineteen thousand, was on the march from San Luis Potosi to attack us. Our small command (now reduced to two Illinois regiments, Washington's Artillery, Colonel Yell's Arkansas Cavalry and a squadron of First Dragoons) moved back from the camp at La Encantado, Colonel Yell's regiment was called in from Potos and stationed at La Encantado, two Indiana regiments, a part of General Butler's division, were quartered in the town, and scouting parties were sent out in every direction. * * * We have been in constant readiness night and day for an attack—the cartridge boxes were filled and each night everything was packed in the wagons except the tents and blankets ready to obey the signal agreed on between Generals Wool and Butler, which was the firing of two cannon in town in case the attack was there, and the same here if they came this way. * * * * Major Warren left Monclova yesterday with three of the companies of our regiment and one of the Second, and will probably reach here in six or seven days. We shall then have all told about five thousand effective men—all volunteers except the squadron First Dragoons and the two companies artillery, and we feel fully competent to whip any number of Mexicans from seven to fifteen thousand.

"If we do get into a fight you may expect to hear a good account of the volunteers, for every man feels the necessity of sustaining the insulted and jeered at character of our citizen soldiers—and this is the first opportunity we have had of testing the question fairly—if indeed we shall have a chance now. * * * * But I feel more like it was genuine than I ever have before and such is the general feeling.

"The 17th inst. was the day fixed upon for a conference between Generals Taylor and Scott at Camargo. We have not yet heard the result of that conference, but rumor—that most constant distribution of camp news—says that General Taylor is coming on here to move forward this column to San Luis. All the regulars being called off by Scott when he ordered Worth to the coast looks like serious operations in that direction. If a vigorous attack upon Vera Cruz is contemplated no doubt this column will be ordered further into the interior with a view to force Santa Ana back into the City of Mexico. Vera Cruz being taken, the road lies open to the 'Halls of the Montezumas' and the city is not fortified to any great extent, so that Santa Ana would be bound to evacuate his garrisons at San Luis or lose his capital. Whether we shall be ordered on this duty is doubtful. Our term of service is so near out that in all probability we will be left to garrison the posts along the line. This I fear more than anything else—for of all lives that of a soldier in garrison in a Mexican town is to my conception the most tedious. Far rather would I be on the march, even if we went with the giant strides that we made on the march from Parras.

"I have enough to keep me busy at all times, but the men having little to do incur habits of idleness and dissipation, and it is more trouble to perform an order than when they are worn down by the fatigues of a long march—and then these numerous cases for court martial, in which it is my duty to act as Judge Advocate, and this accumulates business upon my hands.

"Aside from these reasons, the prospect of seeing new places and getting a sight of as much of the country as possible, which is one of the principal reasons for coming, are additional reasons for wishing to be on the move."

Soon after Wallace writes another letter to his father from the same place.

"January 28th, 1847.

"Since I wrote you last our camp has been thrown into considerable excitement by the capture of Major Borland, of the Arkansas Cavalry, and Major Gaines and Captain Cassius M. Clay, of the Kentucky Cavalry. They were sent out with about eighty men as a scouting party, and while out about fifty miles at a hacienda, were surprised and captured by an armed party of Mexicans. * * * * Colonel Yell, with about two hundred men, went out to the place two days ago, but could hear nothing of the party and sent back for leave to remain and garrison the hacienda, which he said he could defend against one thousand Mexicans.

"General Wool sent word for him to return at once, but the express met him on the retreat. Yell's advance had seen a larger force than he thought prudent to meet. * * * * Major Borland was a gallant and energetic officer, and his being caught asleep is a matter of great wonder to those who know him best. Major Gaines is also said to be a good officer, and Cassius M. Clay is well known for his energy and intrepidity. To be so taken without an opportunity of making a gallant defence is most unfortunate. I think the whole thing occured in consequence of their negligence with regard to guards. I know that great laxity in this respect existed in the Arkansas regiment; for when I visited Colonel Yell at Patos, some forty miles from any of our force, and in the immediate vicinity of a Mexican town, owned by a hostile centralist, Sanchez, he had no guard whatever, and I rode into his camp after dark, without being challenged by a single sentinel. General Wool's strictness in the matter had the effect of making Yell and others careless and indifferent when away from the immediate command of the General. * * * *

"General Taylor is coming on here and will be here in a few days with a great part of his force." * * * * The letter continues:

"January 30th, 1847.

"Captain Henry, who went out with Major Borland, has come in. He is a Texan and went out with the party as interpreter. His account of the affair is this: The party under Major Borland, consisting of forty-three officers and men picked from the Arkansas regiment, went out on the San Luis road on the 19th to ascertain the truth of the rumors that had kept our camp on the lookout for the last few days. They reached the Hacienda Incarnatione on the twentieth and on the twenty-first marched thirty-six miles beyond and saw no evidence of an enemy—on the twenty-second they returned to Incarnatione and encamped.

"They had posted a guard, the night was dark and windy and it rained very hard—a very unusual occurrence in this part of Mexico at this season of the year. About twelve o'clock one of the sentries gave notice that he thought he heard the jingling of armor. The party was paraded and scouts sent out, but nothing was discovered. A great part of the force remained up during the night. * * * * When day dawned they discovered a large Mexican force encamped at about a half-mile distant in every direction. They were completely surrounded.

"General Minion, who is in command of a body of Mexican cavalry, having news of the movement of the party from spies, which he found in every ranchero—had made a forced march and came up with them in the night and quietly surrounded them, leaving till daylight the work of convincing them there was no possibility of escape. A flag of truce was sent in and they were required to surrender. * * * * Majors Gaines and Borland, after stipulating that their Mexican guide, who had been compelled to accompany the party, and Captain Henry, who had been a Mier prisoner and escaped—should be treated with humanity, surrendered as prisoners of war. In five minutes the Mexican guide was shot before their eyes.

"On the second day's march Captain Henry became convinced that they intended to shoot him. The field officers by some whim of the Mexican commander, had been allowed to retain their horses and pistols. Major Gaines mounted the Captain on his mare, a noble blooded animal, and taking advantage of a slight gap in the line of guards, darted through and was out of sight before a gun could be fairly leveled at him. He was pursued for near a hundred miles and succeeded in killing two of his pursuers and eluding the remainder.

"At length his noble mare gave out from fatigue and want of water and died in the mountain, he himself, after being out for five days without food, save a rat which he killed with a club, was at length picked up by the pickets at Aqua Nueva.

"Fears are entertained for Major Gaines lest the Mexicans suspect some connivance on his part and should visit on him the punishment for Henry.

"This afternoon the Second Illinois Regiment and Artillery moved into Saltillo, leaving only eight companies of the First in this camp. Three men of Captain Smith's company (Chicago) taking advantage of the interruption of the guard caused by the move, passed out and went down to a rancho two miles from camp and got into difficulties with some Mexicans about liquor and a fight ensued. I had been on duty in a court martial and did not go out to afternoon drill and was sitting in the tent when one of the men came up in breathless haste and said three of our men were killed. The Colonel was out drilling and had gone with the regiment up the valley two miles. I collected a few men and went out to the rancho and after a short search found one of the men lying in a deep gully with a number of large rocks piled on him. I leaped into the ditch, rolled off the stones and discovered that he still showed signs of life. We lifted him out and arrested all the Mexicans we saw and brought them into camp. By the time we reached camp we had about thirty.

"We assorted our motley crew of prisoners, having detained four of them who were recognized by our wounded men. White, the man whom I found in the ditch, is better, and it is thought he will survive. Fenton and Hodge, the other two, are injured, but not seriously.

"It was a curious scene, that, sifting and selecting by moonlight, each man as he was called on doffing his broad sombrero and turning his copper visage to the moon, dropping his dingy blanket from his chin, to bear the scrutiny of the injured man.

"Among the crowd of prisoners, miscellaneously gathered, was an Alcalde, a haciendado (proprietor of a hacienda) a woman and three young bloods from Saltillo, who had come out with white jackets and silver hat bands to a *fandango,* which was about commencing—an old peon and his four sons, besides a crowd of ragged and filthy looking wretches who showed by their faces they were awfully frightened.

"We had another *stampede* last night, but we are getting used to these alarms and don't mind them much now.

"General Wool has moved his quarters into town and Colonel Hardin is in command of this camp."

On February fifth "General Taylor arrived from Monterey with Jeff Davis' Mississippi regiment, a couple of Indiana infantry regiments, May's squadron, an Arkansas regiment of volunteers, Bragg's and Sherman's batteries. General Worth, also with nine hundred regulars, and two splendid batteries, was at Saltillo, but these just as Santa Ana was known to be swooping down on Taylor with an overwhelming force were strangely and most unaccountably ordered away to join the army General Scott was organizing for his famous march on the City of Mexico. Taylor, who was now left with but a trifle over four thousand men, and these mainly 'unbaptised' volunteers, was consolingly advised to seek safety by falling back on Monterey." (W. Osman).

On the tenth the command in which was Adjutant Wallace, moved to Aqua Nueva, twenty miles south of Saltillo, from which point he writes his father:

"Aqua Nueva, February 14, 1847.

"On the 10th our regiment left the camp at San Juan de Buena Vista and encamped here, where nearly all the troops of the division are now concentrated under Gen. Taylor. General Wool has immediate command of all except the Mississippi Riflemen, two companies artillery and Colonel May's squadron of Dragoons, which remain under the immediate command of General Taylor.

"Our division consists of the two Illinois regiments, two Indiana and one Kentucky infantry. The Arkansas and Kentucky cavalry and a squadron Second Dragoons and Washington's artillery. The force all told, amounts to some six thousand. Wool's division is encamped about a mile from Taylor's."

"February 20th.

"Another *stampede* on hand. The camp is filled with news of Mexicans in the neighborhood. Major Warren, who is in command at Saltillo, has received *certain* information two or three times that a large force was in the immediate vicinity. Night before last he wrote to General Wool that the attack was about to commence simultaneously on Saltillo and this camp. General Wool sent word to General Taylor, who is encamped about a mile from us. The old fellow got up cross, rubbing his eyes and swearing, 'Let 'em come! Let Santa Ana come and I'll whip him like a sack!'

"The only thing that seems to indicate a movement of the Mexicans in this direction is the circulation of these various and contradictory reports. If Santa Ana should come on our rear with a large force and cut off our communication with the Rio Grande, they might give us some trouble."

On the 21st they struck tents and moved to Buena Vista, from where they heard firing in the night. At eleven o'clock they got up and began entrenchments on the right of the pass. The express came in and stated that the pickets had been fired on in pass Aqua Nueva. The battle came on the following day.

CHAPTER VI.

Battle of Buena Vista.

THE battle occurred on February twenty-second. In a letter written a week afterwards to George Green, of Ottawa, Mr. Wallace gives a minute account of the battle:

"Camp Taylor, 20 miles south of Saltillo, Mexico.
"March 1, 1847.

"Dear George:

"I've seen the elephant in every attitude, walking, running, at bay and fighting! You will doubtless, before receiving this, have seen full particulars of the battle of Buena Vista.

"It is a terrible thing, this fighting. And until forty-eight hours before the enemy came in sight, I did not believe we should ever see them. On Saturday evening the twentieth, we were lying in camp just where we now are. Rumors of various kinds were afloat with regard to the Mexican army, but we had had plenty of that sort of thing, I did not credit them until that time. A picket sent out thirty miles towards San Luis, reported that he had seen them in immense numbers. This was the first time they had been *seen* by white men, and for the first time I believed they were coming. It was not fear, and yet it was more like fear than anything I ever felt, during the heat of the action when bullets flew thick as rain around me.

"On the twenty-first we fell back to Buena Vista, which is five miles this side of Saltillo.

"The First Regiment encamped at a narrow pass on the road, where a deeply washed gully approached within a few feet of a considerable hill. That night we threw up a redoubt commanding the pass, which was the only practical road for artillery. On the morning of the twenty-second we commenced erecting a breastwork of stone and earth on the hill in front of our camp. About ten o'clock the head of the Mexican column appeared in sight. They moved up in immense numbers and formed on a hill two miles in front of us—(I send you a rough sketch of the country in the vicinity of Saltillo, also one on a larger scale of the scene of the engagement, to which last I refer you by numbers for a description of the fight.)

"The head of the Mexican column rested near the main Mexican battery. (No. 1). They continued to move up and form on that height till sunset. About twelve M. three horsemen bearing a white flag rode up the road toward our lines. They were met by a like party from us with an interpreter. They met and in a moment one of our horsemen dashed off like a dart toward our lines, rode up to General Taylor, who, with his staff, was then standing by our battery at the pass.

"The messenger brought a very polite note from the great Santa Ana himself, informing General Taylor that he had twenty-one thousand men and forty pieces of artillery, and as a means of sparing the effusion of human blood, he requested old 'Rough and Ready' to surrender!

"To this modest request Old Zack replied, 'Come and take us!' The First Regiment was then in position at the 'breastworks' on the hill, that is six companies—two in the 'redoubt' supporting Washington's battery, six pieces of which were then drawn up in the valley at No. 1, and two companies, A and I, were in Saltillo forming a part of the garrison of that place under Major Warren.

"The top of the hill where the 'breastwork' was erected, is some three hundred feet above the valley, where the camp lay and a very steep ascent. From the 'breastworks' to the foot of the mountain on the east is a rise of about one foot in twelve and generally smooth, except where broken by ravines, as represented.

"The point at the Mexican Battery, No. 3, commands the whole plateau above the ravine. The ravines were deep near their mouths and grew less so as you advanced toward their heads. The ground broken by deep washes is one of the roughest, wildest scenes imaginable; and the Deep Gully running off to the west, opposite the Mexican Battery No. 1, is thirty feet deep and impassable, so there was no danger of an approach from that side, unless the enemy should send a party to cut a road. To prevent this the Kentucky Infantry and Sherman's Battery were sent across and took position at No. 2. * * * * The 'First' was disposed as above described. Colonel Hardin commanding on the hill, and 'Old Buck' in the redoubt.

"The Second Illinois was drawn up at No. 3, the two Indiana regiments on the hill at No. 4, the mounted regiments near them—the Mississippi Riflemen further toward the mountains on the left of the Indiana troops, Bragg's battery in the rear, ready to take any position which might be required. This was the state of things when Santa Ana's note came in.

"For two hours nothing was done. Each lay off and watched the other. Our engineers were scattered about on the different hills taking note of the enemy. About two o'clock they commenced sending a column of light troops toward the mountain and they were seen scattered along the face of the hill. The Mississippi and Indiana Riflemen were sent to meet them on the mountain. At four o'clock the skirmishing commenced on the side of the mountain at No. 5. Santa Ana, who, if he is a coward, has at least some of the attributes of a great general, had seen the advantage of the position at the Battery No. 3—an advantage that had been overlooked by our engineers, though the ground had been frequently reconnoitered. A very large body of light troops under the command of Ampudia was sent into the mountains for the purpose of turning our left flank and gaining this position. The firing was sharp on both sides, but the Mexicans rather got the better of it. They outnumbered us two to one—and clambered up the mountain until they were almost directly over our skirmishers. In the meantime the Mexicans had planted their Battery at No. 1, and three pieces of Washington's, under the command of Lieutenant O'Brien, were dragged up by our men at the head of the hollow by the 'spring' and took position on the plateau. A few shots were fired from a Mexican twenty-four pounder at Battery No. 1, some of the shells falling near our battery, but doing no damage.

"The whole scene during the afternoon was highly exciting. The skirmishing on the mountain was in full view of both armies, and when our party gained any little advantage, the most tremendous cheering would follow from every regiment and corps. This hallooing, some of the Mexican prisoners say, annoyed them terribly, for they thought it useless to fight against men who *fought for fun.* The rattling of the musketry, the wreaths of smoke, the cloud that occasionally gushed from the mouth of the twenty-four pounder, followed at a short interval by its tremendous thunder, the battalioned hosts on either side, and last but not least, a beautiful *rain-bow* in the N. E. almost in our rear, seeming to hold out to us a brilliant hope, all conspired to render the scene inexpressibly grand.

"The skirmishing continued till dark and even after dark, an occasionel flash far up the mountain and the boom of a musket showed that light was all that was wanted to renew the conflict.

"Our regiment remained in its position during the night. I went down to camp and got my blankets and lay down with Colonel Hardin at the Breastworks. About eight o'clock I was up looking around and saw a flash and then a report at the foot of the hill in front of our battery where we had posted a picket. They soon came in with a prisoner —a *real live Mexican soldier*—this was the first one we had seen at close hand—he was one of a small reconnoitering party sent out to look at our position—the others were killed.

"During the night Washington's battery was drawn within the pass and a bank thrown up to protect it. I stood guard on the hill alternately with the Colonel all night. Just before daybreak it was my watch. I saw flashes and heard reports near the gully at No. 6—it was the pickets of the two armies lying close together all night, and firing upon each other as soon as light showed an object. As the light increased the skirmishing recommenced on the mountain.

"A heavy Mexican column was formed and made a movement to march up the road. As they came opposite the ruined rancho and were uncovered by the hill near the deep gully, Washington opened his battery upon them. The first shell fell short but the next fell in the ranks of the heavy column and the effect was terrible. It opened a gap wide and long, and fragments of men and horses were seen flying in the air. The column *deployed to the right double quick* and gained the cover of the hill in front. It moved up toward our left and formed near the mountain. A heavy battery of sixteen pounders was then planted, forming 'Mexican Battery' No. 2. O'Brien in the meantime had been *making it lively* on the mountain—he threw a few shells among the Mexican skirmishers on the mountain and silenced the whole division, which had been playing a lively tune all morning.

"About eight o'clock the engineers reported a heavy column moving up along the foot of the mountain on our left, supported by a large body of lancers and under the cover of Battery No. 2. The Second Illinois was ordered up to support O'Brien, who was threatened by the advance of the Mexican column along the foot of the mountains. Colonel Bissell moved up with seven companies—two of his being in town and the others having gone as skirmishers to support the Mississippians. The Kentucky Infantry were also ordered up from the other side of the deep gulley.

"When the Second Illinois had reached a point near No. 7 the whole Mexican line, battery and all, opened a murderous fire upon them. I was then standing on the breastwork in full view of the fight and watched with intense anxiety the Blue Banner of the Second enveloped as it was in wreaths of sulphurous smoke. It continued to fly, and as the Mexican column advanced firing, they opened their fire, and such a peal as rang along the ranks of the gallant Second had not before been heard on the field. They sustained the fire of that column, which must have been eight or ten thousand, for twenty minutes. Colonel Churchill then rode up and ordered them to fall back, which they did in good order, though their ranks were woefully thinned.

"By this time the Kentucky Infantry had reached the field and commenced their fire. The Second were slowly retiring. Bragg's and Sherman's batteries had come up and opened a fire, but still the Mexican column advanced. All this time Colonel Hardin was keen and anxious to be ordered onto the plateau. A heavy Mexican column, drawn up near their Battery No. 1, threatened the road—but did not advance. At length about nine-thirty o'clock we got orders to move up to support the Kentucky Infantry on the right. Colonel Hardin moved out with four companies, leaving two in position at the breastworks. At the head of the ravine, No. 8, we encountered the first fire. We were advancing toward No. 7 when a heavy force concealed in that ravine, opened a fire on our flank. The Colonel wheeled his command to the right—ordered a 'charge bayonets,' and we moved up in line and soon started the game. They could not stand the cold steel. This was the only time the bayonet was resorted to during the engagement. The Mexicans broke and fled in disorder across that ravine and the next one and our boys following at a run and pouring in a hot fire.

"In that ravine we killed, wounded and captured about one hundred and fifty of the 'Hombres'. Taken in all, that charge was the most brilliant thing of the day.

"In the meantime the heavy Mexican column had turned our left, and a large body of infantry and lancers had crossed the ravine near the Mexican Battery No. 3. The First moved across the plateau to the ravine at No. 9 and were there ordered to support Bragg's battery, which was playing upon a force which was then planting the Battery No. 3. The lancers who had crossed the ravine about this time, made a charge on the Rancho Buena Vista, where they had learned our stores were.

"I am informed that Santa Ana in a speech to his forces that morning before the action, told them that he had nothing to give them to eat, that two hours' fighting would secure all our stores and we had plenty. The charge of the lancers was a most desperate one. They were in a starving condition and fighting for their breakfasts. They were gallantly met by the Arkansas and Kentucky cavalry, who repulsed them with considerable loss, but in the charge Colonel Yell fell. The lancers were divided and a part of them driven down across the gully west of the Ranche. The others were driven back to the foot of the mountains on the east, where their infantry, reinforced by a large number of Ampudio's light troops, had formed.

"The Mississippi and Indiana regiments were ordered to charge them. The Mexican force were, however, hemmed in by the mounted regiments and the Mississippians and Indianians and brought to a stand at No. 10 about one o'clock; while things were in this position a white flag was seen advancing from Battery No. 3. Bragg held his fire and General Taylor rode up to our position at No. 11 and sent out a party to meet and receive the flag.

"In a few minutes two Mexican officers, one of them an elderly man with a blue jacket and a fur collar, and the other a young olive-colored Spaniard, bedecked with green cloth and gold lace, his lower extremities enveloped in a most magnificent pair of fur leggings—came upon foot, doffed their beavers and said Santa Ana wanted to know 'what General Taylor *wanted!*'

"I was standing close to Old Zack at the time and saw his lips quiver. 'Tell General Santa Ana that I want him and his whole army to surrender and I'll treat them as prisoners of war and I'll give him an hour to determine.' Some of his staff here suggested that the movement might be to gain time and that an hour was too much, so he altered it to half an hour.

"The whiskered and furred and laced gentlemen touched their hats 'Adios, Señors,' and left. In ten minutes the Battery No. 3 opened with renewed vigor upon us and their fire was directed particularly at the *white horse* that Old Zack rode. Their cannonading was tremendous. We were not more than five or six hundred yards from them, and the shower of shots, shells, grape and cannister that hurtled over our heads was anything but music to our ears. One of their shots struck and killed a man and two horses at one of our guns.

"At the same time the column of infantry and lancers at No. 10 commenced retreating slowly along the foot of the mountain under the heavy fire of Battery No. 3. A large body was collected in the head of the ravine in rear of Battery No. 3. Bragg threw a few shells among them and they retreated in confusion along the foot of the moontain in rear of their battery.

"But for the delay occasioned by the flag of truce we

would have captured that whole division, for they could not have held out against the fire that was poured upon them from our lines. We continued our fire upon them until near four o'clock the First covering itself from the Mexican battery under the side of the ravine near No. 9—their volley frequently passing only two or three feet above our heads.

"About four o'clock the Mexican batery No. 3 ceased firing and at the same time Captain Chilton, of the Quartermaster's Department, rode up and told Colonel Hardin that he was ordered to the right to make a charge—that the Dragoons were moving up and he must hurry or he would be too late. We were at that time moving up the ravine on the left of Bragg's and a part of Washington's batteries intending to occupy the position at Mexican battery No. 3. I looked round and saw the Squadron First Dragoons moving up quickly in our rear—on the right of our battery were the fragments of the Second Illinois and the Kentucky Infantry at No. 12. We filed right by the heads of companies and passed through the battery which was still advancing, and came into line again on the right.

"The *First* was then some distance in advance of any other troops in the field, but all were moving forward. Just as we came into line on the right I saw the bayonets of a heavy column over a slight rise near the head of ravine at No. 13, and we had not advanced twenty paces before we received the fire of the column. They were a reserve of about six thousand fresh troops who had not been engaged before and were brought up to cover the retreat of their shattered forces. As soon as we received their fire, we inclined to the right, at a run and gained the cover of the ravine at No. 14. The five companies of the *First* and the shattered fragments of the *Second* then opened their fire. O'Brien, with his pieces, began operations—the Kentucky Infantry came upon our right and the most tremendous firing ensued that ever mortal man conceived! To give you some idea of the perfect torrent of shot, the whistling of the Mexican bullets alone was almost sufficient to drown the report of their guns, tho' they were only fifty yards from us. I kept looking over the edge of the hill to see the charge of our Dragoons, as I wanted to see that very much. But instead of that I saw them turn and leave the field.

"The Mexican column, emboldened by their retreat, advanced upon us, outflanking us on both sides. O'Brien was obliged to fall back, having no troops to support his battery—that vast column flanked by eight hundred lancers moved on—we held our position until they appeared on either flank and the shot poured upon us from all sides. Up to this time the *First* had lost only three men killed. Colonel Hardin, seeing that we were entirely unsupported—that we, little more than five hundred men against seven thousand, and that they outflanked us everywhere—at length reluctantly gave the order to retreat. I stood by him at the time—Colonel Bissell of the *Second*, was with us—I saw from Hardin's countenance that he was troubled. When the men had got half way down the hill, which is steep and long, he ordered a halt, himself standing near the top of the hill. Most of our Illinois regiments halted and formed line, and if we had had the whole of our regiment I've no doubt Colonel Hardin would have charged the Mexican column with the bayonet.

"As it was, the Kentucky regiment was running, and we could muster not more than two hundred and fifty men. He turned again toward the top of the hill, and I turned at the same time and saw the heads of the advancing foe within ten paces of us. The Colonel turned and said it was no use, and again gave the order to retreat. We all started and when I got to the bottom of the ravine I turned and looked back—the balls were falling like hail around us—the whole brink of the hill where we had just stood and on either side was lined with Mexican Infantry in their long, tall hats, bedecked with tinsel, and their blue overcoats streaming in the wind;—and what was more interesting to us just then, their long glittering muskets pointing directly at us as if they were really trying to *shoot us*. They are most miserable shots or they would have killed every one of us huddled as we were in utter confusion, officers and men in the bottom of that narrow ravine forming a focus for their shot poured from the top of the hill in rear and on either flank. The bullets struck the rock close about me and one spent ball struck me on the shin—but I did not notice it till next day. I dodged when a few of the first ones whistled close to my ear; but soon came to the conclusion that it was no use to dodge—if I got shot it was my bad luck and if I didn't, it was my good luck. So I determined to run *my luck* and I stood square up to plain, straight-forward running.

"About half way down the ravine I tread upon a rolling rock and sprained my ankle; at the same time I dropped a horse pistol that I was carrying in my sword belt. Just then I cast my eyes up to the top of the hill on my left and saw several lancers riding at full speed toward the mouth of the ravine, and I knew their object was to cut off our retreat. I turned and walked back and picked up my pistol, thinking I might have occasion to use it. I ran on and when I reached the mouth of the ravine, the lancers were pouring over the point of the hill at No. 15, yelling and cussing in Spanish like devils. I had just rounded the point at No. 16 when Washington's battery opened upon the lancers.

"The first shell whistled close to me and burst within fifty yards of me. I've heard many sweet sounds—the voices of lovely women and the melodious breathings of sweet instruments, but the whistling of that shell was the most grateful sound that ever greeted my ear. It was terrible; the main body of the lancers scampered back over the hill, leaving their colonel and several of their comrades dead. A small detachment of forty or fifty took shelter in the mouth of the ravine, and it was they that killed nearly all that fell of our regiment. Colonel Hardin fell by their hands, so did Colonel McKee and Lieutenant Colonel Clay (a son of old Henry's.") [Adjutant Wallace is too modest to relate that when Colonel Hardin was killed he rallied the remnant of the regiment and led it to safety.]

"Colonel Hardin was found half an hour afterwards at No. 17 lanced through the body in four places, his pockets rifled, his sword gone and a Mexican lance, cut nearly in two by a blow of his sabre, lying by his side. All who had been wounded by the heavy fire in the ravine and were able to crawl to the mouth of the ravine were there butchered by those infernal lancers.

"After Washington's battery opened I took it more leisurely—in fact, I was too much exhausted to run further. We had been on the field for more than six hours—the ground over which we had just run was rough, and I was barely able to reach the point at the battery—crawled round the point of the hill and lay down completely exhausted. I had just done so when the Mexican Battery No. 1 opened a tremendous fire of twenty-four pound shot and shells—they flew thick, tearing up the earth and stone on the point of the hill and raising a cloud of dust around me. I lay still, however, until I got my breath, then went to the top of the hill to the breastwork just as Colonel Weatherford was going out with our three fresh companies, to resist the charge of a column that threatened us from a position near Mexican Battery No. 3. He took post at the head of the ravine No. 18 and was soon joined by Colonel Lane's Indiana regiment. A few scattering shots were fired, the sun went down and it grew dark and parties remained in position.

" 'Our bugles sang truce and the night cloud had lowered.' I went down with Colonel Weatherford to our camp to get something to eat and some blankets to lie upon, for I did not expect to sleep much. We found the camp, and especially my tent, crowded with wounded. I was surprised at the coolness of my feelings as I looked upon the ghastly wounds and shattered limbs and heard the deep stiffled groans of my suffering countrymen. But the fight was not yet over. I felt then an absolute certainty that we should have to re-enact the scenes of to-day as soon as light came.

"I got a blanket from a friend and again went on to the hill. There was no moon, a slight breeze rustled the flag close to me, around lay the forms of our wearied men reposing in their blankets on their arms—across the hills to the front the fires of the enemy's camp burned brightly; and occasionally as the breeze rose and lulled, I could hear the creaking of wheels and the noise of some movement. This confirmed me in the belief that we should have another and a harder fight in the morning. I imagined that I could see a column moving down the road, and I was certain they were planting heavy ordnance on the hill in front of us to command our position. I believe that every man of our command had determined to die on that hill. I felt there was nothing for us but victory or death. We had seen enough through the day to convince us we had no quarter to expect. Our wounded friends butchered in cold blood—the savage ferocity of the lancers cut off all hope in that quarter. Retreat was equally impossible. A body of two thousand lancers had entered through the Palomas pass and were hovering about town, and had been slightly engaged during the day with a detachment from town. We had reason to believe that larger bodies had been sent toward Monterey, and what I have since ascertained to be the case, the mountains and valleys on either side of us were filled and covered with rancheros from all the neighboring towns and settlements—even as far as Parras and Monclova, watching the result of the fight and ready to participate in the pillage and slaughter of our defeat.

"Under all these circumstances courage was no virtue, or at least a *virtue* of necessity. With these thoughts and feelings I lay down with Colonel Weatherford. Neither of us spoke. But my fatigue soon overcame me and I went to sleep and slept till near daylight. I got up, the Mexican fires burned dim, and most of them were entirely out. I could hear no noise, but thought I could discover a cloud of dust far up the road. I could not then hope they were gone. I stood upon the breastwork, looking out keenly—day broke—it grew gradually light. I looked to the foot of the mountain at Battery No. 3 and thought I could see the dim outlines of the column that rested there at dark the night before. The light increased and I saw what I had taken for a column to be a row of palmetto. I looked up the road and saw distinctly the dust of their retreating column. Oh, what a feeling of relief came over me. I set up a shout of *victory*—it was a mockery, however, I had the day before felt very much as I should suppose a *whipped* man would feel—and I've no doubt—*inter nos*—had it been just as convenient for us, as for Santa Ana to *vamos* we would have been off for Monterey.

"But no matter for that, we were in possession of the field—the enemy was retiring, leaving his dead and wounded, or a large portion of them, on the ground.

"During the night Major Warren's command had come up from town and taken post with Colonel Weatherford's detachment. After breakfast I walked up onto the plateau. I felt a curiosity to see the effect of our fire at the head of the ravine at No. 14. I thought during the time we were engaged that our men were firing too high, and I gave them orders to 'shoot low.' On the plateau I met with our Ottawa boys. They had lain all night on the field, though not there during the fight. They were all as anxious as tigers, but I'm rather glad they were not there, for we should have had some of them to bury, without materially altering the result. I walked over the field with some of them. Such a scene. I shall not attempt to describe it. At the head of the Ravine No. 14 a pile of dead Mexicans showed the fatal efficacy of our fire, and nearly all were shot through the head.

"We collected the wounded, who were suffering awfully from hunger and thirst as well as their wounds, and sent them to hospitals in town. During the day we collected and buried our dead, amounting to two hundred and seventy. The remains of Colonels Hardin, McKee and Clay were taken to Saltillo and there interred. The wounded, both American and Mexican, were collected and cared for in the hospitals there.

"It was amusing to see our volunteers when the poor miserable famished Mexicans were brought in—for we took a large number of prisoners through the day. 'D— them,' they would say, 'they ought to have their throats cut, but let's give the poor devils something to eat,' and it was a treat to see them eat. They had been in a half starving condition during their forced march from San Luis Potosi. When coffee and biscuit were placed before them they showed even in their famished state some signs of surprise and gratitude. This was the greatest victory of all, a victory unstained by blood and the feelings for its success unchecked by any mournful thoughts.

"The Mexican loss in killed, wounded and missing must

have been at least three thousand. Our loss in killed, two hundred and seventy, in wounded, four hundred and sixty. Taken all in all, it was the Waterloo of the continent. Never were our arms successfully engaged against such fearful odds. And then it was a volunteer fight, and the brightest commentary on free institutions that the age affords. Aside from the artillery, all the fighting was done by the citizen soldiery. May's and Stein's gaudy dragoons constituted the pomp and pride, while the volunteer forces made up the 'circumstance' of the glorious fight.

"An effort is now being made by the regular officers to get up the impression that we had greatly the advantage in position. Whatever advantage of position we had, was the result of our fortification at the pass, and but for Colonel Hardin's earnest request we would not have had that—and that was all lost as soon as the Mexicans gained the position at Battery No. 3. That point commanded the whole field and that battery raked our breastwork on the hill and shells fell and burst in our camp. You will also see by my description that at one time we were nearly surrounded. Where was the advantage of position then? No! nothing but the bull-dog courage and perseverance of the volunteers saved the day.

"And then in generalship, Santa Ána had greatly the advantage. Our forces were sent into action one detachment at a time and might easily have been cut off in detail. The seven companies of the Second Illinois Regiment met the shock of their main charge alone. Was this generalship? Old Zack and Wool both have personal courage, but in all the qualities of generalship they are wofully deficient. Colonel Hardin was more of a military genius than any general on the field. He reconnoitred the ground between our position and the mountain on the morning of the twenty-second, and was engaged in it when the enemy came in sight. As soon as he returned he said to me, 'The fight will be up there' pointing to the plateau, 'the enemy will never attempt this pass while they can come there.'

"They may try to disparage the brilliancy of the achievement by such means, but they can't do it, and this victory is another severe blow on the regular army.

"I have given my feelings and thoughts, freely and unvarnished, and have endeavored to give an accurate account of the whole affair. It is difficult for even an eye-witness to give all the details of so extended a field as that was, especially if he himself was engaged, and then there were frequently impediments to one's seeing all that was going on,—for instance while one was lying in a ravine close to the ground with a shower of grape splitting the air three feet above him, it was difficult to tell exactly what was going on on the other side of the hill.

"But I have gathered items and compared notes with others engaged in different parts of the field, and believe my account to be substantially correct. * * * * * *

"March 13th. I have been writing the above between times as I could snatch a moment from other duties, which are arduous just now. Eaton being in town I have no help and a great deal of writing to do. * * * * *

Most sincerely yours—

W. H. L. WALLACE.

CHAPTER VII.

THE ILLINOIS TROOPS RETURN HOME. WALLACE ENDEAVORS TO REËNTER THE ARMY.

SOON after the battle of Buena Vista new officers were elected to fill the places of those slain in the battle. On February twenty-seventh the command moved to Aqua Nueva by General Taylor's order, but returned to Buena Vista on the tenth of March from where the following letter was written:

"Camp Buena Vista, March 14, 1847.

"DEAR FATHER: I wrote you from this place a day or two after the battle. On the twenty-sixth we had an election to fill vacancies in our regiment. Colonel Weatherford was unanimously elected Colonel to fill Colonel Hardin's place. Major Warren was elected Lieutenant Colonel and Captain Richardson, Major. Our new Major is a prince of good fellows and a man of splendid talents.

"On the twenty-seventh we moved to Aqua Nueva. A day or two afterwards a detachment was sent out to Incarnatione, a hacienda forty miles toward San Luis. They found the place filled with dead and wounded Mexicans, but no armed force. General Taylor sent out wagon loads of provisions as they were in a starving condition. * * * The Mexicans all say Santa Ana's prospects are ruined. He has written to the Governor of Saltillo that he was compelled by Congress to fight this battle against his wishes, without supplies, and that the disgrace of the defeat must rest where it properly belongs—that he would have nothing to do with the future military movements of the Mexican Government.

"I saw our old friend Don Manuel Evara from Parras. He says Santa Ana is moving directly for the City of Mexico, that a rupture between him and the Mexican Congress is anticipated. That battle was a terrible blow to the Mexicans. Santa Ana had displayed the most consummate generalship in the disposition of his troops. He knew to a man our numbers and brought enough with him as anyone would have reasonably supposed to crush us. He had sent strong detachments of horse to intercept communication between here and Monterey and between Monterey and the Rio Grande, and all these different columns reached their destination the same day. Had he succeeded in defeating us here, we would have been cut off from all retreat. The mountains and valleys on every side of us were covered and filled with armed rancheros from even as far as Parras and Monclova, watching the result of the battle and eager to join the pillage and slaughter of our defeat. On the field that day he exhibited the keenest sagacity in detecting and seizing upon the advantages of the ground, advantages that had been overlooked by our commanders, although the ground had been frequently examined.

"We returned here on the tenth and are fortifying our old position. Your affectionate son,

W. H. L. WALLACE."

A letter written by T. Lyle Dickey of Ottawa on March 15, 1847, tells something of the sentiment toward the volunteers in Illinois. After speaking of the rumors they had received of an approaching battle of which they seemed to know nothing definite, he says: "And we are waiting anxiously to hear of your glorious exploits. If you have had a great fight, while we rejoice that you have had a field to shine upon, we tremble lest some of our best loved brothers may have fallen, a few days must tell the story. * * * * There are oft repeated expressions of interest in the welfare of the volunteers. * * * * I don't mean that such interest is manifested by everybody, not so. On the contrary in the minds of most people in the State of Illinois there is a proneness to laugh at and ridicule every man who has entered the army. I attribute this to the jealousy of aspirants who wish to protect against the future popularity of such. The ladies are generally with you and a host of personal friends."

The army remained near Saltillo over three months and on the eighth of May the troops left for Monterey, where they encamped and gradually one regiment after another was discharged and sent home when their year's term of enlistment ended. In June the *First* was discharged, and the soldiers returned north in time to spend the Fourth of July at their homes.

Mr. Wallace returned to his home in Ottawa, Illinois, but his taste of military life had given him a strong inclination to reënter the Army. Before leaving Mexico his friends had written to Washington in his behalf. The following letter from Colonel Sylvester Churchill, Inspector General United States Army, was one of these:

Ins. Gens. Dept. Army.
"Aqua Nueva Mex. March 8th, 1847.

"SIR:—Having been with and witnessed the good conduct of Lieutenants William H. L. Wallace and William Erwin of the First regiment Illinois Volunteers (late Colonel Hardin's) for nearly all the time since I mustered them into service at Alton last July and observed their ardor and gallantry at the battle of Buena Vista the 22d and 23d inst., I have sincere pleasure in recommending them to the favorable consideration of the President for the appointment of lieutenants in any new regiment afoot which may be raised. I have the honor to be
"With great respect
"Your mo. obt. serv't
"S. CHURCHILL,
"Ins. Gen."

"TO HON. W. L. MARCY
Secretary of War
Washington D. C.

Major W. A. Richardson returned home and entered into the practice of law. He was soon after elected to Congress from the Fifth Congressional District by a very large majority. He served eleven years in the House of Representatives and two years in the Senate. Mr. Wallace wrote asking his aid in getting a commission in the Army. Major Richardson answers the letter in August 1847, as follows: "Judge Douglas has promised to write to Washington for you and Erwin and I have written to Erwin to get Wentworth to do the same, which I think he will do without hesitation. * * * * Let me hear from you for I assure you I take interest in all your movements and recur now as I hope I ever shall to our associations with pleasure.

"I am truly your friend
" W. A. RICHARDSON."

Mr. Wallace thinking his applications at Washington for appointment in the army were not being attended to wrote and asked for them to be returned to him, and received the following letter from Judge Young, then Senator from Illinois.

"WASHINGTON CITY, August 19, 1847.

"DEAR SIR:—Yours dated at Mount Morris July 30th, requesting me to withdraw the letters of recommendation forwarded to my care from Mexico, has been received, and I now return them to you as requested.

"I regret to perceive at the close of your letter the belief expressed by you that these recommendations, which were certainly highly creditable to your standing as an officer, had not received from me that attention which was proper on such an occasion, and especially from an Illinoisan.

"The moment I received these communications I hastened with them to the War Department and called the attention both of the President and Secretary of War to the particular merits of your case, and the highly respectable character of the recommendations, and urged the propriety of your appointment to some permanent situation in the army worthy of your acceptance.

"I was answered that there were then no vacancies, but your merits and claim to some such appointment was fully admitted and your papers placed on file, with the promise that you should be provided for, as soon as a suitable situation could be procured for you.

"There was no vacancy in the Quartermaster's Department from our State.

"The only hope therefore was to get you an appointment in the regular army—this I have endeavored to do, but so far without success. * * * * * * There are many applications from our State for office, many more than you would suppose—and but few can be gratified out of the many under existing circumstances.

"The appointments from Colonel down, in our volunteer regiments are made by the volunteers themselves, * * * and when there is a vacancy in the regular army, if it is above Second Lieutenant, it is filled by *promotion*, so that the only place to be had for an original appointment is that of Second Lieutenant—and then we have to contend with numerous applications from the other States, as well as the cadets from the Military Academy at West Point.

"I take this opportunity of sending to you some blank forms for land warrants. A warrant for 160 acres will sell here for $130 only, which may be regarded as the current price in this city.

I am very respectfully
RICHARD M. YOUNG."

Lieut. W. H. L. Wallace,
Ottawa, Ills.

In October Mr. Wallace received a letter from W. A. Richardson in regard to the foregoing affairs:

"DEAR WALLACE:—"I received in due time your last letter and reply I am sorry you said anything to Judge Young that wounded his feelings, for Young is a clever man and has influence at Washington and I am satisfied he did everything to procure for you a situation.

"I received a letter from the Department saying that at present no appointments could be made from Illinois for the reason that we had our full share which was a source of regret to me and the withdrawal of your application may enable some other person to get the first vacancy that may occur. I know that Judge Ralston will resign, if he has not done so, this fall and I had hopes that I could get some friend in his place, and I have no fears but that by spring I could get you an appointment, as vacancies are daily occurring in the line of deaths, resignation, etc.

"The war is not closed and will not be for some time, more troops will be called for and in less than six months you can, I think, get back to Mexico. I may be mistaken I will see what I can do for you.

"Write to me at Washington, as I leave in a few days."

Mr. Wallace answers the letter as follows:

"OTTAWA Ill. Nov. 23, 1847.

"MY DEAR FRIEND:—"I received your last just before you left for Washington and was gratified by the kind attention. I shall write to Judge Young immediately, making apologies for my rashness, as I find I was mistaken in one respect, that the appointment of the officers in the ten new regiments were made before he got my papers and I shall trust somewhat to you 'to make it all right with him.'

"I believe with you that the war is not yet closed, and all I want is an early chance in! I hope you may be able to get me something in the way of an appointment anything from a Quartermaster to a Major General. I'm not particular, though I should prefer a commission in the line.

"I enclose the recommendations forwarded last spring.

"Most sincerely your friend,

W. H. L. WALLACE."

"HON. W. A. RICHARDSON."

The delay in receiving an appointment dragged on until the war with Mexico came to an end so the wish for military service was no longer desired. Mr. Wallace did not dream that when he penned the above asking in jest for a Major General's commission that but fifteen years later in an eminently greater battle than Buena Vista fought in his own country and against his own countrymen he would be in command of a division with the rank of a Major General.

The Mexican war was the school that trained many of the great generals that distinguished themselves in the Civil War, Lee, Grant, Sherman, Bragg, Prentiss, and many others, Lieutenants in one war, Generals in the next.

Mr. Wallace now settled in Ottawa and returned to the practice of the law, becoming a strong man in his profession and in his standing and influence in the community.

He became State's Attorney in 1852 of the Ninth Judicial District, then embracing three or four counties, filling this rather exacting position with honor and ability for four years. He thus became widely known. Hon. Wm. Cullen in speaking of him as a lawyer says: "Having chosen the law as his profession he made it his chief study and he held the cause of his clients a sacred trust. In the preparation and trial of cases he gathered in all the law applicable to the case and was never taken by surprise by the opposing counsel. Because of his close application and ability ere he had practiced one decade he ranked with the first men of the bar in La Salle County then famed for the many able lawyers it embraced."

Mr. Wallace was a devoted member of the Masonic order. He belonged to Occidental Lodge No. 40 of Ottawa, and was Master of this Lodge during the years 1848 and 1849. The first charter given to the Ottawa Lodge was from Kentucky in 1840 with the number 114. When the Grand Lodge of Illinois was organized in 1841, the Ottawa Lodge was dissevered from the jurisdiction of the Grand Lodge of Kentucky and because part of the Grand Lodge of Illinois, as Occidental Lodge No. 40, with John D. Caton installed as Master.*

* From W. L. Milligan's history of Occidental Lodge, No. 40.

CHAPTER VIII.

Courtship and Marriage

ON MR. WALLACE'S return from Mexico he found little Ann Dickey a charming girl of fifteen. He had been as an elder brother in the home of Judge Dickey, coming and going as an esteemed and trusted friend of the family. He always took much interest in the bright little girl, often guiding her in her choice of books and in many ways forming her tastes in conformity to his own. She was of a cheerful, happy disposition, ready for fun and frolic and light as a fawn to run; fearless in sports, riding the pet ponies bare back. But as the eldest child with an invalid mother many duties also developed upon her which she bore as cheerfully and happily as she played, displaying wisdom and judgment beyond her years.

Her father, Judge T. Lyle Dickey, was one of the great lawyers of the Illinois bar. He was for four years a Circuit Judge, which, in the early fifties, comprised ten or twelve counties. In the latter part of his life he was one of the Supreme Judges of the State of Illinois. As a judge he was noted "for the clearness of his discrimination and the facility with which he grasped the real points of a case; the absolute integrity which guided his decisions, and also the absolute freedom from personal feelings or partisan bias in the discussion or consideration of legal questions. His mind was essentially judicial. It seemed to be always in perfect equipoise."

As his friend Judge J. S. Ewing said of him: "He was brave, generous, courteous and kind. He never betrayed a cause or a friend. He spoke kindly to the poor, sympathized with distress, was generous to a fault. There was no false pride born of accidental position. Can I tell of his fidelity to his friends, his urbane and pleasant manners, his hatred and scorn of wrong, his delicate and knightly sense or honor, his integrity of character, which made up a rounded and beautiful character to be loved, admired and honored. He lived with great men and was not dwarfed in their presence. He was a man of thought and action. He lived amidst the stirring times of a great era, and he thought out its problems and acted with its men. His life was a success measured by all the standards of human action."

He was of Scotch-Irish ancestry, a Kentuckian by birth, inheriting the generous impulses of her sons. Hospitality was to him what it was in the south in ante-bellum days, and in a new western country was as freely given. The Dickey home on the north bluff in Ottawa was always open to friends from far and near. When court was in session Judge Dickey usually had eight or ten of his lawyers friends as guests at his home. Abraham Lincoln many times enjoyed this hospitable roof; also many other eminent lawyers of the state.

Judge Dickey was but twenty years old when he married. His wife, Juliet Evans, of Ohio, was about the same age. For a time he taught school in Kentucky,—then moved to Illinois in 1834, he with his wife and year old baby Ann making the journey on horse back. Thus little Ann began her travels very early in life. Judge Dickey first essayed a business career, but soon abandoned it and studied law, making that his life work.

When Ann Dickey was sixteen Mr. Wallace told her of his love, which astonished her very much, as she had thought of him more as her father's friend than as her own, but when she communed with her own heart she found she had loved him unconsciously, although she knew she had always had great esteem and high respect for him.

Not long before their marriage Mr. Wallace's name came up for nomination to Congress at the Whig convention at Joliet in 1850. The other Whig nominee outdistanced him in votes, but was defeated in the election by the Democratic candidate. In a letter from Mr. Wallace to Miss Dickey at this time he says: "You heard your father speaking of the proposition to make me a candidate for Congress. I hope for your sake it may succeed. * * * I own that I am somewhat ambitious,—that to be known and distinguished has its charm for me,—that to be placed in a position where I might wield an influence for myself and friends would be gratifying,—that I occasionally indulge in day dreams which are touched with a tinge of the magnificent,—but, Ann, if all this fancied distinction and influence were to be purchased at the price of one pang to you, or were offered in exchange for one moment of your dear love, it would be found like those men mentioned in the Scriptures who were 'weighed in the balance and found wanting.' "

In February, 1851, the wedding occurred after a two years' engagement, when the bride was scarcely eighteen years of age, and the groom twenty-nine. Their wedding journey was a trip to Chicago. As there was no railroad at that time through Ottawa, they went to Aurora by carriage and from there by rail.

They soon went to housekeeping in their own little home, as the young wife said: "What a proud happy child I was! To me he was all that was greatest, best, truest and most tender in the world,—and this had come to me and I was part of it. Years of pain and ill health came to me, but never an unhappy moment, for every hour of pain disclosed to me the wealth of love, sympathy and self-sacrifice that lived for me in that great heart." During all their eleven years of wedded life never an impatient or unkind word passed the husband's lips.

Mrs. Wallace was brought up a Presbyterian, the Dickey family, far and near, also being of that religious connection. Her grandfather was James H. Dickey, a Presbyterian minister, widely and favorably known in central Illinois for his superior ability and worth. When Mrs. Wallace was sixteen she heard, for the first time, an Episcopalian service, which appealed to her very devout religious nature. She from that time studied into the tenets of that church and later became a very earnest and devoted member.

Mr. Wallace was brought up a Methodist, but always attended the Episcopal church with his wife, although he never became a communicant, but probably would have done so had his life been spared.

Mr. Wallace, in his extensive law practice, was much away from home. In February, 1854, he writes: "Although in traveling I see a great many women I see none that can compare with my own Ann. The knowledge, experience and observation I have in the world but makes me love you the more, and the more highly appreciate the blessing I enjoy in such a wife as you are to me. God bless you, Ann, and may He long spare us both to be a comfort and happiness to one another."

In the summer of 1854, Mrs. Wallace, not being very well, they concluded to take a trip east. They went from Chicago to Detroit, thence by boat to Buffalo, thence to Montreal. Mr. Wallace writes from there to Judge Dickey: "We reached here last evening after a delightful run down Lake Ontario and the St. Lawrence rapids. This is a great city, beautifully located. We have abandoned the idea of going further down the St. Lawrence and will start at 5 o'clock for Lake Champlain and Lake George."

From Albany they took a Hudson river steamboat for New York, where occurred what might have been a tragic ending to their pleasant trip. They were just leaving the boat at the wharf, Mrs. Wallace was on the gang plank, Mr. Wallace still on the boat, when the plank slipped from its moorings on the wharf, throwing all those that were on it into the salt water twenty feet deep. Mrs. Wallace was thrown some distance. The instant she was thrown in Mr. Wallace took off his coat, watched where she came up, jumped into the water and swam to her.

When she found herself in the water, she remembered what she had learned at school, that when in the water, if the arms and limbs can be kept under the face will float. With perfect calmness and self possession she did this. She said afterwards her entire life came to her—she thought she would of course drown, but experienced no fear of death.

Mr. Wallace, as he swam to her, feared she might grab him, and said to her, "steady Ann." She answered, "I am steady." He took hold of her and swam to a boat, clinging to it until a small boat came to their rescue. While they were still in the water, Mr. Wallace said, "Ann took it very cool, remarking it was her first introduction to salt water."

From New York they went to Philadelphia and Boston.

On their way home to Illinois Mrs. Wallace stopped in Ohio for a visit among relatives there. From there she writes to her husband in September: "I long to put my loving arms around your neck and then feel in return your strong, kind arms drawing me closer and closer to your warm heart, those dear arms that saved me from the water, and the brave heart that prompted the fearful leap. Dearest, the more I think of that frightful incident, the more I appreciate your great love for me, and the more I thank my Heavenly Father for giving me such a husband. May He put it into my heart to be a better wife to you than I have ever been before. I can not love you more, but I may be more useful. I am coming to you the first opportunity of company that I have. The day that we are both home together will be one of the happy days of my life. All the days will be long until that one comes."

Mr. Wallace, who had returned home to Ottawa, writes to his wife about the same time: "I went to see Mrs. N— this afternoon. She had heard the story of your fall in the water at New York and had a hundred questions to ask about it. She said when I told her of your putting your hands behind you and holding your face up and how you came to think of it—"God told her." Our little home is still all right except you, its soul and life. How do you bear up under our separation, dearest? I find it harder than I supposed. I find myself constantly thinking of you. I believe I have reviewed again and again every moment of our happy wedded life since I saw you. I believe I love you more dearly now, Ann, than I ever did before, and more fully appreciate and prize your great love for me. What I should be or do without you, God in heaven only knows. I cannot patiently contemplate the possibility of that darkness that would surround me, if you, the light of my life, were extinguished. Come to me, Ann, as soon as you can. I feel distrustful of circumstances, having so great a risk upon your safe return."

Mrs. Wallace had for some years been more or less troubled with rheumatism, and in the year 1857 it was so severe as to make her almost helpless, and Mr. Wallace determined to take her to Hot Springs, Arkansas, then a more formidable undertaking than at the present day with railroad facilities. As Mrs. Wallace said, "He literally carried me in his arms to the Hot Springs and was made happy by bringing me home perfectly restored."

They went down to Cairo by rail, then by boat down the Mississippi and up the Arkansas river to Little Rock, taking four or five days, then going by stage-coach and carriage over sixty miles to Hot Springs, over rough, stony roads, stopping for the night in a log cabin in the woods.

A letter from Mr. Wallace to Judge Dickey will show the primitiveness of the Hot Springs of that period.

"May, 14th, 1857.

"There are two houses here, or rather two establishments, each consisting of several houses—one is called the 'Rector House' and the other the 'Hale House,' named after rival claimants of the grounds containing the springs, the title to which is in dispute. They are situated in a deep hollow between two steep mountains that rise abruptly to a height of about a quarter of a mile, and are covered with pines, the course of the valley is from north to south, and the hot water issues from the mountain east of the hollow near its top and is brought down in troughs to bathing houses near the hotels, where it is applied by pouring, showering, in vapor,—in the ordinary way, and in what they call 'mud baths,' which are what their name imports, mud holes in which the patient is immersed to the throat. There are several springs, differing somewhat in temperature from one hundred to one hundred and fifty degrees, and also differing somewhat in their analysis, though not materially.

"We are pleasantly located at the 'Hale House' with a large comfortable room on the ground floor; the bathing rooms are just across the 'branch.' * * * * The dining room is just across the narrow street from the building in which we have our quarters. The charge for board, lodging and bath, thirty-five dollars a month. There are about a dozen ladies here."

Mr. Wallace left his wife and her little sister at the Hot Springs and returned to Illinois. In Little Rock he writes about meeting Dr. Borland, whom he had known in the Mexican war as Major of the Arkansas regiment, and who was spoken of earlier in this narrative as being captured by the Mexicans surrounding the place where he was with some eighty men one dark, rainy night. He was afterwards United States Senator from his State.

Mr. Wallace, in a letter to his wife, speaks of its taking eleven days for her letter to come, which ought to have come in seven or eight. He says, "If our separation, painful as it is to both of us, results in the realization of my dear hope that you will be permanently restored to health, I shall feel a thankfulness to our Heavenly Father such as I never felt before. My constant prayer to Him that in His wisdom and mercy will so order that you may be restored to me 'whole and sound'."

Mrs. Wallace remained at the Hot Springs for a couple of months, when her husband went for her, bringing her home cured.

An amusing letter was received from Mrs. Wallace's young brother Cyrus, who, with other relatives, was at the Wallace home in Ottawa during her absence. It gives a little glimpse of the life and hospitality of the little cottage home.

"OTTAWA, July 2d, 1857.

"Pa, Mrs. C— and baby and Philander came on Tuesday and went on to Chicago yesterday. John is here, also Alice. Your old friends? Mr. and Mrs. S—, came up on Tuesday and made us a visit en route to Morris—with them and father's troupe we had a pretty full house, but got along very smoothly saving one little accident which I must tell you of. Mrs. S—, being quite tired, concluded to go to bed before prayers, and being of an economical turn of mind, *blew out the gas* before lying down. Meantime, I got one of Scott's Bibles with copious notes. Mr. S— selected a very long chapter in Romans and read and commented on all the notes as he went along—then offered a prayer of extraordinary length and breadth, which I verily believe covered everything on the earth, except the hole from which the gas was escaping in the bed room. But it finally had an end, and if the window in the bed-room had not been up, I fear the old lady would have had an end also."

One thing was lacking in this almost ideal home—the little child—the parental love in the heart was unfulfilled, the place was empty. A tiny babe left motherless appealed to the motherlove so strong in Mrs. Wallace the yearning was irresistible and the little one of three weeks old was taken into their lives and loved and cherished as their own, even jealously so; she grew to womanhood in an atmosphere of the most devoted love, knowing no other bonds of relationship.

For nine years they lived in their little cottage home on "the ridge" in Ottawa. As Mr. Wallace's fortunes improved they built a substantial stone house on the bluff adjoining the Dickey homestead.

CHAPTER IX.

DICKEY AND WALLACE AGAINST LOVEJOY IN 1856 AND 1858.

THE year 1856 saw marked changes in political parties. Slavery was the great question that held all minds and the line that divided all parties. The Missouri Compromise bill of 1820, which admitted Missouri into the Union as a slave state with the proviso that all states formed of the territory west and northwest should be free, was thought at that time to have quieted the slave question indefinitely, if not forever. But with the newly acquired territory from the Mexican war coming into the Union as States, the old sore was opened afresh, especially when the Missouri Compromise was repealed in 1854 and the Kansas-Nebraska bill, furthered by Stephen A. Douglas, passed, giving new States the option of framing their own constitutions as to whether they should be free or slave. The country was in a turmoil and the halls of Congress rang with eloquent and angry speeches on both sides. The people, north and west, were no less loud in their denunciation of the measure which opened up all territories to the spread of slavery. All parties felt as if they must unite to stem this evil, and the Republican party came into being with the marked object of excluding slavery from the territories. It had had its birth in a small way in Illinois in 1854, but was gradually growing in power and strength, absorbing within its fold Whigs, Northern Democrats, Free Soil and Abolition adherents. In 1856 the new party nominated their first Presidential candidate in the person of John C. Frémont, of California.

The American, or Know Nothing Party, put up Millard Fillmore. This party was a secret society much older than the Republican party, but had become a great political power. Their creed was "America for Americans, non-interference of foreigners, or the domination of Roman Catholicism in political affairs." The A. P. A. that arose a decade or two later, was very similar in its tenents.

The Democratic party put up James Buchanan of Pennsylvania for President.

Mr. Wallace was a Whig until this year, when he joined the Republican party. He was a member of the convention who nominated Frémont for the Presidency and one of the committee who went to New York to announce to him his nomination. The following letter was written from Philadelphia at this time to his wife:

"PHILADELPHIA, THURSDAY, June 19, 1856.

"I have been here since Sunday and have been very busy. I write now in great hurry. We have just concluded our business here by nominating Colonel Frémont for President and Wm. L. Dayton of New Jersey for Vice-president. I go to Washington City to-night and back to New York to-morrow night. * * * * I don't feel altogether satisfied with our nominations but hope for the best. I think of you often and sometimes wish you were here, and again am glad that you are not. The houses are crowded —a great crowd of earnest, excited and noisy men."

The Democratic nominee, James Buchanan, won the election, which put the slavery element in power. Kansas became the battle ground of the contending factions in Congressional debates no less than on the actual soil. The slavery element desired to fill the territory with settlers from the South to predominate in the vote for a Constitution favorable to slavery. The anti-slavery or Northern element were equally anxious to bring in the settlers that would make it a free state. Hence, battles, murders and ejections of settlers ensued between the warring factions.

Charles Sumner was the leader of the Anti-Slavery cause in Congress, and Jefferson Davis, the leader of the Southern side. The great men—Webster, Calhoun and Clay—were dead, who had made the halls of Congress ring with their eloquence. In one of Sumner's speeches he reflected on the honor of a Southern member, which so angered this Southerner's nephew that after the session had closed, he assaulted Sumner in his seat with a heavy cane and with such force that his life was almost despaired of, and made him an invalid for some years, so he could not attend to his duties in Congress. This assault aroused a strong feeling in the North. It was taken up as a political question and not merely a personal one. This outrage, added to the decision of the Supreme Court in the Dred Scott case, showing that the highest judicial tribunal in the country was pro-slavery, and with the administration's efforts to force Kansas into the Union with a constitution which recognized slavery, begat an intense feeling in the anti-slavery element that aided the Abolition party.

This party, although ultra and extreme and its adherents hated and persecuted, was gaining ground and receiving more favorable and intelligent attention as the thinking men were coming more and more to see that the slavery question was disrupting the nation. The question must be solved one way or another.

Although the Republicans lost on the Presidential election, Illinois went Republican throughout in the State ticket. Owen Lovejoy, a Congregational minister of Princeton and a rank Abolotionist, was a candidate for Congress in the Third Congressional District on the Republican ticket. Congressional appointments were very important, as it was on the floor of Congress that the great national questions were being battled over and decided.

The desire was to keep a balance of power between the adherents of slavery and those against its non-extension so as to give neither the upper hand.

Scarcely at any time in our history were the debates and laws passed so prominent, so important and absorbing as the decade or more before the Civil War. So to be sent to Congress in those days was no small honor and responsibility.

Lovejoy, as I. N. Arnold says: "Was a man of powerful physique, intense feeling and of great magnetism as a speaker. He went forth like Peter the Hermit, with a heart of fire, a tongue of lightning, preaching his crusade against slavery. He lived to see slavery die amid the flames of war which itself had kindled."

His intense views were not entertained by all people who might admire the zeal and fearlessness of the man, but thought his opinions too radical for the times, as many favored a middle course, or compromise, in hopes that time would help the solution of the vexed question. Many, although not favoring slavery, thought, according to the Constitution, the Central Government could not interfere with States' rights. Some advocated gradual emancipation, certainly a normal and fair way of settlement.

A great evil, however, sometimes demands fanatics in the beginning to educate the public opinion to eradicate it. Abolitionists, with the powerful aid of Mrs. Stowe's "Uncle Tom's Cabin," published in 1852, did much to hasten open hostilities between the adherents of slavery and those against its extension. It seemed nothing but war could finally settle it. Pacific measures and compromise could only for a time stay the impending rupture, but could not stop the violent current rushing on to civil war.

The Republican Congressional Convention met at Bloomington on July 15th and made very moderate resolutions. "They merely denounced the Administration for its course regarding Kansas, stigmatized the repeal of the Missouri Compromise as an act of bad faith, and opposed the extension of slavery into the territories." Owen Lovejoy was put in nomination for the Third District. Many objected and desired another candidate.

An anti-Lovejoy convention was held in Ottawa on July 26th. Delegates were in attendance from McLean, DeWitt, La Salle, Putnam and Vermillion counties, and put Judge Dickey in nomination. An interesting account of this is given by Judge Dickey in a letter to his son John, which gives a clear idea of the middle course advocated by conservative men.

"CHICAGO, ILLINOIS, July 29th, 1856.

"We are in the midst of a political tornado. The Congressional convention of Frémont men met at Ottawa on the 2d of this month nominated for Congress Rev. Owen Lovejoy, a rank old-fashioned *Abolitionist*. About half the delegates bolted the nomination and called another convention to nominate another candidate who would not only oppose the introduction of slavery into Kansas, but would at the same time be *true* to the acknowledged rights of the South under the Constitution, embracing their right to recapture runaway slaves—and who in general would exercise a spirit of fidelity and fraternity to the people of the South and avoid all unnecessary cause of difference. That convention put me in nomination. And I am now a candidate for Congress in the midst of the hurricane preaching peace, fraternity and fidelity. I am stemming a terrible current without any reasonable certainty of success."

His friend, Judge David Davis of Bloomington, realizing the fruitlessness of the contest, wrote him the following very vehement letter, which gives a good idea of the state of public opinion at that date:

"BLOOMINGTON, ILLINOIS, July 18th, 1856.

"DEAR DICKEY:

"I think so much of you and have your interests so near my heart that I know you will consider this *letter* as having been written with the best of motives whether the contents harmonize with your views or not.

"I did not dream that you would have taken the nomination for Congress, else I would have given up my business in Fayette County (where I was on Wednesday) and been present at Bloomington. I had told Gridley that with the feeling in these southern counties that a nomination against Lovejoy would end in defeat. The readiness with which many persons support Lovejoy is surprising. It probably can be accounted for for several reasons. In the first place —the outrages in Kansas, and the general conduct of the Administration, with the attack on Mr. Sumner, have made Abolitionists of those who never dreamed they were drifting into it. These principles and the feelings which underlie them were more active and vigilant than the feelings and principles which you and I entertain, and hence, in a very great measure the nomination of Lovejoy. Many men again express great regrets that he is nominated, but think that he will vote right on the question of the extension of slavery, and are willing that he should vote his Abolition sentiments in other respects rather than send a Democrat to Congress who will vote to uphold slavery further.

"A third class think he was fairly nominated and should be sustained. Again, many would vote for you if the race was between you and Lovejoy alone who will not do it now, believing that Lovejoy is regularly nominated and is the strongest. Again, there are another class of people who think that this fusion war of all elements and whoever adopts the fusion platform should be voted for, no matter how wrong the other sentiments are.

"Now, my dear friend, I am not stating these things by way of any justification for those who act, but simply as reasons (unsatisfactory to us as they may be) why the people are predisposed to vote for Lovejoy. I think the grand reason after all is that his views and opinions are becoming the views and opinions of a majority of the people.

"It is plain that the elements now uniting in electing Colonel Frémont and Colonel Bissell can't coalesce long They will have one feeling in common, but antipodes in everything else. If Kansas gets admitted as a free state the party is *ipse facto* dissolved. What elements will unite in the formation of new parties, time alone can determine. I feel an all abiding faith that you and I will belong to the same political organization.

"This nomination of Lovejoy deadens enthusiasm, dispirits and causes all people who really love the Union of the States to pause. * * * * But it may be asked what you and I and those who think with us are to do. Simply to vote in this canvass for those we can conscientiously vote for, and eschew the others. * * * * We, the old Whig party, will be stricken down during this campaign. Had we not better bide our time, brush up our armor for future operations? * * * *

"You can literally do nothing in these southern counties unless by a thorough and systematic canvass, speaking to be done in every precinct. If Osgood was out of the way by doing this Lovejoy could be beaten.

"To do all these things would require great labor and great expense of time and money. The labor and expense is *not* to be considered where success is likely to be obtained, but should be taken into the account when success, is, to say the best, problematical. * * * *

"If I did not feel a deep interest in whatever concerns you I would not have thus written, and I know you will consider everything as well meant. Do nothing hastily, but after gathering all the facts, decide according to the very right of the case. Your friend as ever,

"DAVID DAVIS."

Judge Davis wrote to Mr. Wallace the following day in the same strain.

"BLOOMINGTON, ILLINOIS, July 19, 1856.

"MY DEAR FRIEND:

"I have written a long letter to Judge Dickey and sent by this mail. I know that he will be beaten and that it is labor, time and talents wasted in making this race.

I did not dream that he would have accepted the nomination, else I would have foregone my business and been here. Pray, prevent him from running.

"Lovejoy was not here last night, but I am told that the ratification meeting was enthusiastic, and about all the old Whig lawyers gave in their adhesion to Lovejoy. * * *

"I want Dickey to withdraw before he gets his feelings so aroused that he would continue on the track through mere pride.

"Excuse the earnestness with which I write. * * * * Read the letter to Dickey if he is out of town and you will see my views hastily written out.

"I wish I could see you and talk with you.

"In haste, your friend,

"DAVID DAVIS."

Judge Davis was a very prominent man in the State of Illinois; for many years a Circuit Judge. He and Lincoln rode the circuit together. Afterwards he was a judge in the United States Supreme Court, resigning to accept a seat in the Senate, and in 1877 was a possible Presidential nominee. He and Judge Dickey were very warm friends throughout their lives.

On September 13th Judge Dickey withdrew his name for Congressman against Lovejoy, who was elected by a plurality of six thousand votes over the Democratic candidate, Uri Osgood.

Judge Dickey, although a Southern born man, did not favor the extension of slavery. He inherited slaves himself, but freed them, although at the time he was heavily in debt through signing the bond of a dishonest partner, when the money he might have received from the sale of the slaves would have been most acceptable.

The following letter from S. B. Buckner to Mr. Wallace is interesting historically on account of the after career of General Buckner, and also showing the state of our militia service in the year 1857.

"Simon Bolivar Buckner was born in Kentucky in 1823. He served in the Mexican war and after the war was assistant instructor of infantry tactics at West Point. He resigned and went to Chicago as Superintendent of Construction of the Custom House in that city. While there, in 1855, he was made Colonel of Volunteers raised in Illinois in that year for the Utah expedition, but not mustered into service. He afterwards practiced law in Kentucky, and at the outbreak of the Civil War entered the Southern Army as General. At Fort Donelson on February 16th, 1862, he surrendered to General Grant with sixteen thousand men as prisoners of war. He was later exchanged and made Major-General, and was in the Southern service till the close of the war. He was afterwards Governor of Kentucky."

The letter reads:

"CHICAGO, January 10th, 1857.

"MAJOR:

"I have been casting about in my own mind for some time past to find some one who, while he would accept the office of Adjutant-General of the State, would enter upon the duties with a purpose to attend to them, and to infuse some life into our military system. You know full well the entire disuse into which the present system has fallen and the dead weight which those who feel any interest in military affairs have to carry. The appointment of an efficient Adjutant-General would strike at the root of the disease which so extensively pervades the military body. Supported as he would be by a soldier for the Commander-in-Chief he could exert an influence on military matters which has long been needed and without which no life can be felt in the extremities.

"For several weeks past, it has been my purpose to suggest your name in this connection to Judge Dickey. I have done so to-day, and it has been after conferring with him that I have addressed a communication to Colonel Bissell in which I have ventured to suggest your name for this position. It may appear to you and to Colonel Bissell, with whom I have only a slight acquaintance, an act of vanity or impertinent assumption on my part to recommend for this position a gentleman so much more widely known than myself, but I have been actuated by a desire to promote the interests of the military of the State; and under the supposition that it probably only required a suggestion of your name to secure your appointment.

"My object in addressing to you this note is to ask you to consent to take charge of the duties of the office. If you do so it will have to be on your part a labor of love. The salary is merely nominal, only $100.00 per year, but I trust you will consider the present lamentable condition of our military affairs, and the necessity of relieving the state from the odium which attaches to its military organization. No time is more propitious to introduce a reform. With both the Governor and his chief executive officer participants in our late war and associated with the state troops in service, we would have reason to expect a salutary change. If nothing can be done during the present session of the Legislature to remodel the military, you could, in conjunction with the Governor, perfect by the meeting of the next Legislature a system whose effects might be beneficially transmitted through long years to come on the military institutions of the State.

"I hope you will take this matter under advisement and for the benefit of those of us who take an interest in military affairs and desire to foster a military spirit amongst ourselves, speedily decide to accept the position. If you do so, cannot you meet me in Springfield? I propose to go there on Saturday or on Sunday night to remain only two or three days. My object will be to do what I can towards obtaining a revision of the military laws. If you have a little time to devote to this it is probable something may be accomplished even during the present legislature. If you cannot meet me, please address me a letter at Springfield. With much regard, I am, Major,

"Very respectfully and truly yours,

"S. B. BUCKNER."

Mr. Wallace did not consider the matter of the Adjutant Generalship, and did not accept the position as advised by Major Buckner. Later Major Buckner, himself, became Adjutant-General of Illinois Militia, but resigned in December of the same year.

Colonel William H. Bissell, who had served in the Mexican war, became Governor of Illinois in 1857, taking the oath of office on January 12th.

* * * * * * *

Although 1858 was not a Presidential year, it is a memorable one in Illinois politics, and without doubt the most famous in her history with far reaching results. The contest between Judge Douglas and Mr. Lincoln for the senatorship, although local, brought the state into national politics and fame and introduced Abraham Lincoln to the entire country, which resulted later in his becoming President.

Stephen A. Douglas was one of the most prominent and best known men in the country, owing to his many years in Congress, first as a Representative, and then for twelve years a Senator. Abraham Lincoln was a country lawyer, little known outside his state. This year Douglas was running for re-election to his seat in the Senate and Lincoln was contesting the place with him. Douglas was a Democrat and was the man who introduced the famous Kansas-Nebraska Bill into Congress, but was against the Buchanan or Southern element of the party who wished to *force* Kansas into the Union with a constitution favoring slavery. Douglas had fought this issue with all his might and on this platform he was running, so he had the split in his own party to contend against as well as his Republican opponent. Lincoln was running on a purely Republican platform —"Non-extension of Slavery into the Territories."

On the 16th of June the Republican Convention met at Springfield and endorsed Lincoln as their choice for United States Senator. At this time Lincoln made his wonderful speech that began his fame and eventually landed him in the White House. It was the few opening sentences that were so effective and powerful and are here quoted: "If we could first know where we are and whither we are tending we could then better judge what to do, and how to do it. We are now far into the fifth year since a policy was initiated with the avowed object and confident promise of putting an end to the slavery agitation. Under the operation of that policy, that agitation has not only not ceased, but has constantly augmented. In my opinion it will not cease until a crisis shall have been reached and passed. *A house divided against itself cannot stand. I believe this government cannot endure permanently half slave and half free. I do not expect the Union to be dissolved. I do not expect the house to fall—but I do expect it will cease to be divided. It will become all one thing or all the other.* Either the opponents of slavery will arrest the further spread of it, and place it where the public mind shall rest in the belief that it is in the course of ultimate extinction, or, its advocates will put it forward till it shall become alike lawful in all the States, old as well as new, North as well as South. Have we no tendency to the latter condition?" This speech made a profound impression; some said it was in advance of the times, others that such sentiments would bring on civil war. Others of his friends, although not favoring the extension of slavery, urged moderation for his own good and that of his party and not to make such utterances in the future. Lincoln was far seeing, brave and true, with patriotic desire for the well being of his country more than political advancement for himself. The truth should be uttered regardless of the consequences to himself or his party.

Leonard Swett, a brilliant lawyer of Illinois, and an astute political observer, said: "The first ten lines of that speech defeated him for the Senate. It was a speech made at the commencement of a campaign and apparently made for the campaign. Viewing it in this light, nothing could have been more unfortunate or inappropriate. It was saying the wrong thing first, yet he saw it was an abstract truth, and standing by the speech would ultimately find him in the right place."

Lincoln challenged Douglas to a joint debate on the issues between the two parties which was accepted by the great Senator, and seven meeting places were named—Ottawa, Freeport, Jonesboro, Charleston, Galesburg, Quincy and Alton. These debates attracted the attention of the entire United States and brought thousands within the hearing of the two "intellectual giants" at each meeting.

The first opened at Ottawa on August 21st in Washington Square in the middle of the town with an eager and attentive audience. After the meeting Douglass walked away almost unattended and returned to his hotel nearby. Lincoln was carried, under his protest, on the shoulders of his enthusiastic adherents to the home of the Mayor, J. O. Glover, but half a block distant. Here he had to make a short speech to the gathered crowd. Mr. Lovejoy was called on for one also, then W. H. L. Wallace closed with a few remarks and the crowd dispersed.

At Freeport, it is said, the questions propounded by Mr. Lincoln to Judge Douglas and his answers to them were the causes that defeated him for the Presidency in 1860, as in these answers Judge Douglas lost the support of the South which divided the Democratic party and gave the Presidency to the Republicans.

Politics all along the line from the Senatorship down was very spirited in the State this year. Owen Lovejoy was up for re-election for Congressman, and while still in Washington sent letters broadcast to his constituents in the district. He still had many opponents, although his abolition principles were gaining ground. Mr. Wallace was desired by his friends to run against him for the Republican nomination, and some letters are here given on the subject and also to show the political feelings of the day on the other stirring questions. Judge Champlain, a prominent lawyer of Ottawa and later law partner of Mr. Wallace, writes the following letter:

"OTTAWA, June 4, 1858.

"DEAR SIR:

"The time is at hand when delegates are to be elected to the State Convention at Springfield and to the Congressional Convention at Joliet, and I think a good deal depends upon the wisdom with which the delegates are selected.

"My own opinion is that this State was lost to Frémont by the Congressional nomination made in this and the Chicago districts in 1856, and if the same course is pursued again I believe it will be attended with the same result. I entertain no doubt that the Congressional nominations now to be made ought by every consideration of justice as well as wisdom, to be from either the Conservative Whig or Democratic portion of the Republican party, and I believe this opinion to be shared in by the great majority of the party. But it will take some exertion to secure this result and hence, I write to you that if you see fit you may use such exertions as you think best to secure a right coming out of this matter.

"So far as public sentiment in this region of the district is concerned I know it to be decidedly favorable to the selection of Mr. Wallace as the next Republican candidate for Congress, and I believe it to be so to a considerable extent in other parts of the district. I also know that Mr. Wallace possesses every quality that is requisite to fill the station with honor to himself, his friends and his country.

"Should these views meet your approbation you are at liberty to show this letter to such of your friends as you see fit, especially Mr. Henning and Mr. Wheeler.

"Truly yours,
"J. C. CHAMPLAIN."

Lovejoy was very active and aggressive in his canvass for renomination at the Congressional Convention to be held at Joliet on June 30th. A letter to Mr. Wallace from Mr. A. Wardlaw of Granville, Putnam County, on May 5th, says:

"I understand that Lovejoy is busy writing letters home

to his friends urging them to see to his interests. I had the reading of one and saw several others. The one I saw stated that he understood that there were efforts being made in the district to defeat him in the convention by calling mass meetings and making it inconvenient for his friends to attend, and saying they ought to have meetings in the different towns and send delegates to attend the convention at Joliet."

A letter to Judge Dickey from C. H. Moore of Clinton, DeWitt County, on June 5th, speaking in the same strain, says:

"I saw a letter from Lovejoy yesterday complaining of the course taken, that the primary meetings were called too soon. He wanted them delayed until he could get home and see the people. Our delegates to Joliet are Jno. Warren, C. P. Ford, L. Welden and C. H. Moore. I am the most of a Lovejoy man amongst them. There is no possible contingency that I can conceive of in which the delegation from this county will vote for Lovejoy in the convention. Our choice is Judge Davis. Our delegation will do its best for him. If it is impossible to nominate him, we will do the next best thing to defeat Lovejoy. As against any man north of the Illinois river, Mr. Wallace, I think, can rely upon this county. I suppose there will be but three candidates, Mr. Wallace, Davis and Lovejoy—Swett, I have not heard spoken of."

From Pontiac, Livingston County, Mr. Wallace received a letter in the same strain from Josh Whitmore, a lawyer there, on June 5th:

"We are thrashed out completely. You never saw Abolitionists flock out so in your life. Lovejoy has sent confidential letters stereotyped to every Abolitionist in the county and probably in the district. I saw one day before yesterday, an appeal to the *Sympathizers* and Abolitionists; every one of them turned out to the rescue. I am not only mad, but tired of this Nigger Worshipping. If Lovejoy is to be the nominee, I am ready to vote for a Douglas Democrat. I have seen some gentlemen from DeWitt, Vermillion and Champaign Counties who say Lovejoy will carry all of them certain. Davis is going to have all he can attend to to carry McLean County. I speak advisedly, I think. I shall be in Joliet on the 30th at all events, and in the event that Davis comes in strongly posted you will get the Livingston delegates, but not if there is any chance for Lovejoy."

Mr. Wallace received a letter from Judge Davis a couple of days later telling of affairs in McLean County:

"BLOOMINGTON, June 7, 1858.

"DEAR WALLACE:—Hill Lamon is just starting to Joliet and Ottawa, to inform you of result and causes of it for our failure, and I can write but a word. I knew ten days ago that the result was inevitable. My friends, however, thought otherwise. The Mass Convention was unfortunate and the weather and roads conspired to defeat us. The main argument used for Lovejoy was that he was entitled to a second nomination. Again they harped greatly upon the fact that I did not vote for Lovejoy.

"The Abolition element is successful here and very proscriptive. They are entirely in the ascendency. The delegates from here are more abolitionized than any you will have at Joliet. The truth is that the county is for Lovejoy. The Whig part of the Republican party is proscribed. I don't think this county could have been saved.

"Is there any hope? The DeWitt delegates are appointed and are true. I don't believe that Champaign and Vermillion can be saved. Consult with Hill and see what you want done.

"If it was not for saving Lincoln for United States Senate a pretty great outbreak would follow. I don't believe Lovejoy can be beaten if nominated and there is no use of bolting. Remember me to Dickey. "Your friend.

D. DAVIS."

On June 9th the La Salle County Republican convention met at Ottawa to elect delegates for the convention at

Joliet; as the Ottawa Republican newspaper of that date says: "Mr. Wallace's name was withdrawn. Many personal friends of Mr. Wallace would like to have had the privilege of sending him to Congress. In this they were not actuated by hostility to Mr. Lovejoy. When they found the majority was for returning Mr. Lovejoy for another term, Mr. Wallace's claims were pressed no further. The friends of Judge Davis have also withdrawn his name from the canvass."

The Ottawa *Free Trader,* speaking of the Joliet convention on the 30th of June, says: "Old Whigs, notwithstanding they comprise two-thirds of the party, are not allowed a voice in the convention. They are the complete slaves of such men as Lovejoy, Wentworth, Dyer and Hawley." Lovejoy was elected by seven thousand votes over the Democratic nominee, George W. Armstrong.

The elections to the Illinois Legislature were important, as the legislators had in their hands the electing of the United States Senators. Even in this year politicians were looking ahead to a time when Lovejoy might run for United States Senate and desired his defeat, as is shown in the following letter to Mr. Wallace from Mr. A. Wardlow of Granville on September 8th:

"The Abolitionists have backed down and have come to the conclusion that it is perhaps best not to monopolize all the offices, and have nominated an old line Whig for Representative and a man by the name of Geo. C. Bestor of Peoria for the State Senate. I do not know what he is, but he will have to give some assurance that he will go for some other man than Lovejoy, for the Senate in 1860, at the end of Trumbull's time, as some of the Abolitionists have said that they intend for him to go into the Senate in Trumbull's place. Consequently he will have to come out on that or there will be bolting. He will not be required to pledge for any particular man, only not to go for Lovejoy. * * * * The Democrats had a mass meeting in Hennepin last Monday and had a complete blow up. The Buchanan men left or bolted and formed another organization; consequently there are two sets of delegates appointed to all the conventions, one set instructed to go for Douglas, the other instructed to go for no man who will support Douglas against the Administration. * * * * * I think Douglas is losing ground here since his Freeport speech, and the Buchanan faction are gaining and the wave is bitter and hot. There is no chance for a reconciliation or a union on Douglas. The only chance for a union of the two wings is to drop Douglas and unite on some one else and I have no idea the Douglas men will do that."

Regardless of the bitter dissension in his own party Douglas won the election in the Legislature to the United States Senate. Owen Lovejoy remained in Congress until 1864, when he died—an eloquent and honest man in his convictions, however extreme.

CHAPTER X.

LINCOLN'S NOMINATION AND THE FEELING IN THE COUNTRY BEFORE HIS INAUGURATION.

THE slave question which had been rumbling for so many years was in the Presidential contest of 1860, the only issue between the parties, State's sovereignty, or each State's right to manage its own affairs with no responsibility to a central union, against the non-extension of slavery. Four parties with four candidates were in the field, each with varying shades of the central question—Slavery.

The Republican party, now growing strong in its advocacy of the evil of extending the bondage of human beings, stood on its original platform of Non-Extension of Slavery, and put forward Abraham Lincoln of Illinois as its leader. The American or Know-Nothing party took no decided ground on the slavery question, but was for a Constitutional Union, nominated John Bell of Tennessee as its standard-bearer.

The Democratic party was divided. The extreme Southern faction headed by Jefferson Davis advocated that the Federal Government must protect slave owners whether in free or slave States in fact that no restriction of slavery was constitutional. This faction nominated John C. Breckenridge of Kentucky. The other wing of the party, not willing to squarely affirm this doctrine, ignored it and nominated Stephen A. Douglas of Illinois, the advocate of popular sovereignty, for President. The real contest was between Lincoln and Douglas, although owing to the disruption in the Democratic party, Douglas did not carry a single state electoral vote, but his personal popularity gave him a large popular vote.

After Lincoln was actually elected in November, and the South knew that a Republican President would be at the head of the nation, and his sympathizers in the officers of state, even if in Congress, the balance of power was still with the Douglas Democrats, they decided to secede from the Union and form a separate Confederation of States that would uphold the system of slavery; which they believed to be necessary to the industrial well being of the South in its principal industry of raising cotton and sugar cane.

On the 17th of December, South Carolina held a convention and decided to secede from the Union. By the first of February six other States had followed suit and by the eighth of the same month delegates from the seceded States met at Montgomery, Alabama, and formed a new government with the name of the Confederate States of America, and elected Jefferson Davis as President, and Alexander H. Stephens as Vice-President.

We now turn to Mr. Wallace and his affairs with some side lights on these great questions that were agitating the entire country.

Mr. Wallace was not only an ardent Republican, but an earnest and devoted friend of Abraham Lincoln, so that it was but natural that all his sympathies were for Lincoln for President for which he worked hard and earnestly. When Lincoln was finally nominated in the memorable Chicago Convention of the 16th of May, 1860, strong men embraced one another, shouted and wept for joy. Mr. Wallace and his friend, Leonard Swett, were together. So elated, so rejoiced were these two strong earnest men, they threw their arms around one another in the exhuberance of their deep feelings. "Come," says Wallace, "let's go and buy our wives some new dresses." The two tall men searched for the latest in pretty dress goods and each took the gift home to his wife. Mrs. Wallace called hers her "Lincoln dress," which is still kept by her family as an interesting relic.

Mr. Wallace's father-in-law, Judge Dickey, was as ardent a Democrat and Douglas man as Mr. Wallace was a Lincoln man—politics could naturally never be discussed between them. When, however, Judge Dickey found Douglas' chances for election out of the question, he returned to Ottawa, went directly to Mr. Wallace's house in the middle of the night told him to get right up and work for Lincoln.

His love of country, and faith in the integrity and ability of Lincoln, for whom he had a strong personal friendship, rose above party feeling.

Judge Dickey, with his daughter, Mrs. Wallace, and a cousin, Miss G—, went to Chicago to be present at the reception of Douglas. Miss G—writes a letter telling of their visit and also speaks of Seward's reception in Chicago at this time:

"October 7, 1860. We arrived in Chicago about six in the evening, put up at the Tremont, and as soon as we got our supper we got a place out on one of the balconies to see the reception of Seward. The reception was on Lake Street, the whole house was illuminated with various colored lamps, two on Lake and two on Dearborn; also two large stars made of large glass beads and fixed in evergreen with gas behind in shape of a star, two on each balcony.

"The street in front of the hotel was crowded with people. About eight o'clock the procession came up with Governor Seward. A company called Lincoln Rangers, mounted on horses, went to the depot to meet him. Then such a sight of torches as there were I never expect to see again. The crowd was remarkably silent. After Seward had eaten his supper he came out onto one of the balconies and made a short speech and then others spoke. Long John (Wentworth) came out to introduce Seward and made quite a lengthy speech. He said here was the man who would rather be in the right than be President, as much as to say that Lincoln was not in the right. He said something about Seward not being an office seeker, which made the people laugh a good deal. They don't seem to think much of Long John the way they laughed at him.

"Tuesday morning there did not seem much going on, but the Wideawakes marching from one street to another with bands of music. About one o'clock a large crowd assembled around the Tremont to escort Seward down to the wigwam to speak. By the way, I forgot to tell you that I saw Lady Franklin Monday night; she was out on the balcony when Seward spoke. She is a fine looking old lady. After Seward had left we all went down to the speaking, we could not get near enough to Seward to hear him; he was speaking out doors. We went into the wigwam and found out that Lovejoy was to speak, so we stayed and listened awhile to him, then went back to the hotel where we met a great many of Cousin Ann's friends. We stationed ourselves again on the balcony to see the Wideawakes.

"Wednesday evening we went to the theatre and heard the great Irish comedian, Collins, in a play called 'Coleen Bawn'—the scenery was fine.

"Thursday morning we went up to call on Mrs. Douglas. She is an exceedingly pleasant lady and very pretty. Mrs. Swift and Mrs. King came to call on us and invited us there to dinner. We went about four o'clock and on our way called on Mrs Judd. We got home from Mrs. Swift's about 7 o'clock. About ten Douglas came; there was an immense crowd collected to receive him. The hotel was all illuminated again and they had fixed up on top of the house, "Welcome, Douglas, Welcome home," in transparancies. Douglas made a short speech that night. Cousin Lyle (Judge Dickey) also made a speech. The Douglas Invincibles were out with their torches and made a brilliant showing.

"Friday the crowd collected around the Tremont to take Douglas to the grounds to speak. There was a long procession of Invincibles to escort him. He rode in a carriage drawn by four white horses with plumes. And stood up with his hat off until the procession had mostly passed, making bows to the people. Just as he was about to start he threw a kiss to Mrs. Douglas."

Popular as Douglas was personally, his cause was not the cause to win. Lincoln stood for the principle that reached the heart of the greater number of the American people so he won over his brilliant rival.

Mr. Wallace was an office seeker to the incoming President, as the following will testify—and also to the regard held for him by his friends.

"To his Excellency Abraham Lincoln:

"The undersigned residents of La Salle County most respectfully and yet urgently request the appointment of

Wm. H. L. Wallace as United States District Attorney for the Northern District of Illinois, for the reasons following, viz:

"1st. We have the most unlimited confidence in his capacity and integrity to faithfully and promptly discharge the duties of said office.

"2d. That we believe that a majority of the legal voters of this district anxiously wish for and respectfully demand his appointment and most determinately yet unitedly protest against the control of the appointing power in this district, by any or all of the Congressional Representatives of Northern Illinois.

"3d. And we hereby again protest against the appointment of a District Attorney from the County of Cook, inasmuch as several most important appointments have already been bestowed upon residents of said Cook County. While La Salle County being second in point of wealth and population in our state has been entirely overlooked and unrewarded by federal appointment."

Then follow many names of prominent La Salle County men.

Judge Davis writes Mr. Wallace on the same topic.

"Bloomington, Ill., Dec. 27, 1860.

W. H. L. Wallace, Esq.,

"My Dear Sir:—"I wrote to Judge Trumbull in your behalf and that of Mr. Weldon for the Southern District. I have just received a line in reply and will give you all of his letter referring to the subject.

"You will perceive that he writes cautiously. He says: 'Personally it will be a gratification both on their account and to conform to your wishes, if I am so circumstanced when the time for action arrives as to be able with due regard to other interests to favor the appointment of Messrs. Wallace and Weldon to the places they seek respectively. I know them both well and favorably.'

"You will perceive that he is entirely non-committal. The above is all he wrote on the subject.

"I am not without hope from him. If I can serve you

any further in the matter, besides writing to Mr. Lincoln and seeing him personally, let me know.

"What did you learn at Springfield? Have you been to Chicago and did you find out who were applicants?

"With the compliments of the incoming year to Judge Dickey and Mrs. Wallace, I am your friend,

DAVID DAVIS."

From Lacon came the greetings and good will of the friends of Mr. Wallace who also desired his appointment to the office.

"LACON, Ill., Feb. 22, 1861.

"FRIEND WALLACE:—"Learning that your friends were presenting your name to the incoming administration for United States District Attorney, I thought I would send you the endorsement of our leading Republicans. I could have got a *thousand names;* supposed it would be of no use to do so.

"We are very desirous you should get the appointment and would do anything in our power to assist you.

"Not having heard from you we do not know that you wish anything of the kind, but we thought we would send our mite at any rate. Respectfully,

"G. L. FORT."

From Springfield Mr. Wallace writes his wife on January 11, 1861, giving a glimpse of the political whirl in this State and the cares accumulating around Mr. Lincoln even before his inauguration.

"There is a great crowd of people here, continually coming and going. I have seen a great many of the most prominent men of the State. I have been so much occupied that I have not yet gone to Jacksonville and don't know that I shall go at all. Political matters are continually changing and no man can tell in this turmoil what the morrow will bring forth. The cause of Major Anderson is generally sustained by all parties here, but all are fearful of the result.

"I have seen Mr. Lincoln two or three times since I have been here, but only for a moment and he is continually surrounded by a crowd of people. He has a world of responsibility and seems to feel it and to be oppressed by it. He looks careworn and more haggard and stooped than I ever saw him. * * * * * There are some amusements here—Mr. Murdock read Hamlet on Tuesday night, a very fine treat. On Monday night I went on Eaton's (R. E. Goodell, son-in-law of Governor Matteson) invitation and spent the evening and played euchre at Governor Matteson's with Mrs. Goodell and Mrs. Maginnis."

The political atmosphere in the beginning of the year 1861 was very similar to the physical before a thunder storm. Many feared the Southern States would secede and disrupt the Union. With this fear was the feeling by the Federal Government of doing nothing to bring on a crisis, hoping matters would adjust themselves and all come out right. Even strong men held this feeling. After Lincoln's election the South was more open in her threats of hostility toward the Central Government and fears were entertained of an attack on Washington City. The following letter of Mr. Wallace shows something of the feeling of conservative and loyal men at this juncture:

"OTTAWA, Jan. 16, 1861.

"DR. S. A. PADDOCK,
"Princeton, Ill.

"DEAR SIR:—Your letter of the 3d inst. in reference to the state of the country and suggesting the raising of a regiment to be offered to the government in case of a rebellious attack on Washington City, was received by me while in Springfield. The rapid course of events which every day seemed to change the aspect of the times, with a press of private matters, has hitherto delayed my answer.

"There was a time not long since when it seemed to me probable that those having charge of the Government would succeed in robbing it of treasure and arms, and leave it an easy prey to the disunionists, and I felt that under that state of things it would become the duty of the States who were loyal to the Federal Government to step forward and by timely tender of men and means save the Union from the hands of traitors. That danger, I am happy in being able to believe, is now past, and with it the necessity of extraordinary efforts on the part of the loyal States. The Administration at Washington, inspired by General Scott's patriotism, wisdom and valor now seems to be able and willing to meet and successfully repel any unlawful attack on the Capital. It is true that the treason of South Carolina seems to be spreading and involving other States—they are mustering military force and preparing for war. But who are they to fight? The Federal Government may content itself with collecting the revenue which can be done only by naval force, to which the disunionists have nothing to oppose. We ought not to force upon these unwilling States the benefits of post offices or courts which are intended as a local benefit. So for all the practical purposes of enforcing the laws; no military beyond the regular army to garrison a few forts and arsenals are needed. With these gangs of rampant fire eaters living upon the resources of a country already on the eve of starvation, these disloyal states will soon find themselves in the position that history shows to be the fate of a small state supporting an unemployed army. The military leaders will soon become the most obnoxious and abhorred of tyrants and before many months the cry will come up to the Federal Government or to the people of the loyal States from all men having material interests in the seceding States to be saved from the hands of their armed mobs.

"Opposition or the show of opposition on the part of the Northern States would in my judgment delay this event and keep up the spirit which has lured our Southern brethern into their present position. For I cannot, Dr., notwithstanding the wild, insane and treasonable course they have pursued, as yet regard these people in the light of foes. They are our political associates, our political brethren, common heirs with us of the illustrious sires of the revolution. We are stronger than they. They cannot hurt us and we ought if possible to prevent them from hurting themselves. If I am right in my judgment of the result, and I sincerely hope I am, what a magnificent moral spectacle would be presented by the Northern States, loyal to the Union as our fathers made it, calm amid the wild storm pursuing the even tenor of their way without being provoked into any show of passion by the threats of their own passion and folly. I think I can see in this the seeds of a stronger and more fraternal union than has ever existed between the North and the South.

"But if in all this I am mistaken, if the war spirit of the South should seek to expend itself upon us, if any attack should be made upon the seat of the Federal Government or upon any of the loyal States, then indeed we should act and act promptly and with vigor. But I hope for better things.

"You will readily infer from these views that I am disinclined in the present posture of affairs to take part in any extraordinary military organization, which might appear like preparation for hostilities against the Southern States. While feeling thus I am not insensible to the flattering opinion you are pleased to express of my qualification as a regimental officer, and should the contingency arise in which the employment of military force was in my judgment requisite, I know of no persons with whom I would be more pleased to act than with yourself and the gentlemen you have named in that connection.

"Yours very respectfully,
"W. H. L. WALLACE."

Cyrus Dickey, the brother of Mrs. Wallace, was in Memphis, Tennessee, practicing law in the closing months of 1860, and in a letter from there dated December 20, 1860, to his younger brother shows something of the state of public feeling in regard to the prevailing political troubles.

"The political troubles which threaten our Union as a matter of course affect greatly all branches of business and the practice of the law is no exception. The state of the Union occupies universal attention here and I am sorry to say among Union men very little hope of its preservation is entertained.

"If all men, North and South, had in times past taken as much pains as our father has, to teach his children to respect and love the people of the whole country, without respect to state lines or state institutions, and had sent them into other States and sections, that they might see the people without prejudice, all the present trouble I firmly believe would have been avoided and the Union have been as firmly rooted in the hearts of all the people as it was in the days of Washington; and a word breathed against it would be regarded as incipient treason. We cannot be too thankful to our father for these educational advantages. He has seen them and appreciated them when we did not. And has made all his children national in spite of the sectional prejudice that hung around our homes."

In a letter of February 7th, 1861, Cyrus writes to his father of a Union demonstration in Memphis which is interesting, as but a few months later this same section seceded, although there was a large element in the State against secession.

"Last night I marched for three hours under the old flag with *thirteen* stripes and *thirty-four* stars and an American Eagle on it and to the music of the 'Star Spangled Banner', 'Hail Columbia' and 'Yankee Doodle.' It is the only procession I have marched in in Tennessee.

"The turn out was in response to a call for a torch light procession of those opposed to immediate and unconditional secession. It was the most successful demonstration of the sort I ever saw, and drew forth all sorts of curses from the disunionists. The procession was fully two miles long. It reached nearly all over the city at one time, and was perfectly wild with enthusiasm. The torches lit up the whole city. The Stars and Stripes waved everywhere, and every drum and fife and brass instrument that could be raised was playing *National Airs.*

"A great many stores and residences were illuminated. Balconies, windows and doors were everywhere filled with ladies waving their handkerchief and huzza-ing for the Union.

"At ten o'clock as much of the procession as could get into one place was crowded into 'Court Square.' The American Flag was so planted that it floated over the statue of General Jackson.

"At least two thousand voices joined in singing the 'Star

Spangled Banner' led by a fine brass band. I never witnessed such unbounded enthusiasm. After this the procession (which was by this time a street full of people) marched to the Exchange Buildings, and listened to patriotic Union speeches until long after midnight.

"This demonstration and other recent events have inspired high hopes that Tennessee will not secede and that the Union may yet be restored. A few days more will shed more light upon the subject. The election is on the 9th.

"I think I had better remain here at all events until the middle of March. It may yet be disagreeable to stay."

CHAPTER XI.

LINCOLN'S INAUGURATION. FIRING ON SUMTER. THE COUNTRY PREPARES FOR WAR. MR. WALLACE MADE COLONEL.

IN February, 1861, Mr. Wallace, sharing with many others great fear for Mr. Lincoln's personal safety at the inauguration, went on to Washington to help in his protection if necessary. From there he writes his wife telling of his impressions on that memorable occasion:

"Washington D. C., February 27, 1861, * * * * * * We first stopped at Willard's, where Mr. Lincoln and many of the Illinois people are, but the sleeping accommodations were such that we could not stand it, so this morning we found a private boarding house. * * * * This political cauldron has been in a dreadful boil since I came. The peace conference has just reached a result and will adjourn today. You will see the result in the papers. (*Note) It gives great satisfaction to all conservative men of all parties. Indeed the crisis seemed so threatening that most good men forgot party and only regarded the safety of the country. Last night I saw Mr. Bell of Tennessee, Governor Hicks of Maryland, Governor Pollock of Pennsylvania, Mr. Gilmer of North Carolina and Thurlow Weed of New York, all strong Union men, in anxious consulation—men or different parties, all content to surrender something of their party's dogmas for the sake of retaining the border states in the Union.

"The result of the conference will cause a fierce contest, but I really believe from the present lights that it is the best thing for the peace of the country. For days men having

NOTE: "The peace conference adopted a peace measure, a modification of the Guthrie plan. The measure is not known except that the matter has to be submitted to State Legislatures. Three-fourths must acquiesce before constitution can be amended to suit compromisers. They favored a resolution to enforce the laws until an amicable settlement can be made."

the best opportunities of knowing have asserted with every appearance of sincerity that unless something of this kind were done Maryland, Virginia, Tennessee, North Carolina and Arkansas would certainly secede. Governor Hicks of Maryland, who has stood in the political breach like Anderson at Sumter, told me this morning that if the conference adjourned without advising anything, as the prospect then was that it would, he should immediately call the Legislature of his State together and the State would at once secede. Mr. Bell of Tennessee also told me that some such result as this was necessary to enable the Union men of that State to sustain themselves and save their State to the Union. I trust it may restore peace to the country.

"I dined on Monday evening with Henry Winter Davis of Maryland. Judge Davis, Charles Francis Adams of Massachusetts, Mr. Uhlman of New York, and Mr. Lamon of Bloomington, Illinois, were of the party."

Mr. Wallace attended the Inauguration and writes of the occasion to his wife.

"March 5, 1861. Yesterday I looked upon a scene which realized my dearest political hopes. I saw an honest and able man stand up before his countrymen in the presence of the representatives of the civilized world and surrounded by the insignia of power, and without mental reservation take the solemn oath to protect and defend the Constitution of our country and to take care that its laws be enforced. It was an imposing scene. By the kindness of Henry Winter Davis of Maryland I was admitted to the floor of the House of Representatives and spent the last hour of the session there and from there went upon the eastern portico from which I could see the assembling crowd, and witness the whole ceremony of the inauguration. You will have read in the papers the full particulars before this can reach you, and I need only say that when the ceremony by Mr. Lincoln kissing the Book and the fine band of the Marine Corps broke forth in triumphant strains of music mingled with the joyous shouts of the vast multitude, it seemed to me that our country had passed the darkest hour of her history and the future was brightened with the dawn of a happier day. * * * * Conservative men of all parties here are gratified with the tone and spirit of the President's address, and the direct and honest manner in which he met and dealt with the exciting questions of the day, marked him at once an honest and capable man.

"He had been so abused and misrepresented that the great mass of people here who did not know him were as much surprised at his ability as they were pleased by the spirit of this his first official act. The fearful feeling of foreboding that seemed to pervade the whole atmosphere is changed to one of confidence and trust in the future.

"I have seen Mr. Lincoln but twice since I have been here. I called to-day with about five hundred other people from Illinois, to pay our respects to Mr. and Mrs. Lincoln in their new home. Mr. Lincoln seemed perfectly at home —that is, he was as awkward and easy there as he always was in Illinois. Mrs. Lincoln seems to support the dignity of her new position with becoming grace. * * * I expect to see Mr. Lincoln to-morrow and put my application before him."

While in Washington Mr. Wallace received a letter from his wife showing she, too, shared in the anxiety held by her husband and her country:

"OTTAWA, Ill., March 6, 1861.

"I have been to church this morning and joined my heart and voice with, I trust, thousands of others in a prayer for the 'President of the United States.' The prayer on my part much heartier than usual. Added to my love for our country was my love for the individual. * * * * * We are very lonesome at our house. I want you to stay as long as it is best and pleasant for you, but know I am longing every moment to be near you. The presence and love of my husband is the great pleasure of my life. It seems to me I would die if I did not hope to see you again."

In answer her husband writes from Washington on March 9th: * * * "What you said about praying for the President of the United States really made me soften at heart. God, I trust, will hear and answer the fervent and hearty prayers that are going up to Him all over the country from such pure hearts as yours in behalf of the President. He needs the sustaining aid of the Almighty in the perilous and ardous duties of his station."

Mr. Wallace continues his letter:

"Mr. and Mrs. Lincoln held their first levee or reception last night. The throng was immense, ladies' crinoline suffered mercilessly. The crowd was thickly sprinkled with the gay uniforms of the Army and Navy and the diplomatic corps. Mr. Lincoln wore white kid gloves and worked away at shaking hands with the multitude with much the same air and movement as if he were mauling rails.

"I do not know yet whether I will succeed in my application, but I am determined not to be much disappointed if I don't. The delegation in congress—the senators and representatives—claim to dictate the appointments for the whole State and if this claim is sustained I suppose I will be counted out. But the indications now are that so far as Illinois is concerned Mr. Lincoln will see to the appointments himself.

"It is rumored that he has already appointed Archibald Williams Judge of Kansas without consulting the delegation, and that they (the delegation) are mad about it. It is also rumored that he has appointed Mr. Alex. Simpson of Hancock County, Marshall of the Northern District of Illinois over the unanimous recommendation of the delegation for another man. As far as regards the attorneyship the delegation are divided. Washburn, Farnsworth, Lovejoy and Kellogg have recommended Joe Knox—Mr. Arnold, the new member from Chicago, is very much opposed to Knox and desires to have Mr. Larned of Chicago appointed, but if he cannot succeed in that he is for me. Mr. Trumbull has not recommended anyone, but tells me he hopes things may turn so that I may get it. If I can keep the delegation divided I think my chances are the best, and even if they should unite on Knox I should still not be without hope."

Mr. E. C. Larned of Chicago won the appointment.

The optimistic views held by Mr. Wallace that the country had passed its darkest hour were not to be realized. On April 12th Fort Sumter was fired on—the fatal shot that began the terrible strife of civil war, homes made desolate, treasure in blood and money given boundlessly to keep a united country. We of a later generation can scarcely realize the excitement and intense feeling that was aroused by this assault on Fort Sumter. We have enjoyed the result in peace and prosperity of a united country all our lives that was given us by the blood and terrible sufferings of our martyred fathers. We scarcely appreciate what was done for us and honor enough the brave men who sacrified so much that we now can have a country to love and one that is honored by all.

To give some idea of the prevailing feeling aroused by the firing upon Fort Sumter, a quotation is here given from Rev. T. M. Eddy's Patriotism of Illinois:

"The Union was assailed; the right of the constitutional majority to rule was denied, and war begun. Perhaps no single thought proved more intensely exciting than the dishonor to the flag. It was the representative of Government; it was the symbol of national majesty; it was the emblem of authority and protection. It had been honored on all seas, had afforded sanctuary in all lands, and now it was insulted and hauled down before home conspirators! 'For the Flag!' 'Defend the Flag!' 'Rally to the Flag' 'Avenge the Stars and Stripes!' were mottoes seen in all places! The Flag was displayed everywhere from stores, shops and printing offices.

"It floated from church spires, and draped alike orthodox and heterodox pulpits. It flaunted from private residences and school rooms and miniature ones were placed upon the cradles of little ones soon to be left fatherless by the fortunes of war. It was mounted on almost every locomotive. * * * In a day old party lines went down, and for a season we were again one people, united in the determined purpose of National Salvation. Nineteen millions of people were intensely excited; moving like vast waves surging before a great wind.

"In the churches, pulpits thundered stern denunciation of

rebellion. The ministers declared that God had set this land midway between the oceans as a great political and religious missionary land. They showed it as the home of a united people, and that when He aforetime determined the bounds of our habitation He gave us this land to be made, in its entirety, the land of free speech, free presses, free schools, free pulpits, free men and women. They said He so built its mountains as to bind together, not divide, the North and the South; and what God has joined together let no man put asunder!

"He has traced the great rivers of the continent so there can not be dividing lines between the States of the cotton, the rice and the sugar and those of the wheat, the corn and the barley, with the beds of coal and the spindles of industry. They said He hath made it one, and never can it be cut in twain. More than one, at the very outset saw the contest was between Freedom and Slavery, and putting on the prophet's mantle, said: 'Slavery hath taken the sword; it shall perish by the sword!' Not in the Crusades was the religious spirit more marked, causative and controlling than in the Great Uprising of 1861.

"The press was active. Political, secular and religious alike made appeal after appeal * * * * Oratory played its part, and from rostrum, from out-door stands, from court-house steps and hotel balconies, speakers addressed masses of people animated with one great purpose.

"The women, knowing that war meant bereavement of husbands, sons, brothers and plighted lovers, said the nation's honor must be preserved, no matter at what cost!

"All eyes were turned toward the National Capitol and the eager question went from lip to lip: 'What will the President do?' The question was soon answered. Before nightfall on Monday, the 15th, was transmitted by telegraph the following proclamation:

"PROCLAMATION.

"By the President of the United States.

"Whereas, The laws of the United States have been for some time past and now are opposed, and the execution thereof obstructed, in the States of South Carolina, Georgia, Alabama, Florida, Mississippi, Louisiana, and Texas by combinations too powerful to be suppressed by the ordinary course of judicial proceedings, or by the powers vested in the marshals by law; now, therefore, I, Abraham Lincoln, President of the United States, in virtue of the power in me vested by the Constitution and the laws, have thought fit to call forth, and hereby do call forth, the militia of the several States of the Union to the aggregate number of 75,000 in order to suppress said combination, and to cause the laws to be duly executed.

"The details for this object will be immediately communicated to the State authorities through the War Department. I appeal to all loyal citizens to favor, facilitate, and aid this effort to maintain the honor, the integrity, and existence of our National Union and the perpetuity of popular government, and to redress wrongs already long enough endured. I deem it proper to say that the first service assigned to the forces hereby called forth will probably be to repossess the forts, places and property which have been seized from the Union; and in every event the utmost care will be observed, consistently with the objects aforesaid, to avoid any devastation, any destruction of, or interference with, property, or any disturbance of peaceful citizens of any part of the country; and I hereby command the persons composing the combinations aforesaid, to disperse and retire peaceably to their respective abodes, within twenty days from this date.

"Deeming that the present condition of public affairs presents an extraordinary occasion, I do hereby, in virtue of the power in me vested by the Constitution, convene both houses of Congress. The Senators and Representatives are, therefore, summoned to assemble at their respective chambers at twelve o'clock, noon, on Thursday, the fourth day of July next, then and there to consider and determine such measures as, in their wisdom, the public safety and interest may seem to demand.

"In witness whereof, I have hereunto set my hand, and caused the seal of the United States to be affixed.

"Done at the City of Washington, this fifteenth day of

April, in the year of our Lord one thousand eight hundred and sixty-one, and of the independence of the United States, the eighty-fifth. ABRAHAM LINCOLN.
"By the President,
"WILLIAM H. SEWARD, Secretary of State."

On April 15th a call was made on the Governor of Illinois by Simon Cameron, Secretary of War, for six regiments for immediate service.

Governor Yates called the Legislature to convene by April 23d to make preparations to obey this call for troops.

All over the country there was nothing else talked of but this treasonable assault on the government, and the measures and means to suppress the outbreak.

Men offered themselves by hundreds and thousands, no lack of men—but there was the equipment to be furnished, firearms and clothing, living accommodations, as President Lincoln said when begged for the necessary equipment for the organized and willing regiments: "The ore is still in the mine from which the guns are to be made and the wool on the sheep for the clothing." The South had been secretly preparing for years and was better equipped in every way. Firearms had been sent to the South from the Federal arsenals. The North, however, though the clouds had been so lowering for years, was thunderstruck and utterly unprepared for the pressing emergency, and it is sad to say it took her many months, aye, almost years, to realize the vastness and the enormity before her in suppressing this unholy rebellion.

Mr. Wallace offered his services immediately with no selfish thought of the personal sacrifice engendered in leaving home, and his lucrative law practice. He had built a beautiful suburban home on the bluff overlooking Ottawa and had enjoyed but one year of pleasure in the new house he and his wife for two years had taken such pleasure in planning and building, when the war came and he left it never again to return there to live. While he was in Springfield making arrangements for the enlistments, his wife writes, and how many a woman's heart yearned the same way:

"Must you really go? I only know now, when it is too late, how much hope I have had that you would think it best to serve your country at home."

It can scarcely be realized with what dispatch, after the President's proclamation on April 15th, the country was on a war footing. But nine days after this Mr. Wallace had enlisted, formed a regiment, and with his men was at the State capitol. From Springfield he writes to his wife on April 24th, 1861:

"The feeling here is tremendous and almost unanimous in sustaining the Government. Mr. Douglas is expected here to-morrow morning and it is thought he will make things quite unanimous. The troops here will probably be required for active service immediately."

A unanimous support by the Legislature to the Governor's request for war appropriations was imperative; a bill was introduced, but was being dallied with from day to day, fearing it could not be carried owing to the southern counties of the State being largely Southern sympathizers. These sections with southern Indiana were devoted to Mr. Douglas and it was thought he could, if he would, bring unanimity of action; so it was important to know where he stood and gain his influence for the Northern side. Hon. Washington Bushnell, then State Senator, drafted a resolution which he presented to the Legislature, and which was passed, asking Mr. Douglas to address that body, thus making it necessary for him to come forward and show his position on the vital question agitating the Nation.

Dr. Eddy says: "Mr .Douglas in the political controversies of preceding years was in favor of compromise, but when the crisis arrived, the parting of the ways between the Southern States seceding from the Federal Government, Douglas rose to this great emergency and with his magical and gifted oratory and personal power urged loyality at all hazards to the Central Government.

"He reached Springfield on the 25th of April and addressed the two houses of the State Legislature in a style of magical power."

He said: "For the first time since the adoption of the

Federal Constitution, a wide-spread conspiracy exists to overthrow the best government the sun ever shone upon. An invading army is marching upon Washington. The boast has gone forth from the Secretary of War of the so-called Confederate States, that by the first of May the rebel army will be in possession of the National Capitol, and, by the first of July, its headquarters will be in old Independence Hall.

"The only question for us is, whether we shall wait supinely for the invaders, or rush, as one man, to the defence of that we hold most dear. Piratical flags are afloat on the ocean, under pretended letters of *marque*. Our Great River has been closed to the commerce of the Northwest. * * * * So long as a hope remained of peace, I plead and implored for compromise. Now, that all has failed, there is but one course left, and that is to rally, as one man, under the flag of Washington, Jefferson, Hamilton, Madison and Franklin. At what time since the Government was organized have the Constitutional rights of the South been more secure than now? For the first time since the Constitution was adopted there is no legal restriction against the spread of slavery in the territories. When was the Fugitive Slave Law more faithfully executed? What single act has been done to justify this mad attempt to overthrow the Republic? We are told that because a certain party has carried a Presidential election, therefore the South chose to consider their liberties insecure! I had supposed it was a fundamental principle of American institutions that the will of the majority, constitutionally expressed, should govern! If a defeat at the ballot box is to justify rebellion, the future history of the United States may be read in the past history of Mexico.

* * * * * *

"It is a prodigious crime against the freedom of the world to blot the United States out of the map of Christendom. * * * * How long do you think it will be ere the guillotine is in operation? Allow me to say to my former political enemies, you will not be true to your country if you seek to make political capital out of these disasters; and to my old friends, you will be false and unworthy of your principles if you allow political defeat to convert you into traitors to your national land. The shortest way now to peace is the most stupendous and unanimous preparations for war. Gentlemen, it is our duty to defend our Constitution and protect our Flag."

Douglas made another speech in Chicago—his last, and worthy of this great statesman. These two speeches were sent by telegraph to all sections of the country and without doubt united the West and prevented the horrors of civil war east of the Mississippi and north of the Ohio river. As Dr. Eddy says: "His voice had such power as had no other. His words were as the prophets of old, falling upon the public conscience and the public heart!"

Mr. Wallace writes of the first speech from Springfield, April 25th:

"Judge Douglas and wife arrived here this morning. The Judge made a manly, forcible and patriotic speech to-night before the Legislature at a unanimous request passed by both branches. He took high ground in support of the constitutional authorities and was loudly and frequently applauded by men of all parties. It is thought that his presence and influence will create perfect unanimity on all measures in support of the Government which may be passed by the Legislature, and the moral effect of his course will add greatly to the force of any measures that may be adopted, by showing an undivided State rallying in support of the Federal Government."

Cyrus Dickey, Mrs. Wallace's eldest brother, joined one of the companies made up in La Salle County, which afterwards made part of the Eleventh regiment commanded by Colonel Wallace. He writes from Springfield to his sister something of the situation in which the new soldiers were:

"CAMP YATES, April 24, 1861.

"We have now been twenty-four hours in camp and are beginning to get the run of the ropes slightly. Our initiation was rather a tough one. We rode all night from Joliet in a train of fourteen cars crowded with soldiers, about four hundred, besides a great crowd of other passengers.

We arrived at Springfield about 8 A. M. yesterday and marched without breakfast to the camp, which is at the old Fair grounds.

"The rush of volunteers, and the haste with which the arrangements have been made to receive them, has given but little chance to make proper provision for our keeping.

"We lay on the grass for over two hours before we had quarters assigned us, and then it was more than an hour before we could get our rations and cooking utensils and get our first camp meal prepared.

"Our quarters are the old cattle stalls with a curtain in front. The wind has been from the west ever since we came in, and the smoke from our camp fires (which are in front) fills all the stalls or quarters with smoke. I rolled myself up in my blanket and went to sleep on the hay last night feeling very tired and with a severe headache, but got up at daylight this morning feeling perfectly well and clear-headed.

"It is a pretty rough life, but not more so than I anticipated. Will was here yesterday and is here again to-day. The election of field officers takes place this P. M. and I think Wallace is probably to be the Colonel of our regiment—we will know before night.

"Our company has adopted a cheer for saluting colors, which commands the admiration of the whole camp and beats the 'Tiger'. It is 'Ottawa' pronounced in three measures—1-2-3- Au-tau-wa. * * * * I write this under a tree in a gale of wind, on the top of Widmer's valise."

The organization of the regiments was slower than was anticipated. Mr. Wallace writes his wife from Springfield on April 28th:

"Our regimental organization is not yet completed. Captain Pope, the mustering officer, went to Cairo yesterday and will not return before Tuesday. I have the most positive assurance from the Governor that our regiment shall be the next formed here. There have been three formed, the Seventh, Colonel Cook; the Eighth, Colonel Oglesby, and the Ninth, Colonel Paine. * * * *

As it was probable he could not leave to go home Mr. Wallace wrote his wife to be in readiness to come to him, but he says:

"You ought to have an escort now, as the cars are full of soldiers; perhaps your father will let Charlie come with you or perhaps John could come, but don't come alone."

The Illinois regiments, out of respect for those of the Mexican war, began numbering from where they left off in the Mexican war; thus, the Illinois regiments in the Civil war began with seven.

The Eleventh regiment was mustered into service on April 30th with Mr. Wallace as the Colonel, and was ordered to Villa Ridge on May 5th. Mrs. Wallace joined her husband and remained with him until the regiment left Springfield. At Villa Ridge Colonel Wallace named his camp Hardin, in honor of his idolized and gallant Colonel in the Mexican war, John J. Hardin. From the new camp Colonel Wallace writes his wife:

"HEAD QUARTERS, CAMP HARDIN,
"VILLA RIDGE, May 12th, 1861.

"One week ago to-day this afternoon I left you at the St. Nicholas Hotel in Springfield and rode out to Camp Yates and took command of my regiment and marched them through the city to the Great Western depot. Amid the hurry and bustle of departure and the sense of responsibility in starting off with nine hundred men, illy disciplined and poorly provided, I still thought of you and the lonely feeling you would have when you found yourself alone, and I prayed inwardly that you might be comforted and sustained.

"When my men were all embarked in the cars, I inquired of the officers having charge of shipping supplies if the necessary means of subsistence and defence were on board, and was told that they were. I had previously given the necessary orders for provisions for ten days and ammunition for our command. We were much crowded, and after the fatigue and excitement of the day I felt very weary and the men near me in the cars were restless. I endeavored to quiet them and soon succeeded.

"The command was divided into two trains, the provisions and baggage being in the advance with Lieutenant-Colonel Filler, while four companies with myself and staff were in the rear train.

"We reached Decatur at 9 o'clock, there were switched onto the I. C. R. R. and went south. At 6 o'clock next morning we reached Carbondale, where I learned that no preparations whatever had been made for our reception. It was then raining heavily and it appeared that we were to be turned out here in the woods without tents or shelter. I stopped at all the stations between here and Carbondale and made inquiry about lumber and carpenters and gathered up all the carpenters we could find and reached here at 1 o'clock A. M. with some twenty carpenters. I got a cup of coffee and some half-baked biscuits at a house near the station—the first I had eaten since I took dinner with you on Sunday at the St. Nicholas—and immediately set out to select a place for encampment.

"I found one on the hill just east of the railroad station, a beautiful spot, combining the advantages of good water, shade and drill grounds, though it was somewhat cramped for a regiment. I laid off the encampment and set men to work, found some lumber here and ordered more from above, and before an hour the place was noisy with the sound of saws and hammers. I ordered a part of the cars we came in to remain on the side track, and took possession of a cooper-shop and one or two other small buildings, so as to afford shelter for the men. In the afternoon the weather cleared off, the sun came out fine and some of the companies moved onto the ground and bivouacked in the woods. I also established a telegraph office here and put Ed Schermerhorn into it, having obtained authority to do so before leaving Springfield.

"Monday night was clear and beautiful and the men got along very comfortably; but Tuesday morning I discovered to my dismay that we were without meat for the men—there being only one day's rations of meat sent along, notwithstanding my orders and the assurances I had received.

This circumstance with its surroundings caused me more anxiety than the presence of an enemy would have done. I took active measures to supply the want by ordering temporary supplies from Cairo, but the rations were irregular for several days. * * * * The work of building sheds or barracks has gone on rapidly and we are all now under shelter and as comfortable as men can be in camp in rainy weather.

"We must postpone the delights of peace till peace is again restored. Then when our government is again established, and the supremacy of our flag again acknowledged throughout the land we will sit down in our quiet home and enjoy the blessings guaranteed to us by Providence and the best government in the world.

"I went to Cairo yesterday, being the first time I have left camp since I came here. I saw General Prentiss, Colonels Oglesby, Paine and Morgan and all the officers of their commands. I dined with Colonel Oglesby and his staff and in the afternoon attended a meeting of the commissioned officers of the three regiments. They had just received notice of the difficulties at St. Louis. They do not anticipate any attack on Cairo, but are expecting orders to advance, particularly if Missouri should secede. A squadron of dragoons will be down to-night and a portion of them will be assigned to me. We need them very much for scouts and outposts.

"We are a great deal more comfortable here, although we landed here six days ago without anything, than they are in Cairo, and I feel that I have my regiment in shape, better disciplined, better drilled than those in Cairo that have been longer in the service and I feel proud of it. I begin to feel assured of my position and if any distinction is to be won in this war I will have my fair share of it. I know there are people who are jealous minded and disappointed who will harp and distract, but I feel with my regiment I am beyond and above all such influence. Discipline comes hard on volunteers, and I am obliged to be severe sometimes, and expect some dissatisfaction, but I believe I have the confidence of the officers and men of my command, and if we should have an engagement, they will find this discipline the very making of their reputation as a regiment. I think I have succeeded in inspiring a proper *'Esprit de corps'* as the French say, and all seem animated with a desire to make this the crack regiment of the service. * * * * We have established regular camp discipline and are drilling constantly. The men are generally attentive to their duties and seem anxious to be instructed. I have a fine regiment. I think they have confidence in me and I am proud of them."

Mrs. Wallace spent a few days in camp with her husband, and on her return home wrote from Ottawa, on May 28th: "My visit to your camp did me so much good to see you and your men entering into their work with such ready self-sacrifice and zeal, has inspired me. I think I can do my little part of the work with a cheerful, hopeful spirit, ready, if the worst that I fear should come to me, to accept it bravely and resignedly as God's will. My many blessings and light sorrows all came from the same tender Father's hand."

Three of Colonel Wallace's brothers followed him into the war. M. R. M. Wallace entered as Major in Colonel Dickey's Fourth Cavalry, organized in La Salle County in August, 1861, becoming later Colonel of the regiment and a brevet Brigadier-General. He practiced law in Chicago after the war, and was for many years Judge of the Cook County Court, filling this office with distinction and ability.

John Wallace went into the Fourth Cavalry, first as Second Lieutenant of Company E, and rising to Captain of Company K. He remained in the regiment until it was mustered out in Houston, Texas, May 29, 1866, the last Illinois regiment in the service. He died soon afterwards in Houston of yellow fever.

Matthew Wallace, a bright, joyous, promising young man of twenty-two, also entered the Fourth Cavalry. He was accidentally drowned but a few months after enlisting, when his regiment was on a transport on the Ohio river bound for service in Kentucky.

A fourth brother, Hitt Wallace, although not enlisting as a soldier, was at the seat of war as clerk in the Commissary

Department under G. L. Fort until he contracted the smallpox and was compelled by ill health to return north. Mrs. Wallace's father, Judge Dickey, went into the war as Colonel of the Fourth Cavalry; her eldest brother, Cyrus, went into the Eleventh Infantry regiment, and her youngest brother, Charlie, enlisted in his father's cavalry regiment. Besides these near relatives, Mrs. Wallace had cousins in both the Northern and Southern armies. Her Confederate cousins were taken prisoners and sent to Camp Douglas in Chicago, where she was able to visit them and give them comforts in their Northern prison.

ST. CHARLES HOTEL, NEW ORLEANS

BATTLE OF BUENA VISTA

View of the Battle Ground and Battle of the "Angostura," fought near Buena Vista, Mexico, February 23d, 1847 (looking southwest). The battle was on the plain to the extreme right

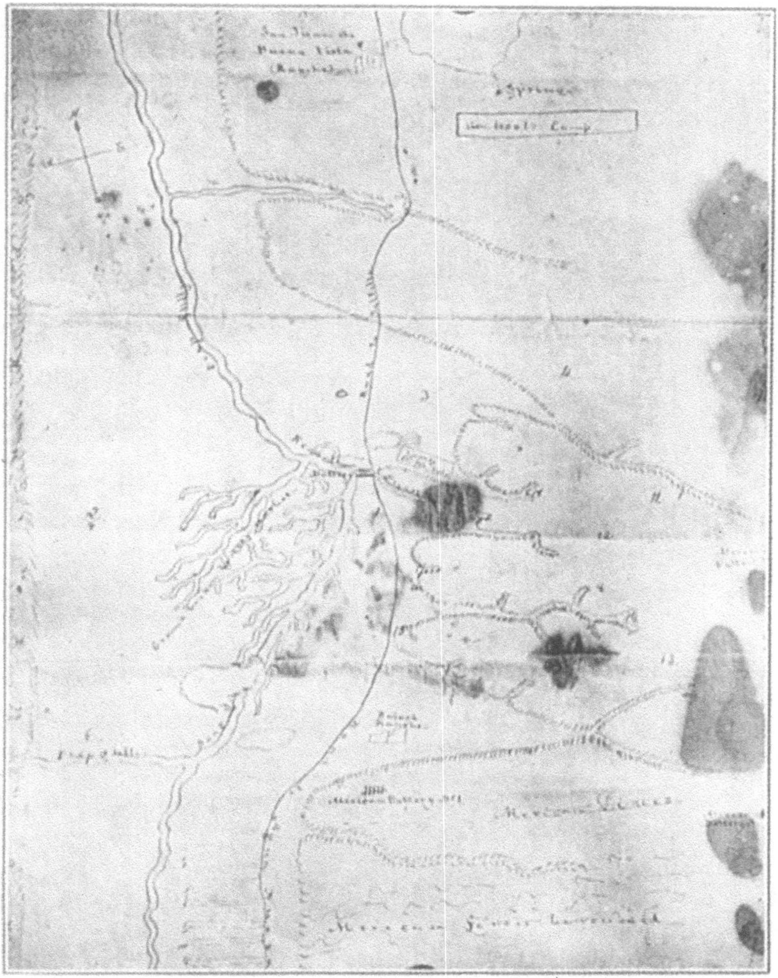

MAP OF THE BATTLE OF BUENA VISTA

THE DICKEY HOME, NORTH BLUFF, OTTAWA, ILLINOIS, 1866

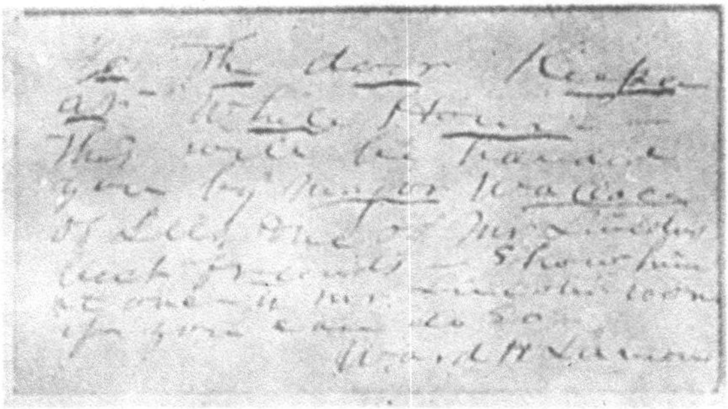

To the door keeper at White House
This will be handed you by Major Wallace
of Ills. one of Mr Lincoln's
best friends — Show him
at once to Mr. Lincoln's room
if you can do so.
Ward H Lamon

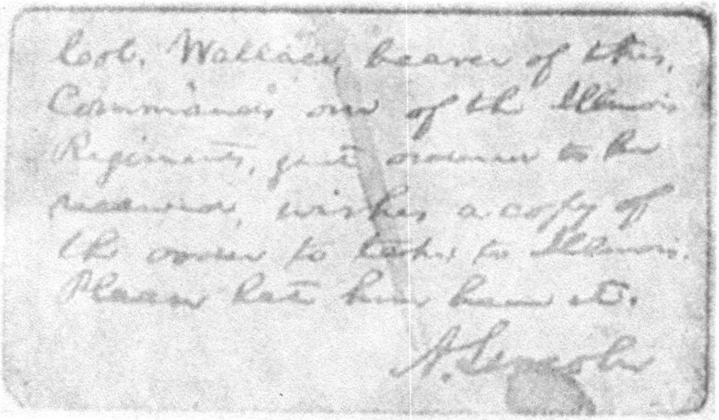

Col. Wallace, bearer of this,
commands one of the Illinois
Regiments, just ordered to be
mustered, wishes a copy of
the order to [illegible] for Illinois.
Please let him have it.
A. Lincoln

AUTOGRAPH CARDS OF WARD H. LAMON AND A. LINCOLN, INTRODUCING COLONEL WALLACE WHILE IN WASHINGTON ON MILITARY AFFAIRS, MAY, 1861

THE OAKS, HOME OF GENERAL WALLACE

FLAG OF THE ELEVENTH ILLINOIS INFANTRY REGIMENT, NOW IN THE LIBRARY AT THE OAKS

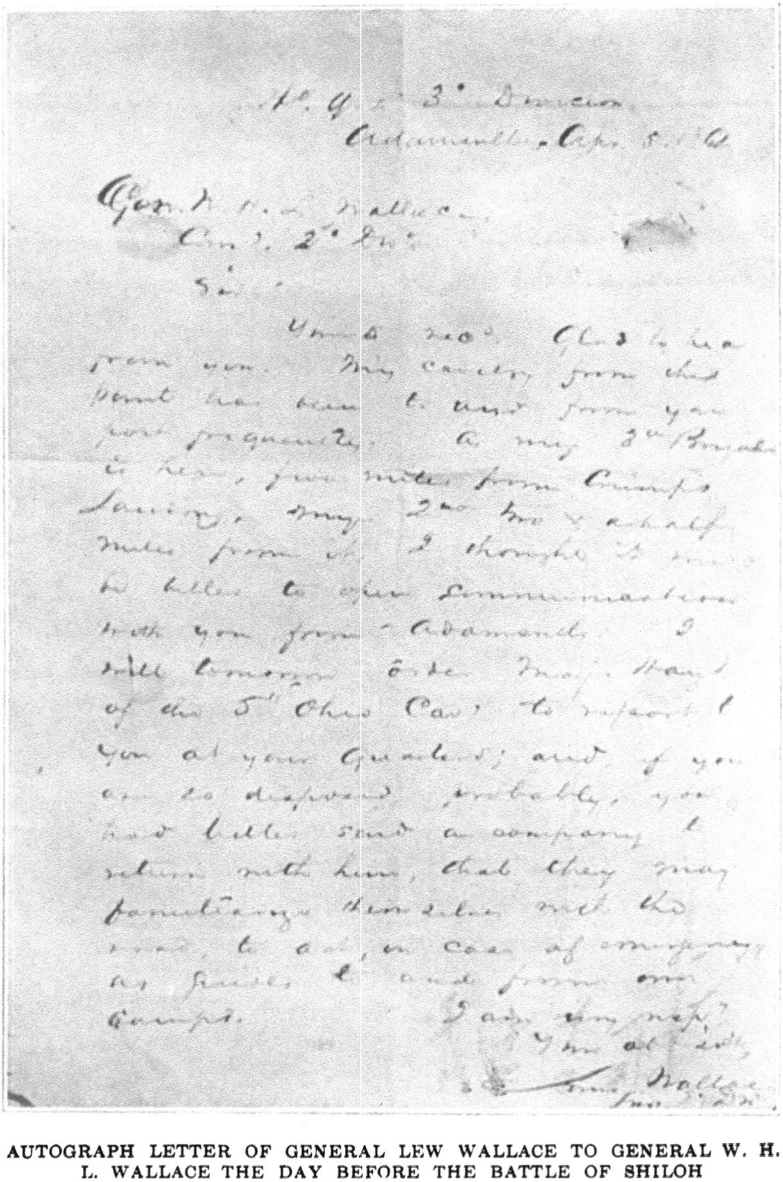

H. Q. 3d Division
Adamsville, Apr. 5 '62

Gen. W. H. L. Wallace
Comd. 2d Div.

Sir:

Yours rec'd. Glad to hear from you. My cavalry from that point has been to and from your post frequently. As my 3d Brigade is here, five miles from Crump's Landing, my 2d two & a half miles from it, I thought it would be better to open communication with you from Adamsville. I will tomorrow order Maj. Hayes of the 5th Ohio Cav'y to report to you at your Quarters; and, if you are so disposed, probably you had better send a company to return with him, that they may familiarize themselves with the road, to act, in case of emergency as guides to and from our Camps.

I am very resp'y
Your ob't serv't
Lew Wallace
Com. 3d Div.

AUTOGRAPH LETTER OF GENERAL LEW WALLACE TO GENERAL W. H. L. WALLACE THE DAY BEFORE THE BATTLE OF SHILOH

THE CHERRY MANSION, SAVANNAH, TENNESSEE, WHERE GENERAL GRANT HAD HIS HEADQUARTERS AT THE TIME OF THE BATTLE OF SHILOH AT PITTSBURG LANDING, TEN MILES DISTANT, APRIL 6TH AND 7TH, 1862. HERE MAJOR-GENERALS C. F. SMITH AND W. H. L. WALLACE DIED

MONUMENT GENERAL W. H. L. WALLACE, SHILOH BATTLEFIELD

MRS. WALLACE, 1877

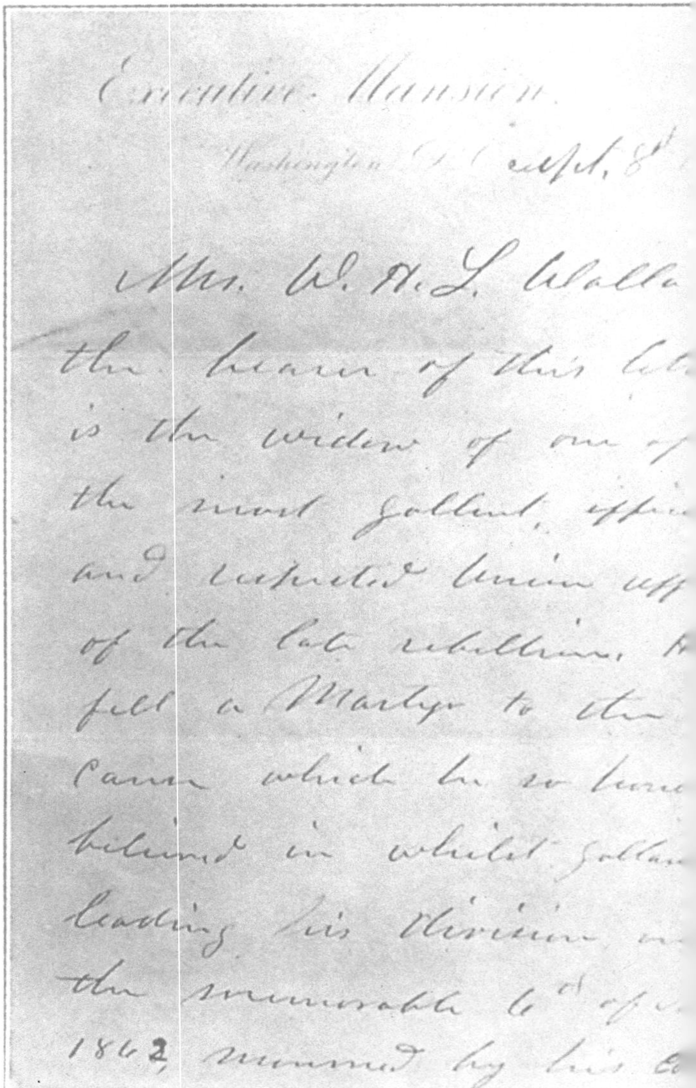

Executive Mansion,
Washington D.C. Sept. 8

Mrs. W. H. L. Walla
the bearer of this let
is the widow of one of
the most gallant, offi
and respected Union off
of the late rebellion. H
fell a Martyr to the
Cause which he so hone
believed in whilst gallan
leading his division on
the memorable 6th of
1862, mourned by his co

AUTOGRAPH LETTER OF GENERAL GRANT

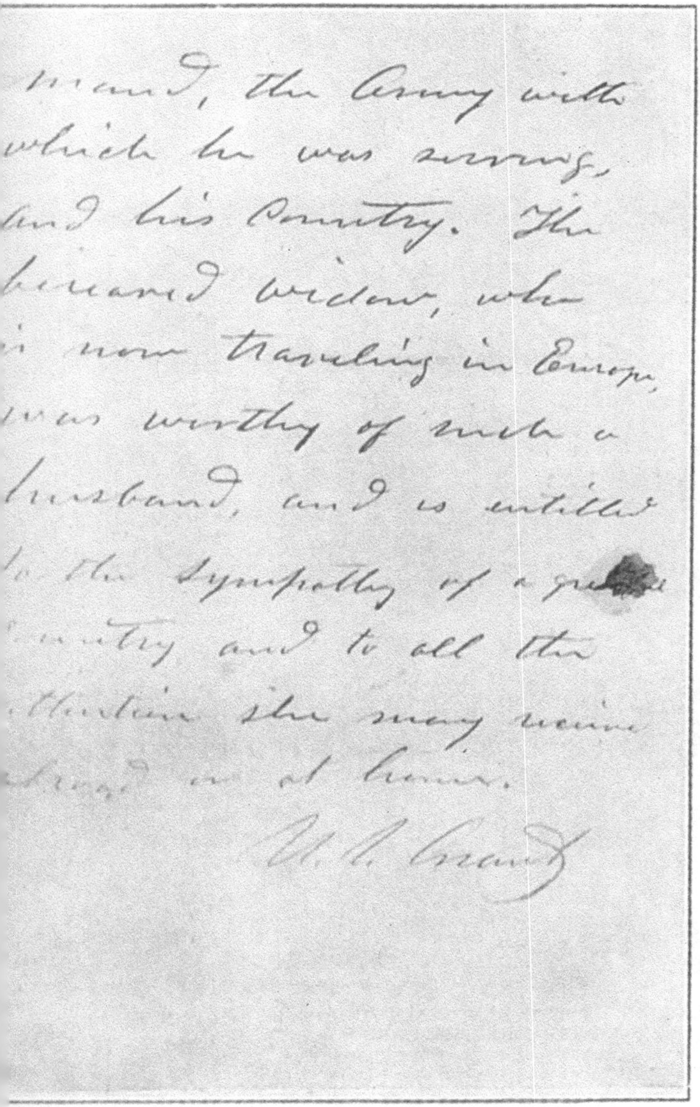

mand, the Army with
which he was serving,
and his Country. The
bereaved widow, who
is now traveling in Europe,
was worthy of such a
husband, and is entitled
to the sympathy of a grateful
country and to all the
attention she may receive
abroad or at home.

U. S. Grant

THE DRAWING OF THE MEMORIAL WINDOW IN THE LIBRARY AT THE OAKS

BIOGRAPHICAL SECTION OF MEMORIAL WINDOW

CHAPTER XII.

Colonel Wallace's Regiment Enlists for the War. His Command Moves to Bird's Point, Missouri.

A LITTLE glance at the general plans of the North and the South will be necessary to understand the movements of Colonel Wallace and his regiment as spoken of in his letters.

The great aim of the contending armies was to protect their respective capitols, Washington and Richmond, from capture, each city building ample fortifications around itself. Each held its own in the four years' struggle, but neither gained the capitol of the other, although the continual struggle in the Peninsular was to that end. But Lee was too great a General and moving on his own ground. The Northern Generals who commanded, from McClellan on would, perhaps, ably plan a campaign to have it countermanded by the authorities at Washington; hence, in the East very little was gained; but in the West it was different, as were also the strategic measures different. "The Confederates desired to make the border slave States, such as Maryland, Northern and Western Virginia, Kentucky, Northern Arkansas and Missouri, the battle ground of the war, hence can be seen the reasons for the invasion of Kentucky, together with the movements of General Price and his associates in Arkansas and Missouri. This was to secure the command of the Cumberland, Tennessee and Mississippi rivers by means of the fortifications of Henry, Donelson, Columbus, and Island No. 10. It was considered important in the beginning of the war by both parties to get possession of the great rivers, because troops could be transported much easier by water than by land. The Confederates saw if they could establish themselves at Cairo in Illinois on the point between the Ohio and Mississippi, they could keep the Unionists from coming down the Ohio and going up the Mississippi, which, below that point, ran wholly through slave States. But the Federalists were also alive to the importance of the place and were ahead of them, establishing a camp there in May, 1861, of several thousand men, throwing up earthworks mounted with heavy cannon commanding both rivers.

"The Confederates, thus foiled, made plans for the capture of Cairo. So in September, 1861, General Polk seized Hickman and Columbus on the Kentucky side of the river, but twenty miles distant from Cairo. Kentucky had remained neutral.

"The Confederates built two strong forts in Tennessee just below the border of Kentucky on the Cumberland and Tennessee rivers, eighty and ninety miles above their mouths, Henry and Donelson, to prevent the Federals from securing these rivers, and with them Kentucky and Tennessee, so their capture was of great importance to the Northern side."

In the latter part of May Colonel Wallace made a hurried trip to Washington City. On his return he wrote his wife of passing through all the lines beyond the river, and how war-like it looked, and also of his errand there:

"CAMP HARDIN, June 2d, 1861.

"I had a very hurried and exciting trip to Washington. I went to Alexandria and Arlington Heights, saw many Illinois friends, all of whom congratulated me. I can now tell you the object of my visit. General Prentiss had tendered his brigade of three months' men for the war, and sent me on to urge its acceptance, in which I was successful. If not more than one-fifth of the men in the regiments decline to go for the war the regiments will be mustered into service for the war. I think my regiment will be almost unanimous.

"I know, dear Ann, what your first feeling will be, but a little reflection will satisfy you that the step I have taken is not only right, but one that I could not avoid. The country demands the service of her citizens in the field. Our regiments are the best drilled and the nearest ready for efficient service of any in the State. Being thus situated and having the opportunity of going into the service for the war, we would justly and doubtless receive censure of all loyal people should we decline.

"The impulses of patriotism and the desire for distinction in the war—the two great incentives to a soldier's calling—lead us to accept the place opened for us—the other considerations I have mentioned impel us to do so. The personal sacrifice of the endearments of home is already partially made, and I hope by this course to aid in rendering those endearments enduring. All business of a civil nature is stagnant and the whole life and energy of the Nation is poured into this war. My position is such that I cannot if I would, decline to enter the path opened before me. My duty as a citizen and a patriot—my true duty to you, dear, requires that I should not leave the service of the country at this time. I trust that the stupendous preparations now making will bring an early end to this miserable treason and ere many months the slumbering loyalty of the seceded States will, under the influence of the present blaze of patriotism, reassert itself, and replant the flag of the Union and re-establish the Constitution everywhere throughout the Republic. Then, when we have again a country to be proud of, when we can feel that we are safe under the protection of the old Constitution, when we can lie down satisfied that the Government has the power and will to protect us in our persons, our homes, and our all, we may turn from the pursuits of arms and enjoy the delights of peace. * * * * I send by Mrs. T. C. Gibson a specimen of a pattern for a havelock, a linen cap cover and cape for soldiers' caps, named in honor of the British General in India. These (the pattern and specimen) I procured from Mrs. Willard of Willard's Hotel in Washington. I wish you would, by subscription or otherwise, procure linen and make up as many as you and the ladies of Ottawa conveniently can for my command, and say to the ladies that their kindness already shown assures us that we may confidently draw on them for any such things which will contribute to the comfort of the soldiers. The soldiers I saw at Washington were nearly all supplied with them, and they were a great protection from the heat and dust. * * * * Yesterday I received a most delightful surprise. Captain W. L. Gibson received a trunk and on opening it he found a package for me. It was little Blossom's dear face, bless her dear eyes and sweet mouth, how I would love to see her and her dear mamma this afternoon. I hung the picture up in headquarters, and it there now represents the daughter of the regiment."

In answer to Colonel Wallace's letter about his trip to Washington and going into the service for the war, Mrs. Wallace writes:

"The Oaks, Ottawa, June 4, 1861.

"* * * * In your letter you tell me you are in the service for the war and give me some of the reasons why it is so. Dear one! my knowledge of you and of our cause told me this would surely be the result. It does not surprise me. * * * * The separation is very hard. God has given me courage and I trust will give it me for the future to let you go cheerfully. Living from day to day on the dear words of cheer you send me in your letters and hoping all may yet be well with our country and you, Will Wallace, I will try to be a true soldier's wife and bear my part in this work bravely."

In answer to Colonel Wallace's request for havelocks, the ladies of Ottawa immediately set to work with sewing bees and havelock socials to raise money and soon all of the soldiers of Colonel Wallace's command were supplied with them. In the following letter Mrs. Wallace tells of the work in connection with making these havelocks or linen cap covers that were needed to protect the necks of the men from the sun.

"The Oaks, June 29, 1861.

"Oh! my husband, I am so glad to write to you again. I know you will have wondered at my silence for the last four days. I have been acting Colonel as far as being busy is concerned. I have been getting those havelocks made. I supposed you wanted about five hundred. We, that is the Ottawa ladies, had already made for three companies. Ottawa has sent five companies into the service and contributed largely to equip them.

"On Monday morning I set out early to begin the work. I knew it would take a good deal of energy on my part and perhaps I should fail. I knew almost everybody that felt inclined to help furnish the means had already given more than they were able. But I thought of your men drilling in that hot sun and that probably the effort on my part would add so much to their comfort and health. So I began it.

"I first looked about for the material and found it at Mr. Halbert's. He was willing to let me have it at cost and wait until the ladies collected the money for his pay. It would probably amount to seventy or eighty dollars.

"Then I got the opinion of a number of gentlemen as to the chance of our being able to raise the money in the course of the summer. Many said they thought we could but did not like to say to me 'go on.' Others (Mr. Cook, Mr. Nash, Mr. Mills and others) said they did not want to discourage me but all that would give had done all they would already, that the men's own neighborhoods ought to supply them. We had supplied our own, that was enough. I said the men were there without the havelocks. I said you would not have made the request if you had seen any chance of their being supplied from any other source. That the Ottawa people had done a great deal and they would never be ashamed of it. I said those companies were probably from scattered neighborhoods where their home folks did not get together as we could in our towns. At any rate, the men were there in the sun; they had given their time and risked their lives for the service and we ought to make the sacrifice of a little more effort to ensure their health. Besides, the safety of our own men depended in a great measure upon the efficiency of those they were associated with. Mr. Thorne, Mr. Warner, Mr. Edward Eames, Judge Champlain and Pa encouraged me and said I had better risk it, and that with my own inclination settled it, and I got the material Monday noon. I telegraphed to you telling you that the work was begun, and asked how many you needed. I thought perhaps, since I had heard in the meantime, you might have got some of the companies supplied from their homes. If so, we would not need so much material.

"I got some of the cloth and got some of the ladies together cutting it out, thinking I would receive an answer by night or early next morning. I stopped the cutting at four hundred until I should get an answer, which did not come until Monday evening. We found we had cut more than you needed. We have enough to furnish Captain Reed's German company at Alton, which we have sent to them, and will have some over for the Irish company. We will send yours on Monday by Mr. Gregg.

"There were lots of willing hearts and hands for the work. They went at it with a cheerful enthusiasm that was very pleasant. Twelve ladies in different parts of town gathered in their neighbors around a sewing machine and the work was done.

"All well at home. I will write more of ourselves next time. ANN WALLACE."

A few extracts are given from Mrs. Wallace's letters, showing what the women were enduring at home with soldier husbands far away. She writes on June 21st when her husband had moved to Bird's Point, opposite Cairo, on the Missouri side of the river, and was in more danger:

"I cannot keep the thought of your great danger out of my mind. Busy as I have to be, I am thinking of it every moment. A prayer for you is in my heart all the time. Oh! Will, Will, this waiting and watching and fearing is dreadful. Forgive me, darling, this was on paper almost before I knew it. You have enough anxiety of your own without mine being added to it. * * * * You are all the world to me, dearest. How can I do without you. God has given me a cheerful spirit. Do not think of me as desponding. I do try to be a brave woman most of the time, but I cannot help but be your longing, loving wife, even if you are a soldier.

"The young folks and I have just returned from attending a floral concert by children. During the evening the Star Spangled Banner was sung and then repeated by the desire of the audience. All the hope and prayer and exultation of that almost worshiped song is in my mind blended with you. 'Thus be it ever,' etc. are no mere words, but a heartfelt prayer from many earnest lips to-night. How our hearts swell and sink at the news of the triumphs and defeats of the troops of the last few days. There are so many heavy hearts to-day over the sad news from Manassas. If this terrible news is true, (the uncertainty of the telegraph makes me hope even yet) how it will lengthen the war. Oh! Will! can we bear it? We can and will by God's help." She again writes:

"You say I must not draw such tempting pictures of home. I did not intend to trouble you in that way. What else shall I write about? Home is not a very pleasant place when you are not in it. I will try not to write anything that will make it hard for you to be a good soldier. If it is not worth a thought, what would be the use of fighting for it. You can be all the better soldier for being a little homesick. I am just selfish enough to want you to think of home and the wife very, very often, and if you cannot come to them, I would feel badly if I did not think you would regret it; but darling, do not think that I would have you jeopardize the cause you are enlisted in for any present pleasure to yourself or me. Your letters before this made me hope I would see you at home for a little while soon, but in the last you do not seem to have thought of such a thing. That, with the telegraph dispatches speaking of the rebels landing below you, has spoiled my bright anticipations in a measure. I have no heart to write you because I do wish to see you and talk to you. * * * * Although my desire to see you is intense, still if it is best for you not to come, I can bear it, as well as you can. Do not let the fear of my disappointment add anything to your burden. What a happy woman I would be if I could lighten your load of care even a little for you.

"You say you pray for me to be blessed as I deserve. Do not pray so. My blessings would be few if that was their measure. God is very good to me. We will praise Him together. He has given me the devoted love of the noblest and best man I ever knew, and given me a heart to prize it."

The husband writes: "How richly you deserve a country and a husband! God grant that both may be restored to you soon! * * * * Around you, dear wife, cluster all the dearest rewards and hopes that fancy pictures as the compensation for success in our stern endeavor. May God in His great mercy keep us both till our country's cause permits us to come together again amid the pleasures of an honorable peace. * * * * Know always that you are the priestess presiding at the altar of *home,* that altar to which next to my Maker I turn with the most reverence, devotion and love."

On June 19th Colonel Wallace's command was ordered to Bird's Point, Missouri, opposite Cairo, then the most advanced part of the army in that part of the country. Here Colonel Wallace was put in command of the post, having besides his own regiment another regiment, seven guns, 140 artillerymen, and a detachment of cavalry. His duties were naturally very arduous and exacting, as he writes:

"BIRD'S POINT, Mo., July 11th, 1861.

"* * * * The business of re-organizing the regiment for the three years' service, (one of the most complicated and perplexing things ever attempted), the attention necessarily required by persons coming in from the country claiming protection as Union men, the general supervision of the command, the constant increasing series of new and difficult questions to meet and decide, the attention necessary to be shown to visitors from the North, of whom there appears to be a legion, the alarms at night by firing of the guards, making it necessary as a matter of precaution to turn out the command under arms and dispose of them so as to meet any attack which might be made—these, added to the ordinary duties of the regiment, have kept me more than usually busy."

To show something of the duties of a Post Commander and his Adjutant or Secretary, a letter is here given from Cyrus Dickey, who was adjutant to General Ransom, then Commandant of the Post, to his sister, Mrs. Wallace, from

Natchez, Mississippi, on August 7, 1863, 10 P. M. * * * "I have attempted occasionally to answer your letter, but have given it up in despair on account of the annoying interruptions. It is utterly impossible to attend to the duties of a post and write a consecutive letter at the same time. In civil life I don't believe any man ever attempted the variety of duties which devolve through his Adjutant on a Post Commander.

"For instance, I was waked up this morning at daylight by an application of a Dutchman who had got tired of the Southern Confederacy and wanted to get transportation for himself and family to the quiet North. I advised him to wait until business hours and fell asleep again. Scarcely asleep when a request came from the Post Quartermaster for a steamboat and guard and a detail of negroes for a foraging expedition down the river on the Louisiana shores. I got up and wrote the necessary orders without dressing, and by this time I was wide awake, went upstairs and took a bath, came down and found two negroes who had come to complain that, 'Ellett's Horse Marines,' who had landed in the night, had come up into town and forcibly taken from each of them a cart load of vegetables and chickens just brought in to sell to the soldiers. I turned the negroes over to the public guard; and sat down to write an order to send out fifteen miles into the country to Colonel Coates in command of a force guarding and hauling C. S. A. cotton. Was interrupted in the midst of it by a modest little boy who wanted an order to purchase some ice from the government for a sick mother—which I couldn't give him.

"General Lee came down to inquire what were the political sentiments of Mr. Lurget, whose house he had taken a fancy to occupy for his headquarters, providing the resident was a rebel. Breakfast was announced and General Lee sat down with us, amusing us meantime with an account of his interview with the Mr. Lurget before mentioned, while looking over his premises with a view of establishing his headquarters there. 'General Lee, what State are you from?' 'Kansas, sir.' 'Aye, what was your regiment?' 'Jennison's Jayhawkers, sir.' 'Have you any of these Kansas men with you here?' 'Yes, about one hundred, and would like stable room for them; how are you off for stables?' 'What! You don't mean to bring these men into my landscape garden, do you?' 'If I establish my quarters here I will camp them near me.' 'Have you any control over these men?' 'Very little.' Lee left him in great apprehension.

"After breakfast the office was full of men, boys and some negroes, all wanting some relief or information. A speculator wanted to know whether he would be permitted to go into the country and purchase cotton; a New Orleans man, if he would be permitted to bring up and sell family supplies to the citizens; a government contractor attached to the revenue department, whether the military would help him to secure abandoned cotton; an indignant citizen wanted some compulsory process to make the negroes haul wood to market; another complained that the soldiers monopolized the vegetable market and that citizens were compelled to live on corn-bread in consequence; a negro wanted to get back his wagon which had been pressed to haul C. S. A. cotton to town; an old woman, whose husband was in the penitentiary for manslaughter, wanted to have us get back from her lawyers her house which they had taken for a fee four years ago.

"A respectable delegation of planters had called to see if some arrangements could not be effected to get the negroes to go back to the plantations and save the crops. A dashing widow drove in with a splendid carriage drawn by a pair of scrawny mules to pray that her carriage horses, which had been seized by mounted infantry, could be returned to her; an elderly lady, with a brace of blooming daughters, wished permission to purchase from the commissary half a pound of tea and a little flour as luxuries for a sick father. Two negroes came in out of breath to report that the guerrillas over on the Louisiana side were burning cotton and shooting all the negroes who refused to go to Texas. Mrs. Nichols came in with a basket of luscious pears, peaches, figs and grapes and a request that her own riding horse may be returned which was taken to mount infantry on.

"Mr. Lurget sends his compliments with a huge demijohn of old sherry, which has been in his garret for twenty-six years, and follows it up with a request that General Lee may be persuaded not to select his house as quarters. Captain Smith reports that he has four thousand and five hundred negroes in his camp of contrabands without a doctor, and some are sick; that the Horse Marines insult his negro camp guards and overrun his camp; an indignant old negro preacher came in to complain that the Major had refused to open the Methodist church for him to hold prayer meetings in; a sour old maid comes to inquire if we will not send letters North for her without inspecting them. The General tells me that I must at once shut myself up in the back room and prepare an order to regulate the 'Jayhawkers' and 'Horse Marines,' also some dispatches for Department headquarters for a boat that is waiting. This is the general style of business this firm is transacting and has been and expects to be for some time. What writing I do which requires any logical connection or arrangement must be done after night or locked up in a back room with some one trying to open the door every two minutes. I break away about once a day and ride away out into the country and call on some planters, I know them all, whom I have met in the office before.

"We, Ransom and I, still hope to get to go to Illinois about the first of September. Ransom is not well to-day, had a chill of ague, not serious, but improves his chance for leave of absence."

Captain Dickey, while in this position, was able to do many kindnesses to the unprotected ladies whose husbands, brothers and fathers were off fighting in the Confederate army. Among these was a family named Winston. Later in the war, when Captain Dickey was shot in the battle of Sabine Cross Roads, near Shreveport, Louisiana, a Major Winston, a son and brother of the ladies in Natchez, found him on the field mortally wounded; finding from some papers on him that he was the same Captain Dickey who had been so kind to his mother and sisters, had him taken to the hospital and cared for until he died, five days after the battle, and then had him buried.

CHAPTER XIII.

General Frémont Takes Command of Western Department. Large Rebel Force Near Bird's Point.

THE South started the contest, having the advantage over the North in being better prepared in the beginning. They had secretly collected arms and ammunition at various strong points; then many of the officers in the United States Army were Southern men who left its ranks to join the cause of the Southern Confederacy, their State love and loyalty being stronger than that for the Union. Thus the South had generals of experience from the beginning, commanders that began the war were the same that continued and finished it, which was quite the opposite in the Northern army. There was no general that was prominent in the commencement of hostilities that was so at the close of the four years' struggle. This constant change of commanding officers was a great detriment to the Union cause and may have had much influence in determining the lack of success in both the Eastern and Western Departments in the early part of the war. The Northern authorities seemed dazed, not comprehending in the beginning the great seriousness of the situation and did not plan and execute with ability, foresight and strength.

"In July, 1861, as Dr. Eddy writes, "Major-General Frémont was given the command of the Western Department then first organized, which included the State of Illinois and the States and Territories west of the Mississippi and East of the Rocky Mountains, including New Mexico. This department was an empire in itself, with an enemy threatening in many directions. Missouri, on the verge of seceding, with a Governor openly for the Southern cause, declaring the State out of the Union, although the people of the State declared to the contrary. War raged within its borders.

"In Western Missouri the gallant Lyon, with scarcely three thousand five hundred men, was confronting McCulloch, Price and Jackson with twenty to thirty thousand. In southeastern Missouri it was equally gloomy. Cairo, Bird's Point, Ironton and Cape Gerardeau were held by Union forces with scarcely seven thousand men, and at New Madrid General Pillow held a Southern force of from fifteen to twenty thousand with a supply of excellent artillery and cavalry and was moving on Bird's Point. Hardee was moving on Ironton with three thousand infantry and two thousand cavalry. Another large force under Jeff Thompson was at Bloomfield.

"The odds against Frémont were tremendous. He was expected to raise, organize and discipline his forces and also to divide the Southern Confederacy by descending the Mississippi river from the Lakes to the Gulf. His plans were well laid and later followed, but after he had been superseded."

Had he been given a better chance with time to work out his plans many lives, labor and treasure might not have been needlessly sacrificed at the altar of inexperience resulting from the frequent changes of commanding officers.

There were rumors of a large rebel force in the neighborhood of Bird's Point, which the capture of the two following letters from the rebel Generals, Pillow and Hardee, confirmed.

"HEADQUARTERS OF ARMY OF LIBERATION,
"NEW MADRID, July 31, 1861.

"BRIGADIER-GENERAL JEFF THOMPSON:

"I have pleasure in acknowledging the reception of your communication of the 31st inst. I am gratified with the spirit and determination expressed in it. Since my dispatch to you I have ascertained that the enemy's forces are concentrating at Cape Gerardeau. It will be absolutely necessary that we unite our forces at some point, and if you can cross the swamp to Sikeston I would advance a portion of my force to that place and make a depot of supplies at it until I have collected sufficient transportation to move the whole column.

"We must have a depot of supplies and we must unite our forces. We shall have a fight at the Cape. This being settled as a necessity, and as our settled policy, you can shape your movements accordingly and take such route as your knowledge of the country may enable you to determine as best. It is more important that you should make Sikeston in order that I may provide you with ammunition and caps, of which I have understood you are in need. Independent of this we are fitting a field battery for your brigade and you must place yourself in position to take charge of it. It is important that we threaten Bird's Point and that the enemy be led to believe that to be our point of attack, and you had better *give out that idea.*

"You will please keep me advised of your movement. I will advise you of the probable time of advance. I shall probably place Colonel Walker's regiment as the supporting force for the battery I am constructing at this place.

"GID. J. PILLOW, General Commanding."

* * * * * *

To General Jeff Thompson, Bloomfield.

"Friday night at Kitheds."

"GENERAL:

"I sent you a dispatch this afternoon inviting your cooperation in a movement on the enemy encamped beyond Greenfield. Fearing that communication may not reach you I write again.

"My command encamps to-night at Reve's Station and to-morrow night will reach Greenville. It is important you should unite your forces with mine without delay. I want particularly to have a personal interview with you before the battle commences. Hurry forward. If possible, throw a part of your force in rear of the enemy.

"WM. J. HARDEE, Brigadier-General."

These rumors of a large rebel force near the camp and amid the reorganization of the regiments for the three years' service, when there was more or less disorganization, was very disquieting, as they were badly situated for an attack. Colonel Wallace writes to his wife from Bird's Point, Missouri, on August 2d, 1861:

"To feel that the responsibility of a battle was upon me without adequate means to meet the emergency gave me great anxiety. For more than ten days past I have not taken off my clothes at night and have slept very little. But to-night I breathe freer. General Frémont arrived this afternoon with eight steamboats loaded with Federal troops and munitions, inspiring us all with a hopeful feeling.

"The General landed about 5 o'clock, and I had a very interesting interview of an hour with him and was pleased to find that the course I had taken met his approbation. His manner and tone inspired me with the conviction that he is the right man in the right place."

On August 5th Colonel Wallace again writes:

"Since I wrote you General Frémont has brigaded the forces at Cairo and Bird's Point, making General Prentiss acting General of division and placing me in command of the brigade here, so that your poor husband is now an acting General in command of the most important point in the West. You hardly expected that you would ever be 'Mrs. General Wallace,' but such you are in fact. Don't you feel proud? You will scarcely believe me, but it is true, that I would gladly lay down the honors of command could an honorable peace permit my return to you and the delights of our home.

"The position I now hold was not sought by me. Indeed, I dreaded its responsibilities with my self-consciousness of inexperience in its tremendous duties. And when I felt that it was coming I earnestly prayed God to give me wisdom and strength to fulfill its requirements in a just and proper manner. Pray for me, dearest, that I may be enabled to do my whole duty, to God, to my country, and to you."

Mrs. Wallace answers the above letter:

"You ask me if I am not proud. I am no more so than I always have been. I just think others are finding out what I have known so long, that you are the noblest, bravest, best man in the world."

Colonel Wallace writes on August 6th:

"I had hoped to see you soon, but you know as well as I that the Colonel of the Eleventh and the acting Brigadier-

General cannot leave his post in the hour of danger. The very danger that you seem to dread makes it imperative that I should remain here. Perhaps your consciousness that this was so, makes it the more to be feared by you. But seriously, I don't think the danger is much. You haven't heard of any Brigadier-General being killed on our side in this war, have you? They seem to have a much greater immunity than Colonels."

The woman and the wife makes answer:

"OTTAWA, August 12th, 1861.

"Your letter dated the 6th took away all hope of my seeing you here. I never felt so sad in my life. I am very proud to know that you have been so trusted, yet my poor heart would rather have you a private, for they all come home for a little while at least. I see no help for it but for you to let me come to you. * * * * I want to come so badly. I am afraid I shall have to come without leave if you do not give it soon. This is not like a good soldier's wife, but I can't help it. * * * * I wish you knew what a comfort and delight your letters have been to me since we parted. They are such an alleviation of the sad, weary days. They each give me strength and fresh courage to take bravely the trial God has given me. If I could see you a little while I could live on letters such a long time again."

A week later Colonel Wallace was able to make a hurried trip home, and spend a Sunday with his family. His wife writes the day after his return of the joy of it:

"OTTAWA, ILL., August 21st, 1861.

"Your visit was so unexpected and short that it seems to look back upon as a happy, happy dream! No one can tell the joy of it until they have known the anxious, weary waiting and sad disappointment that went before. I will try hard not to let myself get so babyish again."

Colonel Wallace writes from his post, comparing the Sunday at home and the one in camp:

"BIRD'S POINT, Mo., August 25, 1861.

"It is Sunday afternoon, just one week since I spent that delightful Sunday with you in your quiet, beautiful home. How different the situation now. There all was serene, beautiful and peaceful—now and here, although quiet for camp, yet on every hand is seen the grim implements of destruction and the stern preparation for war. The few brief hours I spent at home seems now like a delightful dream. But I am glad, very glad I went home, if it was but for a day. I shall now always think of you in that quiet, pleasant home, with its surroundings of beauty, and love and hope. Oh! how ardently I hope that I may soon be joined again to you there. Oh, for peace! an honorable peace that would enable me to return permanently to you and the enjoyments of our home. God grant it may soon come. * * * But 'man proposes and God disposes.' In His hands are the destinies of nations, and He in His wisdom will in His own good time and for His own wise purpose conduct and close this war. We, as humble instruments, have but to discharge the duties we have in hand and leave the issue to Him."

A little incident of camp life is told in a letter of August 30, 1861, from Colonel Wallace to his wife, which probably was a common occurrence later in the war.

"I have had quite an incident to-day. About noon the officer of the day brought in an officer in a strange uniform, who announced himself as the bearer of a flag of truce and a letter from General Pillow. I found General Pillow's letter to be a proposition to exchange prisoners and introducing the bearer of the flag as Lieutenant Herndon of the Mississippi cavalry. He appeared a very gentlemanly fellow, and of course, I treated him civilly, gave him his dinner and detained him in polite confinement while I went to Cairo to consult with Colonel Oglesby in command there, as to the subject matter of General Pillow's communication. It was finally determined to exchange man for man of equal rank. I accordingly wrote a letter to General Pillow to that effect and sent it, with a list of prisoners we now hold, by one of my Lieutenants, Lieutenant Tuft of Captain Noleman's cavalry, who accompanied Lieutenant Herndon on his return.

"After the business was closed and the papers all prepared I rode out a mile or two with the party on their return and talked with the secession officer on politics and the war. He was a stiff secessionist, but we didn't quarrel. When I parted with him we shook hands and he expressed the hope that we might meet under more peaceful circumstances.

"During the first interview I had with him he inquired after one of the prisoners we had and expressed a wish to write him a note, informing him of the health of his family and friends. I told him he could do so and I would see it delivered. I took it over to Cairo, and after getting through with my business, I went to the hospital where the prisoner was and gave him the letter. He took it and commenced reading it, trembling with joy and excitement. He was a member of the same company and seemed overjoyed to get news from his friends. He asked if he could write a note in reply. I told him certainly if he conveyed no information about us. He accordingly wrote a note which he submitted to me, and in it he asked the Lieutenant to send him some money. I delivered the note and when the Lieutenant was about starting he asked me to take charge of some money for 'Frank,' the prisoner. I told him I would see that it was carried to him. He took out two $20 gold pieces and handed them to me. As I took them, I remarked: 'You haven't discarded the Federal coin yet, I see, Lieutenant.' He smiled and seemed perplexed, but answered. 'No.'

"I don't know what the powers that be will say about my action in consenting to an exchange of prisoners, but I am satisfied it must come to that, and I am willing to take the responsibility. I shall report the facts and correspondence to General Frémont to-night."

On September 4th, Colonel Wallace writes that he had received marching orders, and was all ready at the hour designated, "with two regiments, two companies of cavalry and a battery of four guns," As he says: "I had the infantry and cavalry in line with wagons loaded all ready for a march, but the artillery was in Cairo, not subject to my immediate orders, was delayed and before they got across the river my marching orders were countermanded, and we are here yet, but subject to march on an hour's notice."

On the 8th he writes his wife that their intention had been for the march into the interior:

"BIRD'S POINT, Mo., September 8th, 1861

* * * * "It has been rather a busy day. This morning General McClernand, Colonel Buford, Colonel Reardon and Colonel Lawler came over and I rode around the lines with them. About the time they left a boat arrived with a battery of artillery and a regiment of infantry from above. * * * * The move that I expected to have made, and which has unnecessarily caused you uneasiness, did not take place and probably will not, so I may as well tell you what it was. Take a map of Missouri and look at the southeast portion of the State. Pillow was at New Madrid pushing a column up through Sikeston towards Cape Girardeau. Jeff Thompson, another rebel leader, was at Benton and Commerce, with a body of Missouri State troops. Hardee, another rebel General, was at Greenville with another army. General Prentiss was at Ironton with 7,000 Federal troops. There were about 3,000 Federal troops at Cape Girardeau. General Prentiss moved from Ironton with his force and was to be joined at Jackson by the forces from Cape Girardeau and move down towards Sikeston. I was to send a regiment to Belmont, opposite Columbus in Kentucky, and about twenty miles from here, and when I learned that Prentiss had made his juncture with the forces at the Cape and commenced moving on Sikeston I was to move to Charleston with two infantry regiments, two companies of cavalry and a battery of artillery to be ready to co-operate with Prentiss should the enemy make a stand at Sikeston. The regiment sent to Belmont was to join me at Charleston. If the enemy did not make a stand at Sikeston we were to follow him to New Madrid and there try to drive him from Missouri. Prentiss' column reached Jackson and were there joined by the Cape Girardeau forces, but some question of rank

between General Prentiss and General Grant, who was in command at Cape Girardeau, threw things into confusion and the column did not move from Jackson south. I sent the regiment to Belmont and was all prepared, packed up and loaded so far as my limited means of transportation would allow, and had my men in line to start, when my marching orders were countermanded. In the meantime, the rebel forces fell back to New Madrid and have taken boat and gone to Columbus in Kentucky. A portion of them are within twenty miles on this side of the river opposite Columbus and we may have a brush with them yet, but I apprehend we will not move on them at once."

The anxious wife writes on September 5th:

"I find it very hard, in fact, almost impossible to interest myself in this company and this fair. My heart is not in it, but away off sharing your weary camp life, bearing your cares and perils."

In answer the patriot husband at the front writes:

"BIRD'S POINT, September 10th, 1861.

"I am sorry you did not enjoy the fair. Don't let thoughts of me prevent your enjoyment of matters passing around you. *If I am successful and come out safely it is all right. If I fall it is glory enough to die in such a cause, and furnishes no reason for regret.* Man must die sometime, and to die nobly is a boon granted to few. Not that I am tired of life, dearest. The hope of spending the future with you makes me wish for long life more than ever; but in the soldier's existence death is always a contingency that must be regarded. Of course, the ordinary chances of life are diminished in such a calling and it would be folly to overlook it. You may rest assured * * * * that you shall have no occasion to blush for me whatever may befall.

"We are in the midst of exciting events. The occupation of Kentucky by the belligerents is an important event, but I still hope that the share Kentucky may be called upon to act in the drama may be confined to her western borders.

A large force of rebels have occupied Hickman and Columbus. Our forces occupy Paducah and Fort Holt on the Kentucky shore opposite this point. The rebels also have a force on this side of the river some fifteen miles below here, and we have advanced a portion of our force to Norfolk, five miles below here, so that our lines are within ten miles of each other. * * * * I am glad this season of comparative inactivity is over. The sooner we get at our work the sooner it will be over."

Some further extracts are given from Mrs. Wallace's letters, showing the woman's side in the cruel war which has not been so often told as the daring deeds of the men at the front:

"OTTAWA, September 9th, 1861.

"Your letters give me new courage and make me strong and brave for my woman's work, waiting and hoping. What a pleasant picture you draw of the end of it all when God shall have given us peace and given us to each other again. * * * * I think we will be all the happier for the cruel separation. You have made me such a happy woman so many years I can afford to have a few sad days and then have a happier lot than most other mortals.

"This separation is the first real trial that we have had. Maybe we needed it to remind us that perfect happiness can not be known to sinners in this world. Our life together has been very, very nearly perfect happiness. If it had not been interrupted we might have forgotten to strive for heaven."

"OTTAWA, September 10th, 1861.

"I seem very near you in church. We have joined our hearts and voices so often together there. Almost every petition seems to be made in your behalf or in my own by the whole congregation. God will answer such earnest prayers, perhaps not in the manner that we look for, but it surely cannot be in vain."

Not long after this Mrs. Wallace spent a few days at Camp Lyon at Bird's Point with her husband, and writes on her return home:

"THE OAKS, OTTAWA, ILLINOIS, September 30th, 1861.

"I do not feel like writing a bit. I have been beside you and talked so much that I dislike to return to this old medium. * * * * I could not help but see when I was with you at Bird's Point how uneasy you were because I was in such an exposed position. I know it is because you love me so much that you felt so, but don't you know I love you? If I did not feel that I was a burden to you the danger of your place would have no terrors for me so long as I could be near you. * * * * It was so hard to leave you this time. It is not so hard for you. You are engaged in the work that takes you from me, and I am just waiting and watching until you get it done and can come to me and your home. It is a weary watching and looks very hopeless to me to-night."

CHAPTER XIV.

Major-General Halleck in Command of Western Department. Battle of Belmont.

WHEN General Halleck succeeded Generals Frémont and Hunter as commander of the Western Department, he organized his department into military districts, appointing General Grant as Commander of the "District of Cairo," which included "all the southern part of Illinois, that part of Kentucky west of the Cumberland river, and the southern part of Missouri south of Cape Girardeau."

General Grant brigaded his military district as follows:

Headquarters, District Southeast Missouri,
Cairo, October 14, 1861.

General Order No. 11.

For the better convenience of administering the duties of this military district, this command will be brigaded as follows, subject to such changes as may be deemed necessary in the future:

First brigade as now organized, and commanded by Brigadier-General John A. McClernand, with the addition of the Tenth and Eighteenth Illinois regiments, Schwartz's battery of light artillery, and Stewart's cavalry.

Second brigade will be composed of Eighth regiment Illinois volunteers, Seventh Iowa, and Twenty-second Illinois, Captain Houghtaling's Light Artillery, and five companies of Second Illinois cavalry, yet to be assigned, and will be under command of Colonel R. J. Oglesby.

Third brigade will be composed of the Eleventh and Twentieth Illinois regiments, Second Iowa regiment, Captain Taylor's Battery of Light Artillery, and Langen's, Pfaff's, Burill's, and Noleman's cavalry, and will be under command of Colonel W. H. L. Wallace.

Fourth brigade, Colonel John Cook commanding, will be composed of the Seventh and Twenty-eighth Illinois regiments, McAllister's company of light artillery, DeLano's cavalry, and one company of Second Illinois regiment of cavalry.

Fifth brigade, Colonel Plummer commanding, will be composed of the Eleventh Missouri, Seventeenth Illinois, and Tenth Iowa regiments. Headquarters at Cape Girardeau.

The command of the Post of Cairo, including Mound City, will be retained by General McClernand.

Brigade commanders will make their report immediately to these headquarters.

By order of Brigadier-General U. S. Grant, commanding.

JOHN A. RAWLINS,
Assistant Adjutant-General.

There had still been no very serious engagements when General Wallace writes home on October 15th, 1861, telling of some of the passing events in camp at Bird's Point.

"I went to Cairo this morning and while there was introduced to Commodore Porter, the commandant of the gunboat fleet here. At his invitation I went with him onto his boat, the New Era, and he fired two shells from his immense quick guns. They fell in the river two and a half miles off and exploded in the water.

"General Grant has brigaded the forces here and given me command of one of the brigades, the Third. We are to have a general review of all the forces here to-morrow at 10:30 o'clock. General Grant reviews us.

"The flag of truce that came up on a boat from Columbus yesterday, was ostensibly for the purpose of negotiating for an exchange of prisoners. It brought a letter from General Polk (the Rev. Bishop rebel General) asking for an exchange 'upon the principles recognized in the exchange made by General Pillow and Colonel Wallace.' General Grant declined to negotiate, but referred the matter to higher authority. I think he might as well exchange, for it must come to that in the end."

After the review Colonel Wallace writes about it to his wife:

"October 16th. We had a grand review to-day. General Grant was to have reviewed us and I had the whole force in line at 10:30 o'clock, and waited an hour for the General. He then sent word that his services would be postponed till further orders. But I determined that the review should go on and I reviewed them myself. It was a fine sight. Six companies of infantry, five companies of cavalry, and a light battery of six guns. It was as fine a column as I ever saw. The line was a mile long. All were highly pleased with the display." The soldiers probably equally admired their commanding officer, as many have said General Wallace was one of the finest looking men on horse-back they ever saw.

The following day he again writes to his wife:

"BIRD'S POINT, October 17.

"No news and no new movements. What can I write you about. Nothing but the old story. * * * * Old, but none the worse for its age, I hope. That tale, old as Adam's conversation with Eve, but new as the Eden in which they dwelt. I love you none the less, than I loved you twelve years ago, but my love, like a sturdy, vigorous oak, has grown broader and deeper and stronger with its age, until its roots are so entwined and interlaced with the very foundations of my being, that it seems to lose it would be to destroy my very life."

On October 21st, he again writes of details of post life:

"Yesterday I rode with Colonel Oglesby over to Cairo, attended a review of the Eighteenth regiment and dined with General McClernand. In the evening there was quite a collection of officers at headquarters, and it was late before we got through talking, so that I did not feel like writing. * * * * I may be with you as I have applied for a leave of absence. If I get it and all is as quiet here then as now, I shall run home for a few days."

His wife writes:

"OTTAWA, October 22d.

"Come if you can and do right, if not stay at your post. I love you all the more because you can give up your home and all its comforts and endearments when our struggling country calls. Such men as you must win. All will yet be well. Oh! may God give you back to me when this sad contest is over."

General Wallace was home for a few days and while away occurred the expedition and battle of Belmont in Missouri on November 7th. Cyrus Dickey wrote his sister, Mrs. Wallace, as they were starting out:

"COMMERCE, MO., 35 MILES NORTH OF CAIRO,
"November 4th, 1861.

"DEAR SISTER:

"We have started on an expedition at last with two weeks' rations. The object of it or direction of it is not yet made public. About 5,000 men, infantry, cavalry and artillery with ample transportation. We arrived here to-day by river and take up the line of march to-morrow at sunrise. We have only five companies of the Eleventh under Lieutenant-Colonel Ransom. The expedition is under command of Colonel Oglesby. Our companies are C, D, E, G and R, and Captain Noleman's cavalry.

"We are now outside the postal communication with the United States and you will probably not hear from me again until the close of the expedition. I have no notion how long.

"The whole troop is in good health and spirits. I am very sorry Wallace was not at the Point on Saturday, for I think I have good reason to believe that General Grant intended to give him the command of the expedition and waited for him to the last moment."

Colonel Wallace arrived at Bird's Point by the sixth and made immediate preparations to join the expedition. He writes his wife:

"BIRD'S POINT, MO., November 6th, 1861.

"* * * * I found on my arrival here that an expedition has gone under Colonel Oglesby out west, and that Colonel Ransom and Cyrus have gone along with five companies of the Eleventh. I start to-night with the balance of the regiment to join them. I go to Charleston by rail and from thence march by land. I expect to join Oglesby's command at or near Bloomfield. I cannot say how long we shall be out, perhaps several days. * * * My mind is filled with pleasant remembrances of my visit home. These busy scenes and active preparation cannot drive them altogether from me. I write amid the hurried bustle of preparing for our departure with a hundred interruptions to inquire about this and that, but amid it all and underlying all my active thoughts runs the strong, deep current of my love for you, an ever present, all pervading consciousness full of pleasure. God in His great mercy grant that it may always be so, and that we may be restored to each other and to the full enjoyment of our great love for each other."

Colonel Wallace did not arrive in time for the battle of Belmont, which occurred November 7th. "It was a bloody and stormily contested battle, and one that caused much criticism. The enemy was encamped on high ground about two and a half miles from the landing, which they could easily see and command with their guns. The fight was continuous from the landing on the Federal side up to the enemy's camp, which was taken after severe fighting, but could not be held, as heavy reinforcements were coming in and the Federal soldiers fell back to their boats, fighting all the way back against desperate odds."

"The engagement was supposed to be necessary to protect our southwestern army in Missouri from overwhelming forces being rapidly consolidated against it from Arkansas, Tennessee and Columbus, Ky. The struggle was a desperate one."

Colonel Wallace thought it had been unwise to attempt the battle, as he writes: "The advantages were all against the attempt and any permanent or substantial good an utter impossibility under the circumstances. * * * * It is called a victory, but if such be victory, God save us from defeat. True, it demonstrated the courage and fighting qualities of our men, but it cost too much. * * * * I saw Mrs. B's friend, the Right Reverend Major-General Polk. Many of the rebel officers were very pleasant gentlemen, but Polk's manner made me mad when I remembered his former position and profession as a minister of the Gospel of peace, to see him strutting in the livery of rebellion like some vain cadet."

This same rebel, General Polk, and General Wallace met again on the hard fought field of Shiloh, where they were within seventy-five feet of one another when General Wallace fell. General Polk sent one of his officers to find out who "that brave man was."

Mrs. Wallace had been making some visits among relatives down in the central part of the State, and on her return writes to her husband:

"OTTAWA, December 2d, 1861.

"How comfortable and luxuriant our home is. I have been nowhere among our friends that are so well fixed as we are, thanks to your loving care. I have envied happy wives the society of their husbands, but none are so proud as I am. They all seem to apologize and give good reasons why their husbands are not in the army. I am proud and happy to be Will Wallace's wife at home. * * * * Captain Rockwood took luncheon with us at Aunt M's in Delavan. In talking of the battle of Belmont, the Captain said if you had been with Grant the result would have been better. I told him I supposed Grant was in command and would have done as he thought best. He said you had made the lay of the land about there your study and they all knew it and that a suggestion from you went a great ways, even if you were not first in command."

General Frémont was in command of the Western Department but a few months. For a very brief time General David Hunter was in command, to be followed by General H. W. Halleck, who assumed the command on November 9th, 1861, which he held until July, 1862, when he was made Commander in Chief of the armies of the United States, with headquarters at Washington City.

The following extracts from Colonel Wallace's letters will show the feeling in the Western army at the lack of a competent head, and the changing so frequently of commanding Generals so disastrous to a cause:

"BIRD'S POINT, November 26, 1861.

"We have a new General (General Halleck) at St. Louis and there seems to be a new order of things, but whether it will be any improvement on the old remains to be seen. I am getting very tired of this and feel strongly the necessity of some head—some leading mind on whom I can rely, and feel that in so doing I am directed by a mind that conceives the crisis and comprehends the means of meeting it. This feeling of doubt and distrust is terrible when there are such momentous issues at stake."

"December 1, 1861.

"I am becoming discouraged at the prospect. The Government seems to be unequal to the emergency. In spite of the perils and dangers with which it is surrounded, those who ought to adopt vigorous and efficient measures to meet and crush the rebellion seem to be devoting their time and talents to rewarding political favorites and enriching mercenary contractors. * * * * We lack a head—a fatal lack in times like these. Changes constantly recurring in Generals, accompanied by changes of plan, have resulted only in inaction and the wealth of men and means which the patriotism of the country poured out, so far from being moulded and fashioned into an army to crush the traitors are fast degenerating into a mob. Unless some vigorous measures are at once adopted our army will soon be a source of weakness instead of strength to the Federal Government. Men whose capacity is not above that of a regimental Quartermaster, are put into positions where it is their duty to plan campaigns and move thousands or tens of thousands of soldiers to battle. With such counsels governing, defeat and disgrace is certain. * * * *

"Excuse me for inflicting on you these gloomy forebodings, but I write as I feel and think, and as I write to no one else in this spirit you must bear with me. I feel as if I need some other incentive to urge me on in this war.

Your brave words of devotion and patriotism have done much to sustain me, and although I have often had these thoughts I never have expressed them so strongly before. The convictions have been gaining ground for some time. I pray I may be mistaken in my judgment of the signs of the times."

In another letter he writes: "We seem to have won a substantial victory in Kentucky at Somerset. I hope it may be followed by others, and if it is my lot to bear a part in them, I hope, dear Ann, you may not have occasion to blush for me. I know you would, much as you love me, rather weep for me honorably dead, than blush for me living. And yet, I see how a brave man may be so circumstanced that he may be blamed and disgraced even when doing his utmost. Such are the chances of war, and it is under unskilful leaders that I fear more, far more than the personal dangers of the conflict."

His wife answers these gloomy forebodings.

"OTTAWA, ILLINOIS, December 5th.

"If you have conceived a plan that if carried out you think is good and you know of men that can do it and will do it right if they were put in power, would it not be well for you (in fact your duty) to go to Lincoln and Cameron or write it out plainly and have the right man go for you and at least give them the benefit of your thought in regard to the Western Division at least. Do not *ask* for anything for *yourself* and refuse any preferment that should by any chance be offered, and then there is little room to impugn your motives and more certainty to have your views studied. I know you will say and think that your wife's opinion of the dear soldier husband's capacity is too exalted. Your opinion may have more weight than your modesty gives it credit for."

Mrs. Wallace made a little visit to her husband at Cairo the first of the year and on her return resumes her letter writing.

"The Oaks, Ottawa, Illinois, January 7, 1862.

"Here I am again at my old evening's work just talking to you before I sleep. * * * * Our dear little Blossom is growing sweeter and dearer every day. She is like sunshine in the house. She is doing a great deal of thinking nowadays. To-day she asked me in a very thoughtful manner—without anything to introduce the subject that I could see without it was the anatomy of her doll—who made her. I told her God made her and tried for the first time to tell her there was a God that made us all and everything and who kept us alive and loved good and hated wrong, who lived high up beyond the stars and could see us all always. I never will forget the pleasant wonder of her thoughtful face. Then to-night before she went to bed I told her that that good Father in heaven would hear her if she would ask Him to take care of her all night and to take care of papa and bring him safe home, and with the pure faith of a child she lisped her first prayer, me prompting her. Do you not feel strong, dearest, with that little innocent pleading for you? Oh! I do believe you will come back safe to us. * * * * I have not got fairly settled at home again yet. I am living over again in my thoughts so many of those precious hours that we spent together. It looks a long time until the 'eighteenth' but I find I am already enjoying your visit in anticipation."

Colonel Wallace answers the above letter:

"Bird's Point, January 12th, 1862.

"I have read over and over again your dear letter of Tuesday evening last, wherein you give me an account of your first lesson to Blossom about God and her first prayer, and I have been unable to read it without a swelling heart and a dim eye. * * * * I felt a stronger faith in a Divine Providence when I knew that the fervent prayers of two such pure souls were going up in my behalf, and I felt a stronger desire to be worthy of such pure intercession. * * * * Kiss Blossom and tell her Papa loves his little Blossom and prays to Our Heavenly Father for her and Mamma and he wants little Blossom to love him and pray for him."

In answer to this letter of her husband's Mrs. Wallace writes on January 14, 1862: "It seems strange, but very pleasant to me to have you in the midst of all the busy, rough preparations for moving troops stop and read over and over the simple story of a baby's first prayer. Do believe that it is an acceptable service and that strong angels will keep guard over you in answer to it. Oh! if our little one could always keep her simple faith of to-day unaffected by the careless indifference that years so often bring. God helping her, she will."

Colonel Wallace writes of an expedition they are about to make, which shows his care for his men, his faith in God and his great love for his country:

"BIRD'S POINT, January 13th, 1862.

"We are again under marching orders to leave here to-morrow. We cross into Kentucky—where we go I don't know. * * * * It is cold—very cold. It has snowed some to-day and the river is covered with floating ice. The cold weather cannot last long, however, and the men are in fine spirits at the prospect of a forward movement. I have taken every precaution in my power to make them comfortable and I hope we may make the movement without much suffering. * * * * We take five days' rations.

"Going as we do without knowing where or on what particular mission, of course, makes us all feel somewhat anxious, and it makes me feel that I am in the hands of a kind and over-ruling Providence, who will order all for the best. I feel and have ever felt since I embarked in this cause that the hand of God was in it, and that out of all the seeming evil He would evoke the greatest good. Men, even the ablest and the best, are but instruments to accomplish His ends; and if He wills that they perish on the field or live to return to their homes, all is for the best. Man can die but once and to fall in support of the Constitution and the Government our fathers established under so many evidences of Divine favor is no mean ending of this period of existence. But I am looking to the worst contingency. Besides this, there is the prospect of doing what I may to establish the Government and then return unscathed to enjoy all the delights of home."

Mrs. Wallace was naturally anxious at this unknown expedition and writes on January 17th:

"I can think of nothing but the unknown perils of this expedition. I am loving you, and hoping for you and praying for you, and may that knowledge make you strong for your work, able by God's help to win a lasting victory * * * * do not risk yourself unnecessarily. I am proud to believe that you have moral courage to order a retreat if the great cause you fight for would not be benefited by an advance, and I know that no personal danger would turn you back from a known duty."

On January twentieth the expedition was back in their old quarters and Colonel Wallace wrote:

"The trip we have made has resulted in at least one good thing for us—It has demonstrated that we can move over any kind of roads and that we can stand any kind of weather, for it has been very cold and exceedingly wet and rainy ever since we started, and yet our men have been not only well but cheerful. The Eleventh preserved its good name for orderly conduct and promptness in the discharge of duty when some other regiments suffered. The officers and men of the —— were publicly reprimanded by General Grant for plundering, and five dollars for each officer and one dollar for each private in the regiment was ordered to be stopped from their pay."

After receiving Mrs. Wallace's letter, showing her great anxiety at the expedition, he answers it on January twenty-second at Bird's Point.

"I sincerely commiserate the suffering and suspense you endured on account of our recent movement. I felt it would be so, and yet I cannot say I would have it otherwise, because had you not feared and been troubled you had not loved me. Strange, is it not, that such suffering is inseparable from a great love? But you are relieved now. The papers have told you, even before my letters did so, that we are all safely back to our old quarters. I was in Cairo to-day. * * * * I had quite a talk with our old friend Commodore Foote. He always inquires about you, and to-day he wished to be remembered to you. While talking with him in the public room of the St. Charles a naval officer came up and he introduced us and went on to say, 'He is a fine lawyer and soon to be a Brigadier-General and I hope a Major-General before the war is over.' I looked at the officer, thinking the Commodore was talking to *me* about him, but soon saw he was talking to *him* about *me*. Such excessive praise from such a source was too much for my modesty and I actually blushed."

The country was not entirely given up to war. Politics still had a share in national affairs. The friends of Judge Davis of Illinois were anxious to have him placed on the Supreme Bench of the United States, a gift in the power of the President. Mr. Leonard Swett, a devoted friend of both Davis and Wallace, and a very prominent lawyer and politician in Illinois, wrote the following letter to Colonel Wallace asking him to write to Lincoln and also refers to other political matters of the day.

"St Louis, January 28th, 1862.

"Colonel William H. L. Wallace,
"Bird's Point, Mo.

"Dear Sir:

"The friends of Judge Davis are making an effort to have him appointed Judge of the Supreme Court for the new district of Illinois, Iowa and Missouri. I have already sent forward a paper signed by the most prominent men of the present State convention of our State. They signed it very generally and irrespective of party. John T. Steward has also written.

"I wish you would write to Mr. Lincoln upon this subject. It is a sad commentary upon supposed human gratitude that this is required, but it is required. The President is hanging fire between Browning and Davis.

"I wish you would write as soon as you can, for I suppose the matter will soon be decided.

"I don't know anything of moment now. I think the convention will make a good constitution, making comparatively few changes. I think they will extend the jurisdiction of the County Courts and give them to Justices without a Grand Jury the right to dispose of the smaller misdemeanors. They will reduce the circuits to a proper size and give a Judge from $2,000 to $2,800. Also, I think they will create the office of State Chancellor who will have chancery cases which now go to Supreme Court and leave the Supreme Court about as it is.

"No material changes occur here. The secessionists are still able to carry local elections in the city. In the Chamber of Commerce they at first prevailed and since in the elections of the Mercantile Library Association they elected their ticket by 200 majority.

"It seems to me, confidentially, that General Halleck is too much the Governor of Missouri rather than the leader of an army. His administrative faculties seem to be good, but he is the back-office lawyer of the concern rather than an active leader.

"I am informed a large number of troops will leave here for Cairo this week. Yours truly,

"LEONARD SWETT."

CHAPTER XV.

Capture of Fort Henry and Fort Donelson.

NOW began the onward march of events that went steadily forward until culminating in the surrender of Lee at Appomatox in April, 1865. On February second the troops started for the capture of Fort Henry, a stronghold of the Confederates on the Tennessee River. Colonel Wallace writes his wife of the intended expedition:

"Bird's Point, February 1, 1862.

"We are under marching orders if going by steam may be called *marching*. We leave to-morrow morning. We go up the Ohio and Tennessee rivers and you may hear of us near the Tennessee line next. * * * * I can say to you what I cannot say to any here, that these troops with others from Cairo, Fort Holt, Paducah and Smithland to the number of about fifteen thousand go up the Tennessee to take Fort Henry, which is situated on the Tennessee river just above the line. If successful we will have the honor of being the first Federal troops on Tennessee soil. I understand unofficially that I am to command a brigade consisting of the Eleventh, Twentieth and Forty-eighth Illinois regiments, the Fourth cavalry (your pa's) and Taylor's battery and another battery of artillery. Six gunboats accompany the expedition—I hope you may hear a good account of us.

"This move may interfere with my seeing you on the eighteenth (the anniversary of their wedding which they had always spent together), but I yet hope it may be possible—I should regret it very much if I should be deprived of that pleasure. * * * * How much I have to thank you for. My all of happiness of life is clustered around you. The many years we have spent together furnish abundant most pleasant food for memory and inspire hope for the future. You talk of my praise being pleasant to you. * * * * If I could express all your goodness, your loving kindness, your constant, patient attention, your noble self-sacrifice, I would indeed sketch a character worthy of all honor and love. Know that deep down in my heart, underlying all my thoughts, animating all my hopes, lighting up all my fondest and dearest memories, and inspiring all my desires and wishes, is the dear image of yourself. * * * * Without your love or without the love I bear you, I should not be myself. It is a part, the best part, of my life. It has made me and is still making me a better man in the endeavor it inspires to be worthy of that which I prize more than all on earth."

The official announcement giving Colonel Wallace command of a Brigade.

HEADQUARTERS FIRST DIVISION,
CAIRO, ILLINOIS, February 5, 1862.
SPECIAL ORDER NO. 4.

COLONEL W. H. L. WALLACE,
Commanding 11th Regiment Illinois Volunteers.
SIR:

By General Order No. 5 of Brigadier-General U. S. Grant commanding the District of Cairo, dated February 1st, 1862, the following regiments and unattached companies compose the Second Brigade of the First Division:

The Eleventh regiment Illinois Volunteers, Colonel W. H. L. Wallace; the Twentieth regiment Illinois Volunteers, Colonel C. C. Marsh; the Forty-fifth regiment Illinois Volunteers, Colonel I. E. Smith; the Forty-eighth regiment Illinois Volunteers, Colonel I. N. Haynie; the Fourth regiment Illinois cavalry, T. Lyle Dickey.

Taylor's and McAllister's artillery, the latter with four siege guns:

By the same general order you, as senior Colonel of the Brigade, are assigned to the command.

You will please report to these headquarters the strength of your command, the names of the officers commanding—and the date of their rank, preparatory to numbering and classifying them.

After embarkation please communicate with the General commanding for further instructions.

By order of

BRIGADIER-GENERAL JOHN A. McCLERNARD.
M. BRAYMASS, A. A. General.

A general order given to a Brigade Commander.

HEADQUARTERS FIRST DIVISION,
ON BOARD THE "ALPS," February 4th, 1862.
FIELD ORDER No. 10.

In planning the encampment for the troops, the Commanders of Brigades of the Division will strictly adhere to the following rules, viz:

1. The batteries of artillery of their commands to be put in the most commanding positions, giving them a wide range, if possible.

2. The proper support must always be given to the batteries in locating the infantry camps.

3. If the camping ground is wanting commanding positions for the artillery, the encampments of the same ought to have a central position, protected by infantry in front and rear, as well as on the flanks. In this case the guns will not be unlimbered.

4. Cavalry not on picket or other duty ought to be kept in the rear.

5. The infantry camps ought to be located with a view to an immediate formation into line of battle, which must be, at all times and under all circumstances, before the encampments, and fronting the enemy.

6. Public roads and other means of communication must not be obstructed by the encampment or baggage trains.

7. The baggage trains of regiments and independent companies must be kept in the rear of the respective encampments.

8. Brigade headquarters should have a central and most acceptable location, and the main guards should have their fires nearby.

9. Requisitions and returns for provisions and forage must be made in due form, and corresponding to the number of men present on the morning reports. They must be

approved at Brigade headquarters before issues can be made.

10. The guards, including the men for the picket line, composed of 300 men, more or less, will be mounted at 8 o'clock in the morning.

11. By breaking the camps the troops will always be provided with one day's rations, already cooked, to be carried in their haversacks.

By order of

BRIGADIER-GENERAL JOHN A. MCCLERNAND,
Commanding First Division.

A. SCHWARTZ,
Captain and Acting Chief of Field Staff.

On February second, on the journey up the river to Fort Henry, General Wallace had the sorrow of losing his younger brother, Matthew by drowning. As his Assistant Adjutant-General, Lieutenant I. P. Rumsey, says: "We saw the tenderness of his heart when, as we started from Cairo, the news came of the death of his youngest brother, an officer in the Fourth cavalry, who was drowned from their boat as it lay at Cairo, but still the man and the soldier went bravely on with present duty." General Wallace writes his wife of the sad event:

"ON BOARD STEAMER D. A. JANUARY,
CAIRO, February 3, 1862.

"I have sad news to write. Brother Matthew fell overboard off the steamer Chancellor last evening and was drowned. It was a dark cold day and everything was covered with sleet. His company had embarked on the boat and it pushed out into the stream to make room for another boat. He was passing along the guard and slipped. He put out his hand against one of the swinging beams used as fenders—it gave way and he lost his balance and fell overboard forward of the wheel and passed under the wheel, and although he had his saber, carbine and pistol on and his overcoat, he struck out and swam some distance toward the shore, but the load was too much for him and he sank before assistance reached him. Poor Mat! Had he fallen in action I should not have felt it so keenly, as that is the fate a soldier contemplates, but to be thus cut off in the flush of his youth, with a bright career just opening before him, is indeed most sad."

He writes again February 4th:

"We are here four miles below Fort Henry on the east side of the Tennessee river. We can see the rebel flag for the first time floating over their forces. We landed here this afternoon and are now occupying a series of hills running back from the river. * * * * I am very tired to-night. I haven't got used to my new responsibilities as commander of a brigade in the field and feel of course, a great deal of anxiety about details. I trust, however, that all may, with the will of God, work for the best. My quarters to-night are in a negro cabin, with my brigade bivouacked on the hills about me. I have just sent out my last instructions for the night."

Dr. T. M. Eddy tells of the attack on Fort Henry in his "Patriotism of Illinois:"

"The General commanding ordered the First Division, General McClernand's, including the First and Second brigades, to take a position on the roads from Fort Henry to Donelson and Dover to prevent the reinforcement of the fort or the escape of its garrison and to be in readiness to charge and take Fort Henry by storm on the receipt of orders. The Second Division, commanded by General C. F. Smith, was to cross the river and move up the western shore and occupy a hill overlooking the fort which the enemy had begun to fortify, and then to send a portion of his force across the river and reinforce General McClernand. The gunboats were to shell the fort and drive the enemy from the guns. Commodore Foote urged the land forces to start in advance of the gunboats and when he ascertained they would not, said pleasantly, but prophetically, 'I will take the fort before you get there.'

"The two divisions set out as ordered. The First made every exertion to get up into position to intercept the garrison, but the Tennessee mud was too deep. Over slippery hills, through tenacious swamps, the Illinois boys pressed eagerly forward, marching to the music of Foote's deep-mouthed artillery and the reply of the heavy guns from Fort Henry. Suddenly all was still, and the question ran along the lines, 'What does it mean? Is Foote beaten?' They were to learn that the majority of the boasting garrison had fled from their camp and that the remainder had surrendered. In addition to mud McClernand was obstructed by outer lines of defense made by felling the timber for several rods in breadth until the piled trunks and mingled branches made a barrier truly difficult to scale."

General Wallace's brigade was on this march, and on February seventh he writes his wife from the fort:

"We are here, got in yesterday afternoon after the gunboats had shelled the enemy out. We (the Second Brigade) were some three or four miles out, on the march, when the cannonading ceased. It lasted about two hours and was tremendous. The effect of the fire on the fortifications here was terrible. Guns dismantled, earthworks torn up and the evidence of carnage meet the eye on every hand. It was a strong place and could have been held by a determined force for a long time. The enemy seemed to have been seized with a panic and the whole body, some four or five thousand, left, leaving one artillery company in the fort. General Lloyd Tilghman, who is in command of this district or division of the rebel forces, is among the prisoners.' * * * * The Eleventh didn't get under fire, but hope for better luck next time. * * * * The men have been without tents most of the time since we started and were exposed to a tremendous rain the night before we reached here. The roads were horrible, but notwithstanding this they marched and took the heavy trains of artillery over the worst roads I ever saw."

The marriage anniversary of General and Mrs. Wallace was on the eighteenth of February, which they had always spent together, and Mrs. Wallace had hoped her husband would be able to be at home for the day, but this hope was shattered by the following letter:

"HEADQUARTERS SECOND BRIGADE, FIRST DIVISION,
"FORT HENRY, TENNESSEE, February 11, 1862.

"The prospects for being with you on the eighteenth are very poor indeed. In fact, I am reluctantly compelled to admit that it is impossible, and so is the project of your coming to me. We are concentrating a large force here and some important forward movement *ought* to be made at once. But, even if it should not, this is no place for you. I know you would brave all the danger of coming here, but I ought not and cannot permit it."

Mrs. Wallace's disappointment was deep—that they could not spend their anniversary together, the first they had missed since their marriage.

She writes on February 11th:

"The disappointment is almost more than I can bear. To be a good wife for such a good soldier I ought to send you brave words prompted by a brave heart. I am too sad. * * * * The days so filled with sweet memories make me more a wife than a patriot, I ought to be proud that it is your lot to stand successfully between your threatened country and her enemies. I ought to be grateful to the kind Father that has thus far preserved you amid many perils."

Then followed the march on Fort Donelson with the investure and four days' fight, ending in the surrender on the sixteenth.

Before going into detail in regard to General Wallace's movements, some extracts are given from Mrs. Wallace's letters, showing the anxiety and tension of the women at home when a battle was in progress:

"OTTAWA, ILLINOIS, February 13th.

"Our papers to-day tell of no result as yet at Fort Donelson. Oh! that that stronghold was ours as well as Fort Henry. I cannot but dread the battle. God help us and our loved country."

"February 14th, 1862.

"There is a party over at Judge Caton's to-night. The others have gone. Mrs. Caton seemed to want me to attend very much, but the thought of you before Fort Donelson is in my mind every minute. The gay scene could not be agreeable."

"February 17, 1862.

"This Monday morning I give you a word or two hoping, praying it may find you safe. I cannot write, I can only wait, almost holding my breath, wishing, yet dreading to hear the result of the deadly conflict that I feel is going on at Fort Donelson. Oh, God in mercy, spare me!"

"February 18, 1862.

"I believe you are safe. Your name is not in that dread list. A kind Father has heard my prayer. * * * * A week ago I could not have believed that I could have passed this anniversary so happy away from you. But the comparative relief from my anxious dread of danger to you and other dear ones is such that I have felt exhilarated and happy."

Mrs. Wallace had had a new black brocaded silk gown made to grace the occasion should her husband come home for their anniversary. When he did not come it was put away until he should. He never came home again. When he was taken the dress was put away for her own burial. The little package went with her over many miles of travel —over home land and foreign lands—oceans and mountains. Her daughter was told what it contained, and for what purpose it was to be used, but never saw it until the sad time that it was needed. It had been folded away twenty-seven years.

On the twelfth of February the forward march began on Fort Donelson, twelve miles distant from Fort Henry, with a force of about fifteen thousand troops divided into two divisions under the command of Generals McClernand and Smith. The fort was invested, but no fighting, except skirmishing on the lines, was done until the arrival of the gunboats on the thirteenth and another division under General Lew Wallace, and the battle was begun on the fourteenth by firing from the gunboat fleet of Commodore Foote, but the boats after a couple of hours were disabled when Grant attempted to invest the fort and take it by siege. This was frustrated by the enemy making a sortie and attacking the Union forces. A terrible battle raged for several hours.

The rebel Generals in command of Fort Donelson were Generals Pillow, Floyd, Buckner and Bushrod Johnson. Pillow and Floyd deserted their friends, leaving the command to S. B. Buckner, who on the sixteenth, addressed a communication to the Federal General commanding for terms of capitulation, to which Grant, then General commanding, made the answer that has passed into history.

"HEADQUARTERS, ARMY IN THE FIELD,
"CAMP NEAR DONELSON, February 16, 1862.

"TO GENERAL S. B. BUCKNER, CONFEDERATE ARMY:

"Yours of this date, proposing an armistice and appointment of commissioners to settle terms of capitulation is just received. *No terms other than an unconditional and immediate surrender can be accepted. I propose to move immediately upon your works.*

"I am, sir, very respectfully, your obedient servant,
"U. S. GRANT, BRIGADIER-GENERAL. U. S. A.
"Commanding."

General Buckner had but to surrender or subject his men to unnecessary carnage. He answered as follows:

"HEADQUARTERS, DOVER, TENNESSEE.
"February 16, 1862.

"TO BRIGADIER-GENERAL U. S. GRANT, U. S. A.
"SIR:

"The distribution of the forces under my command, incident to an unexpected change of commanders, and the overwhelming force under your command, compel me, nothwithstanding the brilliant success of the Confederate arms yesterday, to accept the ungenerous and unchivalrous terms which you propose.

"I am, sir, your very obedient servant,
"S. B. BUCKNER, Brig. Gen. C. S. A."

This magnificent victory gave the Union army nearly fifteen thousand prisoners of war, one hundred and forty-six guns of the largest caliber, with a fort of great strength. As Dr. Eddy says: "It broke the line of rebel defence; compelled the evacuation of Columbus and placed Nashville at the mercy of Federal bayonets. Grant and Foote desired immediately to move upon its works, but General Halleck refused permission. As the telegraph flashed the news of the surrender the country was wild with excitement. Bells rang, bonfires blazed, strong men embraced each other on the streets and wept and shouted."

From a Southern standpoint John A. Wyeth, M. D., in a magazine article of February, 1899, said: "The struggle at Fort Donelson was the first decisive battle of the Civil War. In many respects it proved to be the most important engagement between the contending armies of the North and the South. There were to follow many more desperate encounters where greater numbers were engaged and the slaughter more fearful. But in all probability the careful historian will yet decide that in shaping events which step by step wrought the downfall of the Southern coalition, Fort Donelson stands preëminent. It was a blow which staggered the Confederacy, and from which it is safe to say it never wholly recovered. A disaster that led into captivity thousands of its best and bravest men and thus early in the contest weakened the *morale* of one of its armies in teaching it the bitter lesson of defeat."

Dr. Eddy in speaking of W. H. L. Wallace's brigade says: "The Second Brigade of the First Division was commanded by Colonel W. H. L. Wallace, a gentleman, a brave man, a noble leader. * * * * Again and again was this brigade in whole or in part in the deadly fray, and nobly was upborne the dignity and glory of the State."

Captain I. P. Rumsey of Taylor's Battery and Assistant Adjutant General on General Wallace's staff and now an honored resident of Chicago, in speaking of General Wallace and Donelson, says: "At Donelson—that terrible night—as we were stationed there in front of the rebels, notice came from the picket to General Wallace that there was a good deal of motion and noise in our front, and that the enemy were probably moving out from their works. General Wallace and I were lying in a tent when the report was brought. He instructed me to order the brigade into line, remarking, 'It is too bad to turn the boys out of their blankets.' It was a terrible night, with its sleet and its snow.

"Nothing, however, developed in our front, and after one hour I again passed along the line with orders to lie down. On the next day as McArthur's brigade was broken, and Oglesby's brigade was falling back, the rebel bullets began to come along between us and our troops, paralleling our line, showing they were working around in our rear; I made the remark, 'they are flanking us and will get around in our rear." General Wallace was a man of few words and made no immediate reply, but presently said, 'Rumsey, you go to McClernand, tell him McArthur has broken, Oglesby is breaking and it is necessary to withdraw and change our front, and form a new line to the left and rear.'

"I found McClernand and repeated what the General had told me, that it was necessary to withdraw and change our front, and try to hold the enemy while Generals Oglesby and McArthur rallied. He said, 'Tell General Wallace if it is absolutely necessary, to withdraw and form the new line.' General Wallace then gave me the order to move the troops by the left flank and form the new line changing front to the right. I did so, and he immediately started for the right, where Colonel Ranson with the Eleventh Illinois was fighting hand to hand with the rebels.

"He then sent Davis of his staff with word to Lew Wallace, who was lying to the left and rear with fresh troops, that had not been engaged at all. Captain Davis finding General Lew Wallace, gave him General W. H. L. Wallace's message to which Lew Wallace replied, 'I would be glad to see Wallace and any suggestion he has to make will be gladly received and acted upon.' Receiving this answer W. H. L. Wallace rode rapidly to Lew Wallace—ignoring General McClernard, his Division Commander— and pointing out the situation suggested what seemed to him necessary to save McClernand's Division and perhaps the day; which was that he, Lew Wallace, should bring his fresh troops to our front and hold the rebels while we replenished ammunition and General Oglesby and McArthur rallied.

"Forward they came, filed into the right, about twenty-five yards in front of our brigade, also one section of Battery A, which Colonel Taylor placed on the left of Battery B; they had no sooner unlimbered than the rebels reached our lines and the leaden hail flew wickedly but found more ready ammunition than they expected. This suggestion of General W. H. L. Wallace and acted upon by General Lew Wallace so promptly was the means of saving great disaster and the escape of the rebel army down the river that night. All of which is due to General W. H. L. Wallace's prompt action, even without orders, but realizing the situation and that with proper action the right could be saved and the enemy held, he acted and accomplished what was the means of compelling their surrender on the next morning."

In General Lew Wallace's account of the battle of Donelson given in his autobiography he speaks of this interview with General W. H. L. Wallace as follows: "I saw, finally, an officer riding slowly toward me, one leg thrown over the horn of his saddle, and four or five hundred men with a flag behind him. I galloped to meet him.

"Good morning', I said, 'May I ask who you are?'

"My name is Wallace,' he returned, stopping.

"Oh, you are Colonel W. H. L. Wallace. Well my name is Wallace.'

"Lew Wallace, of the Eleventh Indiana?'

"The same.

"We shook hands, he saying: 'Our names and the number of our regiments—mine the Eleventh Illinois—have been the cause of great profanity in the post-office.'

"Mixture of letters, I suppose?' 'Yes.'

"I noted him hurriedly, a man above medium height, florid in face, wearing a stubby, reddish beard, with eyes of a bluish cast and a countenance grave and attractive.

" 'I take it, Colonel, you are getting out of a tight place.' " 'Yes, we are out of ammunition.' 'That's bad,' said I, 'But I can help you. Down the road by the big tent, which is mine, and at your service, you will find two wagons. They, too, are mine and loaded with ammunition. Help yourself, and tell McClernand to do the same!'

" 'Thank you, I will do it.' His men were halted; facing them, he called out in a cheerful voice, 'Forward!' 'A moment, Colonel,' I said, 'Are the enemy following you?' 'Yes,' 'How far are they behind?' Just then the head of my column hove in view. The Colonel saw it. 'Are those yours?' 'Yes.' 'Well'—his face took on an expression of calculation,—'you will about have time to form a line of battle here.' 'Is that so? Then please give my men room to come—and good-by, Colonel, I'll see you again.'

"We shook hands and parted. A word from one so cool and thoughtful as Colonel W. H. L. Wallace was enough. The moment called for action. I am sorry to say I never met him again. His light went out at Shiloh."

An Ottawa paper of February, 1862, says: "W. H. L. Wallace's brigade bore the severest charge of the enemy and to him, his officers, and men under command eye witnesses give the credit of doing most to stay the desperate onslaught made by the rebels to break through the lines."

Captain Rumsey continues: "Sunday morning we expected a general charge, but report came that the enemy had surrendered. General Wallace ordered me to form the brigade and move it forward down the road toward the enemy's lines while he went forward to satisfy himself as to the truth of the report. When I met him at the enemy's works he said, 'Rumsey, it is true; their arms are stacked and they stand behind them', and the look on his face showed a feeling far deeper than words could express; seldom have I seen a more expressive face than his.

"At the head of our brigade General W. H. L. Wallace moved through the works, and on toward the river fort, when several staff officers were sent to him trying to halt him; one with great assurance and pomp rode up in great haste, and saluting, stated that he was from General Smith, who ordered him to halt his brigade; General Wallace moved on with great dignity, remarking to the officer, 'General Smith is not my commander' and to me he said, 'I am going to the fort; I commenced this battle, and it is my right.'

"And he did go and took Battery B with him to fire the salute from the high and strong river fort, when the gunboats came steaming up the river firing their salute. And he said to me as we sat on our horses, his face glowing with satisfaction, 'Rumsey, this is glorious,' to which I replied, 'Yes, General, but my heart aches as I think of the many comrades and true soldiers lying on the field who, forty-eight hours ago, were with us," to which he replied, 'Yes, but they died in a noble cause.' So all through that dreadful three days' battle, he showed his tender and loyal soul."

Chaplain B. H. Pearson, of the Eleventh Regiment, writin to the *Christian Times* from the battlefield of Donelson, said:

"MESSRS. EDITORS:—I take this opportunity to inform my friends of what my eyes have seen, and my ears have heard, and my heart has felt, in the few days just passed. I have realized all that I ever could imagine could be on the field of battle. I now know, what I have believed, that our men love the old flag, and would rather die around it than see it dishonored. Could you have been with us on the day of the recent great battle at this place, you would say. 'Can it be possible that this long extended line of men have no love of life, no fear of death? How firm they stand, while the leaden hail is flying like snow-flakes all around them!'

"I was with the surgeon and music of the Eleventh a few paces in the rear of the regiment where I could see our whole line, with the Twentieth and Thirty-first. The latter was the left wing of the First Brigade. The Eleventh was the right wing of the Second Brigade under command of W. H. L. Wallace. I have always thought the Colonel was a cool man; but could you have seen him that morning, on his black steed, moving from one point to another, directing the conflict as composedly as if on dress-parade, watching every movement, you would have said that prayer from some pure heart had been answered on his behalf. We all love him, and believe that God owned him and protected him that day. And he was not only one—Lieutenant-Colonel Ransom and Major Nevius, though younger in years, exhibited skill in the art of war equaled by few. In a word, I may say that the officers and soldiers of the Eleventh surpassed the most sanguine expectations of their most ardent admirers."

In a letter soon afterwards Mrs. Wallace writes to her husband: "I hope good Colonel Ransom and Cyrus are better. Tell them I am thinking of them and I think it is more honor to be one of the 'Eleventh' after the battle of Donelson than to be General McClellan himself. All Ottawa and all Illinois are proud of you all. * * * I should judge by the papers that you are to really be made a Brigadier-General. I am glad that you are to have the rank as well as the work of the office. I think you deserve the honor. I want Colonel Ransom to be promoted, too. Mr. Earl said this morning he would not be content until you were made a Major-General."

Colonel Wallace writes his wife the day after the battle:

"Fort Donelson, Tenn., Feb. 17, 1862.

"This has been a day full of sad offices, collecting and caring for the wounded, burying the dead and doing all that could be done to allay the distress of those who suffered in the terrible fight. * * * *

"I will not attempt to give you any details of the terrible conflict through which we have passed. The papers will fully advise you of that. It was the greatest battle ever fought on this continent. I hope the fruits of the victory may be the speedy restoration of peace. Our victory, great as it is, and great as I hope it will be in results, has been dearly bought. The *Eleventh* suffered terribly, much more than any regiment engaged. We buried on the battlefield to-day sixty-eight belonging to the *Eleventh.* * * * * *

"The colors of the regiment are riddled with shot and the staff was struck twice with bullets, breaking off the spear at the top. The Color-Sergeant, McCaleb, was shot down and Color-Corporal Armstrong of Co. H seized it and bore it from the field. Tell Helen Fisher that the pledge I made to her when she in behalf of the Ottawa ladies presented the flag to Co. I. has been redeemed. The *Eleventh* lost nearly everything but their flag and their honor. It was the first flag planted on the inner fortification of Fort Donelson.

"The scenes here yesterday and to-day have been the saddest and strangest ever seen on this continent. The prisoners amounting to nine or ten thousand or perhaps more have been marched in long lines from their camps to the landing to be sent to Cairo. They are a strange and motley crowd, but they shoot terribly sharply. * * * *

"Dear wife, God has indeed heard your prayer and that of our little innocent. I little expected when amid the fierce storm of lead and iron that beat around me for hours, striking down my men by hundreds, that I should come off unscathed, but I never thought of the surrounding dangers without a mental prayer for mercy for myself and for you, darling."

The flag of the Eleventh which had been given by the ladies of Ottawa, a beautiful large silk one and made by them, to Co. I. and taken as the regimental flag, was used after the battle of Donelson at the burial of sixty-eight men in one grave. It was there presented to Colonel Wallace as a personal gift, which he sent home to his wife to be cared for by her. She considered it as one of her most valued possessions. It is now in the library at "The Oaks"—General Wallace's late home.

Mrs. Wallace speaks in her letters about the feeling in Ottawa towards the flag.

"The Oaks, Ottawa, March 6, 1862.

* * * * * "Helen Fisher says to tell you that all the Ottawa ladies were proud of the honor bestowed on that flag. I am told there has been a large subscription taken up in town to get the *Eleventh* a new flag—one to be purchased in Chicago, worth ninety dollars."

In another letter she says: "I will take good care of the precious old flag. It on account of its brave defenders is almost worshiped by the Ottawa people."

On March 12th she writes:

"The old flag of the Eleventh stands against the arch in the dining room and is an object of great interest to all; it is touched with a feeling akin to awe. The new banner that Cyrus is to take stood side by side with the old one and to-day many times the hope has been expressed that its honor might be preserved without the fearful cost of life of the old one. * * * * The new flag is a beautiful blue silk one, but not the Stars and Stripes. I suppose it is all right, but it was not what I expected. There is to be some speech, making over it. The old flag was taken down to exhibit with the new one. The promise was made me that no harm should come to my charge—the precious old flag, and I am to have it again as soon as the ceremony is over."

Her brothers, Cyrus and Charlie, were home for a few days on leave. She writes her husband on March 21st: "I have laid in a new stock of courage these few happy days—I cannot be in contact with the spirit of glorious self devotion that seems to inspire my soldier brothers without catching a part of the inspiration that sustains them."

The following letter from General Wallace to his wife is a relaxation from the tension of battle, but is interesting as showing other sides of army life at the front:

"FORT DONELSON, TENN., Feb. 20, 1862.

"It is eleven o'clock at night. I have just returned from a trip up the river to Clarksville. Generals Grant and McClernand with several of their staff went up and I took two companies of my brigade (Co. D. of the Eleventh and a company from the Twentieth) with the band of the Eleventh. It was a pleasant trip and a great relief from the constant and heavy cares incident to our dearly bought victory. Clarksville is a beautiful village or town of five or six thousand inhabitants on the north side of the Cumberland, forty miles above this and within sixty miles of Nashville. We marched through the streets, but met no welcome except from the negroes. Most of the white inhabitants have left. One house, where there were pleasant looking ladies at the door, had the British flag hung out.

"On the way up we met one of our gunboats with Flag-officers Foote on board. I went aboard his boat with the Generals. The Commodore met us on crutches. He was slightly wounded at the bombardment of Fort Donelson. He inquired about you and I gave him your congratulations on his success at Fort Henry. He wished to be remembered. * * * * *

"When you write your Cousin Rose in Kentucky tell her that I had the pleasure of seeing Colonel Roger Hanson of Paris, Kentucky, a prisoner. He is a rank traitor of the Buckner school—the worst possible kind.

"I have not completed my official report of the battle. The list of killed and wounded is fearful. It will reach six hundred in my brigade alone. The *Eleventh* lost seventy-five killed and two hundred wounded and several missing I felt indeed when looking at the fragment of the regiment with its tattered banner like Napoleon did after one of his disastrous battles, that 'all was lost but honor.' I do not underrate the importance of the victory. I think it is the death blow of the rebellion if rapidly and judiciously followed up—but I cannot but feel when I look at my own regiment, whose long front I have so often looked upon with pride, now shortened of more than half its length, that it is a dearly bought victory. May the sacrifice we have laid upon the altar of our country be acceptable to the God of battles and of Nations and may He smile in mercy and peace upon us in the speedy restoration of our old loved Union."

CHAPTER XVI.

Congratulatory Correspondence. The Troops Move up the Tennessee River to Savannah.

THE fellow townsmen of Colonel Wallace and Colonel Dickey sent the following letter of congratulation to them over their achievements at Fort Donelson:

"Ottawa, Feb. 22, 1862.

"To Col. William H. L. Wallace, Eleventh Illinois.

"Acting Brig. General: and

"To Col. T. Lyle Dickey, Fourth Illinois Cavalry.

"Sirs:—On Monday morning last the gratifying intelligence of the capture of Fort Donelson was flashed to us along the wires. As you well imagine, so important and pregnant an event threw our citizens into the wildest excitement, and men soon gave themselves up to mutual congratulations, rejoicings and thanks to the brave men by whom it was accomplished.

"All seemed to regard this crowning victory as a sure guaranty of an *enduring Union.*

"Our rejoicings were dampened, it is true, by intelligence of the loss of many brave men who have fallen in the contest, conspicuous among whom was Lieutenant-Colonel Erwin, whose remains were deposited in their last resting place here on yesterday with appropriate funeral ceremonies.

"Dulce et decorum est pro patria mori.

"We embrace this earliest opportunity of congratulating you and the gallant soldiers of your respective commands, upon the late brilliant achievements in which you and they have well acted so conspicuous a part.

"Rest assured that in our rejoicings to-day the soldierly deeds of our Illinois Volunteers are remembered, and our prayers shall be offered, that on other fields they may gather new honors, and when the contest shall be ended (as end it must) in 'unconditional surrender' to the Old Honored Flag of the Union, you may all return to your homes to receive from numberless friends the welcome due the soldier, who has fully answered his country's call.

"With emotions of pride, we subscribe ourselves, your fellow citizens and friends.

S. W. Cheever.	G. S. Stebbins.
Wm. Reddick.	J. V. A. Hoes.
H. F. Eames.	H. M. Swift.
Wm. Osman.	J. D. Caton.
T. Hampton.	L. Leland.
D. Walker.	W. E. Hollister.
O. C. Gray.	W. Bushnell.
E. L. Waterman.	A. W. Cavalry.
J. O. Glover.	J. Avery.
P. K. Leland.	A. B. Moore.
E. C. Henshaw.	J. F. Nash."
J. C. Champlin.	

In answer to this letter Colonel Wallace writes:

"SAVANNAH, TENN., March 18, 1862.

"J. V. A. HOES, H. M. SWIFT, and others, Ottawa.

"GENTLEMEN:—Your letter of the 22d ult., addressed to myself and Col. Dickey, congratulatory of the victory at Fort Donelson, is just received. If there is anything more gratifying then the consciousness of having fulfilled a duty, it is the commendation of those to whom we are best known, and whose good opinion we prize. I thank you sincerely for your timely remembrance of this fact, and the graceful and patriotic manner in which you have conveyed your congratulations.

"Illinois indeed has reason to be proud of her soldiers. In every field in which they have had an opportunity they have added new laurels to those the State already bore; and when the Union is again perfect, and the old, honored flag again hailed as the national ensign from the shores of New England to the banks of the Rio Grande, and from the Falls of St. Anthony to the capes of Florida, the part that Illinois has borne in the sacred work will be just matter of pride to every loyal citizen in the state.

"Hoping that the consummation we all so devoutly wish

for may soon come and that we in the field may return to receive those thanks you promise, I remain,

"Very respectfully,
"Your friend,
"W. H. L. Wallace."

Colonel Dickey also answers the letter.

"In Camp, near Pittsburg, Tenn., March 27, 1862.
"S. W. Cheever, J. V. A. Hoes and others:—

"Gentlemen:—By reason of my absence from camp on account of illness brought on by exposure during the siege of Donelson, your kind letter (of the 22d of February addressed to Colonel Wallace and myself) was not put into my hands until this day. I assure you the approving words of 'fellow citizens and friends' and their congratulations (to me and the brave men of my command upon the achievement in which we bore an humble part), fell gratefully upon our hearts.

"It did not fall to the lot of my command to take a very active part in the scenes of the heaviest fighting. Their principal service was rendered in leading the first advance upon the ground in forming our line of battle, and in frequent reconnoissances; and on the afternoon of the last day of the fight it turned out that our presence upon a leading road in front of the enemy held him in check until our infantry reinforcements were brought up, before which the enemy at last retired within their trenches.

"For the encouragement of my command in bold and gallant deeds, I will cause your very kind letter to be read at the head of the regiment. Hoping that the old honored flag of the Union may soon wave triumphant over every foot of our whole land, and that God in his mercy will unite the hearts of all our people in fraternal affection, I remain very respectfully, your fellow citizen and friend,

"T. Lyle Dickey."

Colonel Wallace writing to his wife tells of an interesting trip to Nashville and conditions there as the result of the victory at Donelson.

"FORT DONELSON, Feb. 28, 1862.

"I have just returned from Nashville. I went up on the steamer W. H. B. with Generals Grant and McClernand and staffs, Colonel Lauman of the Seventh Iowa, Captain Taylor of Chicago and others. The weather was beautiful and the trip a very pleasant one. We found Nashville a most beautiful city with a magnificent capitol building and, better than all, the old flag waving over it. The city had been occupied two days before by a part of General Buell's army, the last of the 'secesh' army moving out as our troops came in sight. There were unfinished fortifications below the city, the guns were left standing.

"Our victory here is a very great one. Bowling Green, Clarksville and Nashville, all strong places, have all been evacuated as the result of our success here at Donelson, and it now seems probable that Columbus will fall from the effects of the same blow. *Te Deum laudamus. Let the people praise Him.*

"At Nashville I found some eighty-five of our wounded soldiers who had been taken prisoners and carried away by the enemy. Among them were about forty belonging to the *Eleventh.* It would have done you good to see the poor fellows' faces brighten when they saw me. Scarce one of them but shed tears when I shook hands with them. I found them comfortably quartered and well cared for, although some of them were suffering for want of surgical attention to their wounds. Few of them are dangerously wounded and they all agree that they received kind treatment from the enemy. I made arrangements for medical and surgical attendance at once. * * * * * *

"In company with General McClernand I called on Mrs. Polk, the widow of President Polk. She is "secesh," but a very ladylike person. I plucked a daffodil from her garden and enclose it to you in this letter."

An interesting letter is here given from General Wallace to his friend, Judge *Champlin,* who had written to him of the affairs agitating the public mind, and also refers to the wish for General Wallace to run for Congress when his other duties permitted.

"FORT DONELSON, TENN., March 3, 1862.

"HON. J. C. CHAMPLIN,
"OTTAWA, ILL.

"DEAR CHAMP:—"I ought to have replied to your long letter long since, but a press of other duties has prevented—and now I am again under marching orders to leave at seven o'clock to-morrow morning for a point on the Tennessee river seven miles below Fort Henry, so that I am in no condition to write an answer to your elaborate letter. Having a few moments leisure, however, I drop you a line for 'Auld Lang Syne.'

"You seem to be anticipating a state of facts which may soon arise, i. e., what to do with the rebels after we have conquered them. That same question seems to be troubling our secession friends just now. A few weeks ago, the assertion was—'You can never subdue the South!' Now they ask—'What are you going to do with us after you have conquered us?' They are not conquered yet, though they have received some heavy blows lately. But they want to be more thoroughly and soundly whipped. They hate us sufficiently, but they do not fear us enough yet. They do not despise us as much as they did, but we must whip them harder before they will have a decent respect for us. When we have once more convinced them that we can whip them, we may then live on friendly terms with them, but never till then. If the successes of the last few weeks are vigorously followed up, we will soon reach a point where peace is possible, but if we falter here, or hesitate even, all that has been gained by the recent victories will soon be lost. I trust in God that the men at the helm will push things vigorously to the desired consummation.

"Among the many projects for disposing of the traitors and punishing the treason that have been broached, yours is perhaps as perfect as any. It may be open to the objection that it is too complicated, but this is a complex business and much machinery may be necessary to work it off successfully. The project of instituting territorial governments for the rebel States as fast as they are conquered is open to the objection that such governments would be required to be supported by armed force forever. Perhaps however, that would not be the case if the people were thoroughly subdued now. A few such damaging blows as this at Fort Donelson would bring the mass of the people to submit to almost any government that gave them security and protected their property. I do not find in the masses here any lingering memory or a love for the old flag and the old Government. In fact the present generation has been reared in hatred to the government, and I think no reliance can be placed on any supposed suppressed Union feelings here. Nothing but the stern iron rule of the strongest can ever give anything like security. It is bound to be a 'Union pinned together with bayonets.' The picture is gloomy enough, but it is too truthful.

"But enough of this—how are you all getting along? How is Bush and Gray and Lindley and the boys generally? Didn't we whip them gloriously here? Beat 'em on their own ground—hunted them to their holes—whipped 'em behind their entrenchments—22,000 of them protected by earthworks and cannon, whipped out of their own trenches by less than 30,000 outsiders. No wonder the scare extended all over the South and sent the army of Bowling Green rushing back through Nashville, and never halting until it got into the Gulf states. Another blow or two like this will destroy their reliance on their boasted chivalry.

"You ask me to give you a programme. I have none. I am, as you know, no politician, and what's more, I haven't any politics, except to restore the old order of things as speedily and effectually as possible. If in the course of the next two or three months the necessity of active military operations is gone and I can rightly return home, I think I shall enjoy above all things staying there. Never have I known such a longing for the peace and quietness of home. If then it should be deemed proper and right that I should go to Congress and nobody would be hurt by my so doing, why I would go, but I think I never shall enter into the intrigues and double dealing which has been necessary for political success. The game isn't worth the candle.

"Give my regards to all our mutual friends. Write me

when you have leisure and feel inclined. I agree with you perfectly as to Bush.* He has brains and what is a rarer and higher virtue, he is *reliable*. Give him my very best regards.

"Yours truly,

"W. H. L. WALLACE."

The larger part of the Western Army embarked on transports and went up the Tennessee river, and in less than a month occurred the great battle of Pittsburg Landing. Colonel Wallace writes his wife of the movement of the troops.

"STEAMER BELLE MEMPHIS, Tenn., River,
"5 Miles above Ft. Henry, March 8, 1862.

"We were two days getting here from Donelson, a very rough, disagreeable march. Here the Eleventh and Twentieth regiments embarked on this boat and have been lying here ever since. My whole brigade is embarked, the Forty-fifth on the *J. H. Dickey,* the Forty-eighth on the *Henry Choteau,* Taylor's battery on the *Silver Moon,* three companies of the Fourth Cavalry on *T. L. Magill* and two other companies of the Fourth on the *Aleck Scott.* Colonel Ross's brigade is also embarked and Colonel Oglesby's brigade is expected here to-night or to-morrow. Generals Hurlbut's, Smith's and Wallace's divisions will also embark here, all bound up the Tennessee river.

"I have been quite ill for two or three days. A bilious attack coupled with lumbago induced by the severe exposure of the last two months. I am getting better, however. The weather is becoming more pleasant and I hope a day or two will restore me completely. The prospect is now that we will be aboard of the boats for two or three days yet and by that time I hope to be able to stand the exposure. I pray God for strength and wisdom to enable me to do my whole duty toward the country in this her hour of peril. I shall endeavor to discharge that duty with a firm reliance on God's all wise providence, that it will result in good in carrying out His Sovereign will.

*Washington Bushnell was a prominent lawyer of Ottawa, a member of the Legislature, State's Attorney and the first Attorney General of the State of Illinois.

"I learn unofficially that I am to be a Brigadier. I do not feel like exulting. I know the added responsibility of the position and pray for strength to fill it. I feel the need of Divine aid more than I ever have done, and feel a more living active faith in God's protection than ever. Pray for me * * * * I feel that your prayers can aid me when most I need aid. I know your fervent piety and appreciate the fulness and purity of your love for me and our cause."

In a letter of March 20th, he writes again:

"It is eleven months since I left home. In that time I have spent six or seven days at home. I have felt the deprivation much as you have. It has shown me, however, some lovely phases in your character that I might otherwise never have known. May the Good God in whom we trust so overrule events that this unhappy war may soon be honorably and rightly ended and we be permitted again to enjoy the pleasure of our home together. In His hands are the issues of life and death. He raises up and puts down nations, and however individuals may be disposed of I feel an abiding faith that the end will be the furtherance of *His will on earth. Our Father who art in Heaven* will take care of His children and do with them whatever is best."

After the transports arrived at their destination on the Tennessee river Colonel Wallace writes of their new surroundings to his wife:

'SAVANNAH, TENN., March 14, 1862.

"You will wonder where I am when you look at the heading of this letter. Take a map of the United States and follow up the Tennessee river till you get within twenty miles of the Alabama line and there on the east side of the river you will see marked Savannah, the county seat of Hardin County. It is a quiet, sober looking old town, with a single street, a square brick court house, a number of buildings scattered along the street, with some pretty and rather stylish residences in the suburbs. There is a majority of Union people here. Most of the people have remained at home and not run away like they did from Clarksville and other places on the Cumberland.

"We got here two or three days ago and lay on the transports till yesterday, when Colonel Ross' brigade and mine landed and went into camp just back of the town. I have my headquarters in a house in the outskirts of the town. It is occupied by a young man named Seaman, with several blacks. He is a very civil, gentlemanly fellow and offered me his house and the use of his servants for myself and staff. * * * * We hear a great many rumors here as you doubtless do at home, but I suppose the truth to be that the enemy are in force at Eastport or near there, which is twenty-five or thirty miles above here. Some of our forces have gone up the river and we may go soon, but that will depend on circumstances of course. General C. F. Smith is still in command of the expedition but I understand General Grant will be up in a few days to take command. * * * * I do hope this wicked war is nearly over and that I may soon return to you. It is pleasant to receive the commendations of the public for services rendered, but I would more enjoy a kind word and loving caress from you than all the honors that military service could win." In a later letter he writes: "I want to see you and the dear ones at home, but I know you don't want to see me, if to do so I must leave my post here when I ought not to. I really hope I may see you consistently with duty before very long."

On March 21st Colonel Wallace received his commission as Brigadier-General of Volunteers. But no sooner did he acquire one position than he was advanced to another, as was his fate in the Mexican war in lesser degrees. On the following day after receiving his commission he writes to his wife, March 22d: "There will probably be some changes in our organization. General Grant to-day intimated that he intended to put me in command of a division. This may or may not be done. I should be gratified on some accounts and sorry for it on others. * * * * In any event I shall strive to do my duty relying on Our Father for strength, courage and wisdom to aid me.

"When the changes are made I will advise you as to what my command is and under whose direct orders I act, so that you may keep the run of things as they may appear in the newspapers."

Mrs. Wallace writes from her home in Ottawa:—

"March 21st.

"Sometimes, Will, I can hardly restrain myself, I feel as if I must go to you, more so when I think of you sick. It seems wrong to enjoy every comfort of a good home and you sick in tents. Is it indeed my duty to stay so far back and wait so anxiously?"

On March 24th she writes again in the same vein: "I am thinking earnestly of trying to go to you with Eaton. * * * * If he does not throw cold water on the project I will go with him." When she heard that her husband was likely to be put in command of a division she wrote:

"OTTAWA, March 28, 1862.

"* * * * I am surprised to know of the chance of your commanding a division. I know, dearest, you will honor the position as you always have those you have held heretofore."

When Colonel Wallace received his commission as Brigadier-General he asked his old friend, R. E. Goodell of Joliet, who had campaigned with him through the Mexican war and was a very close friend, to take a position on his staff. Mr. Goodell's business affairs were such that he could not accept. He writes General Wallace the following letter:

"ST. LOUIS, March 31, 1862.

"DEAR WALLACE:

"Your kind letter of the eighth came to hand yesterday. I regret exceedingly that my business matters are now in such a shape that I cannot accept the position you have so kindly tendered me. Although I have had several positions offered me in the army, none have so tempted me as the one you now offer, not so much the position as the association. Your command has many of my warm friends in it and to think that I would be with you and Colonel Dickey again and renew in the same field the old ties which were made so strong there, and it seems to me grown stronger every day since; it is really hard for me to decline.

"When I met you at Fort Donelson I supposed our contract here would close in a short time, and had I not taken another before I had an intimation of your tendering me the appointment, I should have at once closed this one and joined you, but on my way home my partners insisted upon my going to Louisville and try to get the contract there for furnishing Buell's department with forage, which I succeeded in doing, and that ties me up close for some time.

"I regret that your letter did not come to hand earlier. It was forwarded to me at Louisville, but I left before it arrived; it was forwarded here and I did not get it until I returned here Saturday evening. I hope it has not put you to any inconvenience.

"Allow me to congratulate you on your promotion. Your prophecy of the last summer was true. You said to me *you* would not receive a promotion until it was earned. No appointment in our State has given more general satisfaction than yours.

"You have undoubtedly noticed that the Congressional convention has separated our county (Will) from La Salle in Congressional apportionment. I am sorry they have. I met Judge Davis here yesterday, who says you are the man to run there, and you must do it, if the war ends so you can attend to it. He thinks there would be no question about your election. Swett will be elected in that district and I think Norton in ours. If possible, I shall visit you during the coming month. Truly your friend,

"R. E. Goodell."

CHAPTER XVII.

General Wallace's Command Moves to Pittsburg Landing. Mrs. Wallace's Journey to Pittsburg Landing.

ON March twenty-fourth, General Wallace with his command left Savannah for Pittsburg Landing, ten miles above on the Tennessee river. From there he writes his wife of his new camp surroundings.

"In Camp Near Pittsburg, Tenn., March 25, 1862.

"* * * * There is a large force here and the camp covers several miles in extent. General Sherman's division is the most advanced, ours next." * * * * On March twenty-seventh he writes: "This has been a most lovely day, like May or June, except that there are no leaves. The early wild-flowers are in bloom, but otherwise all is yet dead in the woods. I spent all the fore part of the day in my tent writing and attending to the thousand details that constantly require attention. I have my headquarters in tents in rear of my brigade. The brigade is encamped on a gentle ridge in front—that is, the four infantry regiments. Just in rear of them is a depression in which there is a stream of water in wet weather, and there is water enough now in it for the men. This side of the quarters is another gentle ridge on which is my headquarters in four tents—two Sibley tents, one for myself and one for the Adjutant's office. A Frémont tent to eat in and a common tent for the orderlies. My military family consists of Captain Hotchkiss, Assistant Adjutant-General, Lieutenant Davis; Quartermaster, Lieutenant Rumsey; Aide-de-camp, Beckwith; Secretary, Church; Brigade Postmaster and Chief of Orderlies, a sergeant and five men from the Fourth cavalry for orderlies; Jim, the cook; Hartley (body servant), and Ned, the Irishman who takes care of my horses.

"To the left of headquarters and nearby is Taylor's battery, and immediately in the rear is Colonel McCullough's camp with five companies of the *Fourth* cavalry. My brigade is in the center of the division, Colonel Oglesby's being on my right and Colonel Ross' on my left. It is the prettiest camping ground we have had since we have been in the service and we are improving this fine weather in drilling and fitting the men for service."

General Wallace writes his wife on April third of his being placed in command of a division.

"PITTSBURG, TENN., April 3, 1862.

"* * * * I have just been ordered to assume command of General Smith's division, he being sick—I suppose this is merely temporary, but it may be otherwise. The division consists of fourteen regiments of infantry, four batteries and two battalions of cavalry. It is a compliment to be placed in such a command, though I feel a good deal of embarrassment in attempting to fill the place of such a man as General Smith. * * * * I have not sought the place and am disinclined to take it, but I suppose there is no help for it. I assume my new command to-morrow. I take with me my staff, Captains Hotchkiss and Davis and Lieutenant Rumsey. Cyrus is going on my staff as soon as he can be spared from the *Eleventh*. No sight on earth would afford me more pleasure than that of your face, but I feel that I must not now expect that pleasure and if you were here I should feel that every moment devoted to you was stolen from my duty. * * * * You must not think of coming here. We are in camp, very busy with preparations to leave and liable to be ordered off at any hour."

Mrs. Wallace's young brother, Charlie, writes from Pittsburg Landing; he was in his father's (Colonel Dickey's) Fourth cavalry regiment:

"PITTSBURG LANDING, TENN., April 4, 1862.

"I have been here just about a week and am now with Major Bowman's battalion bugling for him. It keeps me pretty busy, as there is no bugler to relieve me, and I have to be on the lookout all the time for fear of playing a call out of time. The weather is rather uncomfortable warm in the daytime, but the nights are delicious, just cool enough to sleep well. * * * * It must be very healthy here, for the sick boys are all getting well and the doctors have scarcely anything to do. Nothing of interest is going on except reviews. This battalion has been reviewed three times in the last three days, and to-day Major Wallace's battalion is going through the same. It is very tiresome and seems to me to be useless. * * * * There seems to be movements of troops going on up the river, Buell's troops I believe, but everything is kept secret and of course, nothing is certain.

"There will be a fight very soon and not far from Corinth, I expect."

The day before the battle of Shiloh, General Wallace writes to his wife:

"PITTSBURG LANDING, April 5, 1862.

"* * * * I have assumed command of General Smith's division during his illness. It is a great responsibility and does not set easy on me yet. Last evening there was a skirmish in front of General Sherman's division, a few wounded and a few prisoners taken. It caused a good deal of excitement in camp. The long roll was beaten and several divisions formed in line. I had my division ready, but did not turn out. The night was dark and rainy, and about 11 o'clock I rode out three miles to General Sherman's quarters with Colonel McPherson of General Halleck's staff. We found everything quiet and the General in fine spirits. He had driven the enemy back some three or four miles when his advance came onto their battery. He lost no men killed, three or four wounded, and ten taken prisoners or missing. He killed several of the enemy, wounded a good many and took some ten or twelve prisoners. All is quiet this morning.

"There has been a re-assignment of cavalry and artillery —eight companies of the Fourth cavalry are attached to General Sherman's division, and I suppose your Pa will have command of them. Three companies of the First battalion remain in General McClernand's division. Martin (Major Wallace) will be with General Sherman. Taylor's battery is also assigned to General Sherman's division. I feel very bad at leaving my old brigade, and especially the *Eleventh*. It seems like breaking up of a family. But I suppose the good of the service requires it, at all events, it is *ordered*, and that is law.

"* * * * It is very bright and warm to-day after the rain and storm of last night. Vegetation is coming forward very rapidly. The leaves on the trees are forming, but not yet fully developed. I suppose it is a great ways ahead of things at home in that regard. I wish I could see that pleasant home for a while, but I must not think of it now. I trust in God that it may not be long ere we are again united in that quiet, pleasant home, sanctified by your love and to which I turn constantly as the place of all others on earth the most desirable."

While this letter was being penned General Wallace's wife was but a day's distance from his camp, speeding up the Tennessee river as fast as steam could bring her. But how she came to be there will be told in her own words, written at the request of a friend many years after the events noted:

"After the battle of Donelson my husband was miserable and ill from the care, exposure and fatigue of that four days' battle, unprotected in inclement weather, and confined to the bed some days. He soon got out and able for duty, but headache and lumbago hung around him. I heard of his indisposition both from his letters and from those of other relatives. His absence and danger was a constant source of trial to me all the time, and for the first time ill health was added—I could scarcely bear it. In answer to my often expressed wish to spend my time in camp at Bird's Point, he had often said that had he not been in command he would have had me there as often as he could, but at times the efficiency of the service was hindered by the presence of the families of the officers, and he could not forbid their presence if he had his own wife in camp. So only on rare and exceptional occasions when he was detailed for court martial or something like that, I was telegraphed for and met him and made a trip with him to Springfield or St. Louis.

"My regard for him and pride in him inspired me to be a *brave soldier's wife* and endure cheerfully. I had never gone to camp except when telegraphed for. But when these continued sick days came, and quick communication was impossible and the tone of my husband's letters showed weariness and depression, the feeling took possession of me that if I could go to him and spend a few hours with him that it would make a break in his mind-burden, and rest and relieve him. I knew he would not think it consistent with his duty to send for me, though I found it mine to go to him. Though he would be glad to see me he would blame me and think me babyish and probably send me home at once.

"I wrote him I would come with Mr. R. E. Goodell (then furnishing supplies to the army), if I could. I wrote Mr. Goodell at Joliet that I wanted to go to the front with him, and received a telegram that starting that night I could join Elder Button, Chaplain of the Twentieth at Bloomington, who was going right to his regiment, then in my husband's brigade. My brother John, the only brother not in the army, who was a telegrapher, urged me not to go, said I was 'crazy'—'I never would get to the front, all civilians were turned back, etc.' I argued that Mr. Goodell occupied such a position as contractor, that he would know what could probably be done, and would not have despatched to me if he did not think I could go. Nearly all my friends talked in the same way.

"Judge Caton, my near neighbor, telegraphed to Cairo for me to see if I could pass. The answer came, 'none but soldiers were permitted to go up the Tennessee river!' But I determined to go anyway. General Strong, then in command at Cairo, was a personal friend of Judge Caton and the Judge gave me a letter of introduction to him.

"I had to take a night train to La Salle. When it was time to go to the depot, about midnight, there was a most fearful wind and rainstorm raging, so bad that the half-grown Irish boy said he could not drive; so I sent off half a mile to the foreman of our farm, who came and drove while the boy walked ahead of the horse with a lantern down the hill to the depot.

"We were in an open buggy, but I was so covered with wraps that I did not get wet. When I arrived at the depot I felt triumphant, and thought if I could surmount such a storm, I certainly can any other difficulties that may obstruct my path. At La Salle I had to wait some hours. Mr. Hardy, the hotel-keeper, I knew well, told me it was utterly useless for me to go. I could not get beyond Cairo, that every train brought back disappointed people who could go no further than Cairo. Regardless of these discouraging remarks, my faith in Mr. Goodell's judgment was unshaken, besides I intended if I could not pass the lines at once to remain at Cairo until there was an opportunity.

"At Bloomington Elder Button came to me on the train and introduced himself. He had been home on sick leave after the exposure and exhaustion at Donelson. When I asked him questions about Mr. Goodell, he informed me that he was not at home, nor had been for a week, and that his wife had sent the telegram to me and signed it *R. E. Goodell* because he had a *telegraph frank*. Now indeed, I was discouraged. I would not have left home if I had known that Mr. Goodell had not advised it. But I could not turn back.

"At Cairo Elder Button took a note from me with Judge Caton's note to General Strong's headquarters and came back in ten minutes with a permit to go up the river in a transport that was to start up next day loaded with Iowa regiments."

Judge Caton's letter to General Strong.

"OTTAWA, ILLINOIS, March 31, 1862.

"BRIGADIER-GENERAL STRONG.

"DEAR SIR:

"Allow me to commend to your kindest consideration Mrs. Wallace, the wife of Brigadier-General W. H. L. Wallace, who is my near neighbor and particular friend. Mrs. Wallace is on her way to join the General on the upper Tennessee. By affording to Mrs. Wallace every facility in your power you will lay General Wallace and myself under very great obligations.

"With great respect, I am yours truly,

"J. D. CATON."

To continue Mrs. Wallace's letter:

"It seems General Strong himself was in St. Louis and his Adjutant said, 'I know General Strong would want to do anything he could that was requested by Judge Caton.' He thought a moment, then went to his desk and wrote the permit. As he handed it across the desk to Elder Button, he said: 'There is the permit, but I have gone beyond my orders.'

"My idea is that the Adjutant knew that General Strong's wish would agree with the act and would not be severe to blame him; when if the General himself had been there his strict orders and responsible position would have prevented him from giving the pass.

"At different points along the river officers came on board, and as they approached me evidently intended taking me ashore, but my permit was law to them and I was not molested. There was a kind woman nurse that belonged to Colonel Ross' regiment on board with sanitary supplies. There were also two regiments of Iowa volunteers. Belknap was the Adjutant of one of the regiments. He was kind, patriotic and brave, and I admired him, and was astonished and sorry when disgrace came to him in later years. I do not believe he was to blame.

"These regiments had drilled some at Keokuk, but only received their muskets as they passed the St. Louis arsenal and had never even loaded them until they were marched right from that steamboat into the fire of the enemy at Shiloh; of course, panic was the result. Who blundered I do not know.

"As we steamed along I was perfectly jubilant. I had indeed surmounted all difficulties and would soon see my husband; yet I had a faint fear all the while that by some chance his orders might send him to Illinois and he would pass us and so I might miss him. I could not help feeling that I was going through a similar experience to Longfellow's 'Evangeline,' my surroundings were so strange and unusual. All the officers and soldiers were kind, courteous and attentive to me. At different times the boat turned into the shore and the soldiers landed and cooked up their rations. Many of them brought me bunches of wild spring flowers, so that the ladies' cabin was glorious with them.

"At midnight of April fifth, we touched at Savannah, where General Grant had his headquarters, ten miles before we reached Pittsburg Landing. My last letter from my husband had been written from Savannah, though I had heard from an officer that he had returned to Pittsburg Landing. I asked the officers who went ashore to report to inquire whether my husband was now at Savannah. General Grant himself was up, and sent me word that my husband was with C. F. Smith's division and in command of it at Pittsburg Landing.

"Some of General Grant's staff were on board and I was careful to let them know that I had come without my husband's knowledge, fearing he might be blamed for my presence there.

"We arrived before daylight at Pittsburg Landing. Captain Coates of the *Eleventh* Illinois was on board, returning after a leave of absence. He proposed to walk with me to my husband's headquarters. We heard a great deal of firing, but it was accounted for as the return of the night pickets and the discharge of their guns. I had put on my hat and gloves when Captain Coates suggested that perhaps it would be better for him to first find out how far it was, and perhaps I had better ride, if very far.

"So I remained on the boat. Before half an hour Captain Coates came back wounded in two places, one painful wound in the hand, but neither of them dangerous. I also learned that a big battle was in progress and that my husband had moved with his command to the front, so it was not possible for me to reach him. The only thing then for me to do was to wait where I was, so that any of the dear ones on that field could, if they wished, communicate with me.

"That long day on that steamboat, its scenes and sensations are beyond any description. The wounded were brought by hundreds onto the boat. Some could sit and stand about and talk, others helpless and pallid; but all without exception heroic in their fortitude. I did not hear a groan or murmur except those unconscious under the influence of chloroform or in sleep. I passed from place to place holding water and bandages for the surgeons until it became so crowded that I felt I was in the way and I went on the upper deck and sat there instead of in the cabin.

"The steamer was used most of the day to transport some of Buell's men across the river. Over and back, over and back. The cabin floor was full of wounded, inside and out, by the guards laid close and in rows like bricks in a brick yard. The lower deck was used to transport the troops. Buell's men had to dig a road down to the river's edge to move cannon down to the boats, and the rebels threw shell and shot to stop them, and also shelled the transports. As I sat there I saw these shells strike the sides of other steamboats and cut off limbs of trees near where the road was made, and pass buzzing across our deck. I felt dazed and horrified, yet enthused by some means, so I was not afraid, but felt like a soldier. I knew the danger, but felt lifted above fear of it.

"The panic-stricken raw troops seemed perfectly insane. The steamer had to keep a slight distance from shore or it would have been swamped by the rush of soldiers. At one time an officer got aboard and ordered the pilot to touch shore and take his men on board. He threatened the pilot with his pistol. I sat near by, the only person on deck except the pilot and this officer. The pilot pretended to obey him, but really did not, thus giving the frenzied man time enough to come to his senses. As the shot and shell whizzed about I felt it would be safer below, but the feeling that exhibition of fear on my part would make it a little harder for that pilot to stand at his post kept me from going down."

On that fatal field of Shiloh Mrs. Wallace had besides her husband, her father and two of her own brothers, and two of her husband's brothers, besides a number of more distant relatives. They all came safely through except her husband.

CHAPTER XVIII.

Battle of Shiloh.

THERE was no battle of the Civil War over which there has been so much written, with more discussion, and perhaps more criticism, than the terrific battle of Shiloh at Pittsburg Landing, Tennessee, beginning early in the morning of April sixth, lasting the entire day and the greater part of the following day.

Major-General Halleck was in command of the Western armies, which at this time were composed of the army of the Ohio and the army of the Tennessee. For a short time Major-General C. F. Smith was the commander of the army of the Tennessee, but, owing to an accident to his knee, had to relinquish the command. On March seventh General U. S. Grant was reinstated in command of this army with headquarters at Savannah. General Halleck's orders were to destroy the railroad connection at Corinth, twenty miles away, where the Confederate army was in force, but to do nothing towards bringing on an engagement until the army of the Ohio should arrive under General Buell from Nashville.

The army of the Tennessee commanded by Major-General U. S. Grant was on the fifth of April composed of six divisions:

The First commanded by Major-General John A. McClernand.

The Second by Brigadier-General W. H. L. Wallace.

The Third by Major-General Lew Wallace.

The Fourth by Brigadier-General S. A. Hurlbut.

The Fifth by Brigadier-General W. T. Sherman.

The Sixth by Brigadier-General B. M. Prentiss.

Of infantry, artillery and cavalry, officers and men concentrated here at Pittsburg Landing and Crump's Landing there were over forty-seven thousand. The Confederates numbered about forty-four thousand men.

Pittsburg Landing at the time of the battle was merely a

landing for steamboats. From here a good road ran southwesterly to Corinth. The bluff rising from the river is about eighty feet; the ground on the bluff, and where the battle was fought, along the Corinth road, is about the same level, but is cut up on either side by deep ravines and water courses leading into Snake and Owl Creeks on the north, and Lick Creek on the south. Lick Creek empties into the Tennessee river about two miles above Pittsburg Landing, and Snake Creek about one mile below. These streams, therefore, formed an excellent protection against an attack upon either flank of an army encamped between them. The land near them was low and marshy and at this time of the year the creeks could not be crossed except by bridges. "In 1862 this plateau was covered with forest with thick undergrowth and an occasional clearing of a few acres surrounding a farm house." *

General W. H. L. Wallace's division was near the Landing; that of General Lew Wallace was beyond Snake Creek at Crump's Landing, six miles north of Pittsburg Landing. From Adamsville General Lew Wallace wrote the following letter to General W. H. L. Wallace dated the day before the battle.

A copy of this letter of General Lew Wallace was sent to General Grant when writing his Memoirs, in reference to which he makes the following note in his book:

"Since writing this chapter I have received from Mrs. W. H. L. Wallace, widow of the gallant General who was killed in the first day's fight on the field of Shiloh, a letter from General Lew Wallace to him, dated the morning of the fifth. At the date of this letter it was well known that the Confederates had troops out along the Mobile and Ohio railroad west of Crump's Landing and Pittsburg Landing, and were also collecting near Shiloh. This letter shows that at that time General Lew Wallace was making preparations for the emergency that might happen for the passing of reinforcements between Shiloh and his position, extending from Crump's Landing westward, and he sends it over the road running from Adamsville to the Pittsburg Landing and

* Major D. W. Reed, historian of Battle of Shiloh compiled from official records.

Purdy road. These two roads intersect nearly a mile west of the crossing of the latter over Owl Creek, where our right rested. In this letter General Lew Wallace advises General W. H. L. Wallace that he will send 'to-morrow' (and his letter also says 'April 5th,' which is the same day the letter was dated and which, therefore, must have been written on the 4th) some cavalry to report to him at his headquarters, and suggesting the propriety of General W. H. L. Wallace's sending a company back with them for the purpose of having the cavalry at the two landings familiarize themselves with the road, so that they could 'act promptly in case of emergency as guides to and from the different camps.'

"This modifies very materially what I have said, and what has been said by others, of the conduct of General Lew Wallace at the battle of Shiloh. It shows that he naturally, with no more experience than he had at the time in the profession of arms, would take the particular road that he did start upon in the absence of orders to move by a different road. The mistake he made, and which probaly caused his apparent dilatoriness, was that of advancing some distance after he found that the firing, which would be at first directly to his front and then off to the left, had fallen back until it had got very much in rear of the position of his advance. This falling back had taken place before I sent General Wallace orders to move up to Pittsburg Landing, and, naturally, my order was to follow the road nearest the river. But my order was verbal, and to a staff officer who was to deliver it to General Wallace, so that I am not competent to say just what order the General actually received.

"General Wallace's division was stationed, the First brigade at Crump's Landing, the Second out two miles, and the Third two and a half miles out. Hearing the sounds of battle General Wallace early ordered his First and Third brigades to concentrate on the Second. If the position of our front had not changed the road which Wallace took would have been somewhat shorter to our right than the river road. "U. S. Grant.

"Mount MacGregor, New York, June 21, 1885."

On the afternoon before the battle Captain I. P. Rumsey, aide on General W. H. L. Wallace's staff, with his brother, Lieutenant John W. Rumsey, rode out to reconnoitre, as he says: "We rode to the front of General Prentiss' division and were cautioned by the sentry not to ride farther to the front, as he was the outer guard. Calling his attention to the cavalry we could see in the woods beyond, he stated, 'They are not ours.' Farther along the line to the right, in looking across an open field where the day before the fresh arrivals of troops were being brigaded and drilled, we saw a small squad of cavalry apparently taking in the situation. We then rode to Sherman's division and called on my battery, 'Taylor's,' which was camped near the Shiloh church, and told the boys what we had seen and that they might have a chance to use their guns without even hitching up.

"Starting back we met Colonel T. Lyle Dickey of the Fourth cavalry and told him what we had seen. He asked me to tell General Sherman; therefore, we rode to the General's tent, dismounted and I told him what we had seen. 'Yes,' he replied, 'they have been up on the right three times and fired on McDowell, but I have positive orders from Grant to do nothing that will have a tendency to bring on a general engagement until Buell arrives.' And in his quick, nervous manner he continued, 'Have you heard from Buell?' I answered in the negative, and he went on to say, 'Strange, strange, he ought to have been here ten days ago; ten days ago.' Then taking his map and placing it on the ground, he pointed out the route of General Buell's army, the streams to cross, etc., repeating 'ten days ago.' We then rode back to our camp. I reported to General W. H. L. Wallace who, while surprised, said but little, hardly making any reply."

The advance of Buell's army began to arrive on the evening of the fifth and in another day's time the Union forces would have been consolidated. The Confederate leaders were cognizant of the state of affairs and were anxious to bring on an engagement before the Union forces should be united. General Albert Sidney Johnston was Commander-in-Chief of the Southern forces, with the able Corps Commanders Beauregard, Bragg, Polk, Pillow, Hardee and Crittenden. They succeeded in their wish to engage Grant's army before reinforcements should make it stronger, and did so with such tremendous force and suddenness as to carry all before them for a time, and it looked as if they might carry out their boast of watering their horses in the Tennessee river after the total annihilation of Grant's army.

Prentiss' line was the first attacked and soon after, part of Sherman's division. When they found they were being attacked in force they asked for reinforcements from divisions in the rear. McClernand sent part of his division forward, as did also Hurlbut and W. H. L. Wallace. General Grant sent an order to General Lew Wallace at Crump's Landing, beyond Snake Creek, to hasten, but he did not arrive until seven in the evening, from misunderstanding of orders.

General W. H. L. Wallace's division was composed of three brigades of infantry, four batteries of artillery and four companies of cavalry. His staff officers were Assistant Adjutant-General, Captain William McMichael; his aides were Captain T. J. Newham, Lieutenant I. P. Rumsey, of Taylor's battery, and Lieutenant G. I. Davis and Cyrus E. Dickey of the Eleventh Illinois infantry.

Captain I. P. Rumsey writes:

"The morning of April sixth was quiet with us back near the landing until as we sat down to our mess-table we heard a sudden roar of musketry in the front and the next moment the boom of cannon. All horses were quickly saddled, division ordered under arms, and soon after we were moving in column toward the front, with General Wallace at the head of the division, marching toward the Shiloh Church on the Corinth road, to the Duncan Field, where we found a gap between General Prentiss' right and General McClernand's left,* where General Wallace placed General Sweeney, commanding Third brigade, on the right covering the Shiloh road and Duncan Field, and General Tuttle's First brigade on the left, joining General Prentiss' right. Our Second brigade, commanded by General McArthur, and Battery A, Captain Wood commanding, were

* To the left of Prentiss was Hurlbut's division, to right of W. H. L. Wallace's division came McClernand and to his right Sherman's division.

diverted by General Grant and taken to the left to the support of General Dave Stewart, or to fill a gap between Generals Hurlbut and Stewart.

"In some unaccountable way General Sweeney's brigade was broken to pieces. As I sat by General Wallace in rear of General Tuttle's brigade, who were heavily engaged, General Sweeney rode up and reported to General Wallace, saying, "I have broken the center; if I can be supported, I can hold it.' Without orders, I rode to the right and found great disorder in Sweeney's brigade, then rode rapidly to Wallace and reported the same, at which time Wallace was watching with great interest heavy fighting on our left by Tuttle in what is called 'The Hornet's Nest.' General Wallace could not believe or understand my report, for he had great confidence in General Sweeney and his brigade. What had become of Sweeney I never knew until after the battle of the first day I found him without a command with General Sherman on the extreme right, he having passed clear across General McClernand's front, whose division lay between Wallace and Sherman, and one of Sweeney's regiments moving to the rear on the Corinth road without orders or commander.

"In this ride and investigation I found General McClernand had withdrawn his left half a mile to the rear of Wallace's right, leaving his right exposed. I plead with McClernand to throw his left forward, but he refused. I rode rapidly to Wallace, but it was too late. As I reached him General Hurlbut, who was on the left of General Prentiss and at right angles with Wallace, broke in a rout. This left Prentiss and Wallace flanked both on right and left and it was from the enemy on our right coming into the gap made by Sweeney and McClernand, from which our noble, brave, cool General received his fatal bullet as he was falling back in command of his troops.

"General Prentiss, who was captured with a portion of his division, told me after he was exchanged, that General Wallace advised that he, Prentiss, wheel his division to the left and he, Wallace, would about face his command and then moved onto the enemy's flank who were then crowding General Hurlbut back to our rear, which shows the cool deliberation and generalship of W. H. L. Wallace's action. It was while executing this move that General Wallace received his death blow from Rebel General Polk's troops, who were in General McClernand's front."

By 2:30 o'clock McClernand's division had fallen back and most of Sherman's division. Parts of the division of Hurlbut, with those of Prentiss and Wallace, as Eddy says, "Stood between the enemy and destruction—stood like ocean beat rocks." William Preston Johnston, in his life of Albert Sidney Johnston and the Shiloh Campaign in the Century Magazine of February, 1885, says of this part of the battle, from his Southern standpoint:

"On the Federal left-center W. H. L. Wallace was massed with Prentiss' fragments in a position so impregnable and thronged with such fierce defenders that it won from the Confederates the memorable title of the 'Hornet's Nest.' Here behind a dense thicket on the crest of the hill was posted a strong force of as hardy troops as ever fought, almost perfectly protected by the conformation of the ground, and by logs and other rude and hastily prepared defenses. To assail it an open field had to be passed, enfiladed by the fire of its batteries. No figure of speech would be too strong to express the deadly peril of assault upon this natural fortress, whose inaccessible barriers blazed for six hours with sheets of flame and whose infernal gates poured forth a murderous storm of shot and shell and musketry fire which no living thing could quell or even withstand. Brigade after brigade was led against it. Hindman's brigades, which earlier swept everything before them, were reduced to fragments and paralyzed for the remainder of the day. A. P. Stewart's regiments made fruitless assaults. Then Bragg ordered up Gibson's brigade. Gibson, himself a knightly soldier, was aided by Colonels, three of whom afterwards became Generals. The brigade made a gallant charge, but like the others, recoiled from the fire it encountered. Under a cross fire of artillery and musketry it at last fell back with heavy loss. Gibson asked for artillery to be sent to him; but it was not at hand and Bragg sent word to charge again. The Colonels thought it hopeless; but Gibson led them again to the attack, and again they suffered a bloody repulse. Four times the assault proved unavailing.

"About half-past three o'clock the struggle which had been going on for five hours with fitful violence was renewed with the utmost fury. Polk's and Bragg's Corps, intermingled, were engaged in a death grapple with the sturdy commands of Wallace and Prentiss. * * * * General Ruggles judiciously collected all the artillery he could find, some eleven batteries, which he massed against the position. The opening of so heavy a fire and the simultaneous advance of the whole Confederate line resulted first in confusion, then in the death of Wallace and the surrender of Prentiss at about half-past five o'clock. Each Confederate commander of division, brigade and regiment, at his command pounced upon the prey, believed it entitled to the credit of the capture. Breckenridge, Ruggles, Withers, Cheatham and other divisions which helped to subdue these stubborn fighters each imagined his own the hardest part of the work.

"These Federal Generals have received scant justice for their stubborn defense. They agreed to hold their position at all odds and did so until Wallace received his fatal wound and Prentiss was surrounded and captured with nearly three thousand men. This delay was the salvation of Grant's army."

In a Philadelphia paper of June 13th, 1885, a member of the Mobile bar writing an account of this battle as a participant on the Confederate side, says:

"Towards four o'clock the troops of Bragg and Polk engaged in a death struggle with Prentiss and Wallace. These Federal Generals were delivering blow for blow. They felt keenly their responsibility. On them depended the safety of General Grant and the rest of the army. Wallace fell mortally wounded, the hero of this battle on the Federal side. The table of losses at Shiloh will show this. Many Northern writers have sought to make Sherman the hero of this fight. It is the old story of the living dog and the dead lion."

Eddy says: "General Hurlbut's division became exhausted and fell back, leaving Wallace alone. In consequence of losing his support the division of General W. H. L. Wallace thus in isolated advance was compelled to fall back, the last to leave the field. Just at this moment the brave commander was mortally wounded."

As Charles Carleton Coffin says: "It was like taking away the strength of his division. The men lost heart in a moment. The power which had inspired them was gone. General Wallace was a very brave man. He was cool, had great presence of mind and possessed the rare qualification of making his soldiers feel his presence. He could bring order out of confusion and by a word, a look, or an act, inspire his men. * * * * He could hold his ground, but could not push the superior force. His coolness, endurance, bravery, stubbornness, his quick perception of all that was taking place, his power over his men, to make each man a hero, did much towards saving the army on that disastrous day."

Night came on and the battle ceased. The Confederate hosts spending it in the deserted camps of their Northern foes. The Union army was huddled together near the Landing in the camp of W. H. L. Wallace.

When General Wallace received his death wound his brother-in-law, Cyrus Dickey, was riding by his side, and when he fell supposed him killed. He, with the assistance of three orderlies, endeavored to carry him from the field, but were only able to get a short distance when the firing became so heavy on all sides they were compelled to leave the General's body. They laid him near some ammunition boxes, so he would not be trampled on by the flying horses and sadly left him and in five minutes the enemy was between them.

The battle was renewed the next day, but it was an uneven contest. Generals Buell and Lew Wallace had arrived with twenty thousand fresh troops. The Southerners were exhausted and early in the afternoon began to retire from the field and sought their old camping ground at Corinth, leaving slaughter and carnage behind them, and the great battle of Pittsburg Landing was at an end.

CHAPTER XIX.

Death and Burial of General Wallace. Pathetic Letter of Mrs. Wallace.

THE tide of battle turned on the sixth, the Confederates were driven back, and the Union forces recovered their lost ground of the day before. About nine o'clock in the morning General Wallace was found still alive. The enemy had covered him with a blanket, but it had rained in the night and he was wet and cold. He was taken down to the Landing, placed on a transport and taken to Savannah to the headquarters of General Grant in the Cherry Mansion. A bed was put in the library for him and everything was done that skill and love could accomplish.

In the same room General Walter Q. Gresham, as Commandant of the Post of Savannah, had his office with only a curtain division, and a continual stream of men poured in for orders. General Gresham did everything in his power to maintain quiet so as not to disturb the sufferer.

A pathetic letter is here given, written by Mrs. Wallace some time after the battle, to her aunt, Mrs. Templeton, in which she describes the scenes on the boat, the recovery of General Wallace's person and his last hours.

"The lower deck of our boat and that of others was used to ferry reinforcements over. Over and back, over and back we moved. I was earnestly watching these scenes, more hopeful than most around me. Elder Button came up the steps with a worn, depressed look, for he had been partially disabled by a spent ball while caring for the wounded on the field. I felt sorry for him, knowing he had looked on so many loved faces that day for the last time and that he was suffering somewhat from his own injuries.

"Looking still more depressed, he came near me and a little behind me and said, 'This is an awful battle.' I replied, 'Yes, but these fresh troops will yet win the day.' He said, 'You have a great many relations on this field, you cannot hope to see them all come in safe.' I answered,

They all came safely through Donelson, and to-day my husband is in command of a division and is comparatively safe.' He repeated from behind my shoulder, 'It is an awful battle.' My heart was touched by his depressed tones, but I thought his exhausting day's work had caused them. I turned to console him and raising my eyes to the face of Hartley, who sat in front of me, and whose countenance reflected horror as he gazed full in the face of Elder Button, the dread truth fell on my heart like a thunderbolt, like the cold hand of steel.

"Words needed not to tell it; 'twas before me! I was stunned, chilled, almost paralyzed. Suffering came hours afterwards. Very soon Brother Cyrus came to me, self-charged with the duty of telling me my life had been darkened. He was spared the task; his work was already done. He gave me some of the details. Will's division was falling back under orders and in order, he leading them. They had been outflanked by the enemy and at the time were under a heavy cross-fire of rebel musketry. Cyrus had just directed Will's attention to some move of the enemy and he raised in his stirrups apparently to see better; but a shot had reached him, and the next moment he fell upon his face on the ground. He was in full view of the whole division at the time, and from that time confusion reigned. Their hopes of success were gone; Cyrus and an orderly, (one who loved Will) carried him—whom they supposed dead—over a quarter of a mile. They had passed by their own lines and the enemy was madly upon them. To remain was to court death, and with no hope of finally saving their precious charge, they laid him tenderly beside some ammunition to shield him from the tramping feet, and tearfully left him, narrowly escaping with their own lives.

"My husband was dead, and the enemy had possession of the ground where he lay. 'Twas all they could tell me, and it was enough.

"In a few minutes Cyrus left me to go to Colonel Ransom of the Eleventh, who lay wounded on the steamer near-by, and he was by mistake carried down to Savannah. So I was quite alone that fearful night. God gave me strength and I spent much of the night in bathing the fevered brows and limbs of the sufferers around me. Action was a relief to me, and it was slight help to aid men who were suffering in the cause for which Will had given his life.

"On Monday morning about ten o'clock, as I was sitting beside a wounded man just brought in, Cyrus came to me with the word that Will had been brought in (after the rebels were put to flight) and Oh! joy, he was breathing. I flew to the adjoining boat, where he was. There on a narrow mattress on the floor in the middle of the cabin he lay mortally wounded. His face was flushed, but he was breathing naturally, so like himself, save for that fearful wound in his temple. A ball had passed through his head in a manner that made it marvelous that he could still live. But the greatest joy was yet to come—Will recognized my voice at once and clasped my hand. I was thrilled and exclaimed, 'He knows me; he knows me!' Others said that could not be, but Will's lips moved and with difficulty uttered, 'Yes.' Words fail to tell how sweet it was. I believed my husband dead; and he is alive and knows me; Father, I thank Thee! I could appreciate all the feelings of Mary and Martha at the tomb of Lazarus.

"The boat was now taken to Savannah, and we were permitted to place him in a large room at Post Headquarters. Brothers Cyrus Dickey, Martin Wallace, Hitt Wallace and several of Will's staff were there, and all was done that ready hands and loving hearts could do. He seemed so happy and satisfied to have me near him, but lay in calm self-control even in death, conscious that his moments of life were continued only by this rest. Hope with us grew brighter until after periodical delirium, caused by excessive inflammation, passed away and his pulse began to fail; we knew his moments with us were few. My darling knew he was going and pressed my hand long and fondly to his heart. Then he waved me away and said, 'We meet in Heaven.' They were the last words upon those loved lips, and he faded away gently and peacefully and hopefully.

*"My father snatched a moment to come to my side

* Colonel Dickey sent four miles Monday night to ask leave to go to the bedside of General Wallace, he was not only refused but ordered by General Sherman to report to him Tuesday morning with his entire command. For two days he was in the saddle constantly in pursuit of the enemy, as he says: "No surroundings of my life were ever more painful, Ann had been in the neighborhood for three days and was hanging over the bedside of her dying husband and I could not come to her support."

Thursday evening as he was breathing his last. I had now lost him in very deed, but the blow was not so heavy as when I first heard he was killed on the battlefield. Those last days had been so cherished, so unexpected, I raised my heart in grateful thanks for this, and also that the dearest friends of both were with him at his death. God had led me there, so that I should not meet the great sorrow alone. He had permitted me to soothe the last hours of my husband and had given him appreciated knowledge of the fact.

"After he could no longer see me, he would pass his fingers over every hand he touched to assure himself by the ring that he held mine. In his restlessness he would drop the hand for a moment, but the next instant he would search for it and for the ring. If he took the right hand and found no ring, he would pass quickly to the left hand, and touch the ring as evidence of my presence."

An extract from a letter of Colonel M. R. M. Wallace written at this time to his sister, gives a little more of this sad scene:

SAVANNAH, TENN., April 8, 1862.

He tells about the battle and of his brother, General Wallace's fall, and of the arrival of Mrs. Wallace on Sunday morning. He goes on to say:

"She was the first and only person our dear brother recognized until to-day. He evidently knew her by her voice, and manifested his delight at her presence by patting her on the waist and the pressure of the hand, which was a great comfort under the circumstances. This morning he recognized me, and asked where we were. To-day, also, he asked for some ice and soup. He suffers a great deal but is growing more and more conscious, and we confidently hope and expect if his strength holds out a sufficient length of time, that he will finally recover. Ann is by his side constantly. Her being here softens the sad calamity amazingly.

"The rebels have been driven back to their breastworks at Corinth, and I think we have them about whipped, though we may have another sharp conflict at Corinth. It seems as if the whole Confederate army had collected at this point, for they are thicker than the sands on the seashore and fight like soldiers. The slaughter has been terrible on both sides."

A letter from a private, H. M. Parker, of the Eleventh, written to his father on April ninth, says in regard to General Wallace:

"Our beloved former Colonel W. H. L. Wallace, lately appointed Brigadier-General and assigned to General C. F. Smith's division, fell Sunday afternoon, it was thought mortally wounded. He lay on the field until Monday morning when he was taken to Savannah and to-day we hear he is alive, but there is little hope of his recovery. His fall, I understand, came near losing us the day, but I cannot trust myself to speak of so good a man and soldier. Only those who have served under him can realize our country's loss in his fall."

General Halleck, then Commander-in-Chief of the Western armies, said when he heard of General Wallace's death: "We have sustained a great loss, as he was one of the truest, bravest men this country ever knew."

Mrs. Wallace's brother, John Dickey, writing from Ottawa, tells of the feeling there when the news was first received of General Wallace's death:

"Ottawa, Illinois, April 11, 1862.

"On Tuesday night we received the news that there had been a terrible battle at Pittsburg Landing and resulted in a grand victory. Of course, the whole community was thrown into a tumult of enthusiasm and joy. Every flag in the country was at the mast's head and every one shouting the tidings of victory. About ten o'clock on Wednesday we got a dispatch that Will was killed, giving no particulars whatever. The news ran like wild fire through Ottawa, and in ten minutes every flag was at half-mast and the streets were covered with groups of tearful eyes. I never witnessed such a change in my life. It cast a gloom over every heart, and we heard no talk of anything but poor Will. It was really a day of sorrow with everyone in this vicinity."

The local paper at Ottawa speaks in the same strain:

"The rejoicing of our citizens on Wednesday morning over the great news in Tennessee was suddenly turned to mourning on the receipt of the news a few hours after that General Wallace was among the slain. Of the hundreds of brave patriots who have left our city and joined the armies of the Union, there was perhaps not one on whom the affections, pride and hope of our people were more firmly fixed than General Wallace. A long resident among us, a leading member of our bar, a loved and valued citizen, amiable, liberal, kind-hearted, with a character adored by all, the noble and manly qualities, and *sans peur, sans reproche,* his loss indeed, aside from all considerations of his great service to his country in the field, was felt by our citizens as locally an irreparable calamity."

General Grant sent General Wallace with his staff, relations, servants, horse and equipments all North on a navy dispatch boat.

The remains arrived in Chicago on Sunday evening, April thirteenth. The Chicago paper says:

"The remains of General W. H. L. Wallace, who so bravely sacrificed his life at the late battle of Pittsburg Landing, arrived in this city Sunday evening about 9 o'clock on a special train from Cairo furnished by direction from General Strong. The body was in charge of Colonel T. Lyle Dickey of the Fourth Illinois cavalry, accompanied by Major M. R. M. Wallace of the Fourth cavalry, a brother of the deceased. Lieutenant Cyrus E. Dickey, Lieutenant I. P. Rumsey, Aides-de-Camp to General Wallace, Captain C. Y. Hotchkiss, Acting Adjutant-General. The wife of General Wallace, who arrived at Pittsburg Landing the same day her husband received his death wound, also accompanied his remains.

"At the depot they were met by a detachment of about fifty men composed of Companies D and H of the Irish brigade. The detachment was in charge of Captain Simpson, Company D.

"The body was placed in a hearse which had been provided by order of Mayor Rumsey and about half-past nine the procession started from the depot in the following order:

"Two files of soldiers with reversed arms. Hearse attended by six commissioned officers, four from the Irish brigade, and two from the Scotch regiment, as pall bearers. A rear guard of six men with fixed bayonets.

"The procession proceeded up Lake Street to Clark, up Clark to Van Buren and thence to the Rock Island depot, and notwithstanding the lateness of the hour, was attended by a large concourse of citizens. The tolling of the Court House bell as the procession passed through the streets startled the whole city, many not being aware of the death of the General.

"It was impossible to attend the remains of the dead with public demonstration of sorrow which would have been done had earlier notice of the arrival of the train been received. Combined with this, the arrival of a large number of prisoners at Camp Douglas, rendered it absolutely necessary that but few of the comparatively small force stationed there should be withdrawn for the purpose of escort duty."

At Ottawa the paper speaks of the arrival of the funeral cortege:

"OTTAWA, ILLINOIS, April 19, 1862.

"General Wallace was brought to this city Monday morning, April 14th, at 4 o'clock. The tolling of the bells of the various churches announced at that hour the arrival of the body. An escort of the Knights Templar and a delegation of citizens was at the depot to receive it and accompany it to his late residence. At 2 o'clock P. M. the body was laid in state at the Supreme Court House and visited by thousands of citizens and strangers. Tuesday morning, attended by the members of the Masonic fraternity the body was carried to the Episcopal Church. At the church the usual rites for the burial of the dead were performed by Mr. Benedict, the rector, assisted by Reverend M. Clark, also of this city, and who was formerly chaplain of the famous Eleventh regiment. At the conclusion of the ceremonies in the church the procession was re-formed and escorted the remains to the family burial place in a beautiful spot near his residence on the bluff. The funeral ceremonies were entirely of a civic order, there being no military organization in this vicinity. They were under the immediate control of the Masonic fraternity, in accordance with a wish frequently expressed by General Wallace, while alive, to be buried with Masonic rites. The only military in the cortege were Captain Hotchkiss, Lieutenant Dickey and Lieutenant Rumsey, General Wallace's aides. The charger of General Wallace was led in the procession by his body servant, and the old flag of the Eleventh Illinois regiment, which had been so fearfully riddled at Fort Donelson, was borne by one of his orderlies.

"The day of his burial was one of unusual gloom externally. Yet, notwithstanding rain and mud, the citizens thronged the streets, swelling the funeral cortege. Business was suspended and stores and offices closed. It is not often an entire people are brought to such a general and sincere mourning. Indeed, it is seldom that the removal of a single individual affects so many minds with a sense of personal loss.

"The occasion and circumstances were peculiar. The deceased had occupied a prominent position in this county, and held a high place in public esteem. He had fallen with distinguished honors in devotion to his country, in a cause in which our sympathies are one.

"General Wallace was universally respected, by many loved. Naturally noble and generous, always courteous, his life in most respects far above that of ordinary men, was a model of manly dignity and honor, and yet of engaging simplicity and unaffected modesty.

"One would hardly have supposed that a spirit so gentle, a disposition so modest and retiring, was meet for the warrior and chieftain. Yet Wallace was at the head of his column unabashed, calm and dauntless of soul. His men had all confidence in him. Under such Generals men do not run. They realize the value of the life of their leader, the soundness of his judgment and the justice of his cause.

"But he is gone. He sleeps with the heroic dead. He has closed an honorable career. He leaves an untarnished reputation."

Another newspaper article in an Ottawa paper speaks of the service rendered by the Knights Templar:

"The occasion of the funeral obsequies to General Wallace in this city on Monday and Tuesday brought prominently to the notice of our citizens a branch of the Masonic order about which more deserves to be known. In the absence of any military organization in this region there was a real embarrassment felt at the meeting of citizens how certain formalities at which military of some sort seemed indispensable, were to be arranged. They were happily relieved, however, by an officer of the Knights Templar, who assured them the order was abundantly able to meet the exigency. And they did it nobly. From the moment the body arrived it was surrounded by a guard of honor, thoroughly trained and understanding their duty to the last minute. They escorted the body in true military order to the residence of General Wallace, guarded it faithfully while there, escorted it to the Court House and guarded it while it lay in state and surrounded it with brilliant military escort in the funeral cortege. They deserve all honor, yet it was with them a labor of love. General Wallace has occupied the highest position in the order and ever the first place in the hearts of the brotherhood. The order was commanded by Sir Knight Henry C. Ranney of Chicago, Grand Recorder."

Here are given some extracts from a discourse on the death of General Wallace preached by the Reverend Z. Colman at the Baptist Church, Ottawa, April 13th, 1862, from the text II. Samuel, 13:2. * * * * "And the victory that day was turned into mourning unto all people." * * * * "Our text is especially appropriate to our own city. These victories in which our people, and the people of this State, have so direct, immediate and large an interest, have really been turned into mourning to us. Our banners that would gladly have floated from the top of their staffs, have been draped with weeds of woe and mournfully hung at half-mast. The shout that would have gone up from many patriotic hearts, has given place to the solemn knell and the mournful dirge. Countenances that would have been radiant with joy, have been covered with sadness and gloom. Tearful eyes and bowed heads have told the grief of our people. Surely the victory this day is turned into mourning to this people. And these demonstrations of grief are not without a cause. One of the noblest forms that has moved among us for years has been borne through the streets to its final resting place. Marred, bruised and broken by the bloody hand of treason, one known to all—pure and honorable in all the relationships of life, in manhood's noble prime, he has been smitten down by the cruel traitorous hand of slavery. His place at the bar—in the political assembly, at the Nation's anniversary, in the social gathering, in the family circle, the place of worship, shall know him no more forever. Not only has the grave closed over our gallant dead, but it has opened at our feet and closed over one of the bravest hearts that responded to his country, in the hour of the Nation's peril. A friend, a neighbor, a citizen, a patriot, a hero, with the well earned honors of his country fresh about his brow, has been brought from the distant bloody field and borne to his long home; and the mourners go about the streets. Surely the casualties of war have turned this victory into mourning to this people. * * * * When victories vindicate the Government in its legitimate work they accomplish their proper object. When the murderer is apprehended and brought to justice, it vindicates the Government, it sends a feeling of security to every inhabitant.

"When treason lifts its murderous hand against the Government, lets loose the scourge of civil war, the Government that suppresses the treason, punishes the traitors, restores peace, spreads its protecting shield over the feeblest individual, and humblest calling; such a government vindicates itself. Unless this Government accomplishes this, we shall have other causes of sorrow and mourning besides the dreadful casualties of the battlefield. When the news of this last battle in which our own gallant Wallace fell reached me, the dead, the dying, the wounded, the desolate homes and hearts for a time completely filled my mind, shutting out everything else. I seemed for a moment to forget my country and the cruel treason that sought its destruction. My soul was filled with strange and solemn emotions unlike anything I had ever experienced before. As I recovered from the shock, my first thoughts were: 'Must so much precious blood be shed to wash away the Nation's sins?' My soul filled with grief. I have watched to see the results upon the public mind. These dear bought victories ought to purge the national politics. They ought to quicken into life the national conscience. They ought to arouse every patriot's heart to the fixed determination to banish human bondage from this land. Unless these bloody victories lead to these results we have many bitter tears yet to weep. Unless the time of the end draws nigh, the time when the people, freed from party shackles, long and long outraged by this monstrous iniquity, shall rise in their majesty, and by the God of justice swear that slavery, the cause of all this woe, shall die. Stopping short of this our victories will be turned into mourning more grievous than we have yet experienced. * * * * We do well to mourn. This victory has cast a gloom over this city. Here Wallace pursued his professional studies when a youth. He has grown up to noble manhood in this community. We all knew him well. Of all the brave men who rallied to the standard of their country, not one possessed a braver or more patriotic heart. But fearless as he was, his modesty and gentleness and heart were equal to his bravery. On the bloody field of Donelson after that sanguinary conflict the fragments of the gallant Eleventh were mustered again. I am told that when the small number that survived that dreadful day was announced, Wallace, brave, calm, cool and collected as he always was, shook with emotion and wept like a child. The dead, the dead, his own companions-in-arms, who had chosen him for their leader, lay strewn around on the battlefield. I shall never forget one incident that revealed the man. None but those who were at the National Capital on the fourth of March, 1861, will ever fully know the state of the public mind in the metropolis of the nation at that eventful time. The President-elect, from considerations of safety, had stolen into the Capital under the curtains of night; the city was patrolled with armed men, many looking forward to the inauguration day with fearful forebodings. Many entertained serious fears that the streets would flow with blood, and the President-elect would be assassinated on his way to the Capitol or upon the platform. This may seem like folly; but it was no folly then and there. Wallace was a personal friend of the President's. He thought of proposing to those having charge of the arrangements to allow himself and a few known friends to be admitted to the platform secretly armed and ready for any emergency, ready to throw themselves between the President and any stealthy foe that might in spite of all precautions suddenly fall upon him. He said to me: 'Will you be of that number?' 'Certainly,' was my reply. On inquiring he found that every precaution that friendship, prudence or patriotism could dictate would be provided. That proposition truly revealed the man. He was just as ready then to grapple with treason, though in the assassin's garb, as he afterwards was to meet it upon the field. It is meet that we should weep, for he was our neighbor and our friend as well as a noble man.

"We at least should resolve never to leave in peace the great iniquity that has kindled this rebellion, and smote down our friend and one of the Nation's patriots and heroes. Let others feel as they may, there should be but one determination with us—that we will never cease till the great crime that nerved the arm that laid our loved and honorable Wallace low is destroyed, root and branch. I laid my hand on his coffin, and with emotions unlike any that ever agitated my bosom before, made a solemn vow—that while God gives me breath I will not cease to wage a war against that great wrong that has shed the blood of our friend, and now seeks the destruction of our country."

In a Masonic paper is the following.

"IN MEMORIAM.

"Sunday, Fourth Month, Twentieth Day, A. L. 5862.

" 'Let the bell toll, a saintly soul
Floats down the Stygian River.'

"Fourteen years since, while residing in Central Illinois, we were so favored as to enjoy the intimate companionship of one on whom 'Every God had set His seal, to give the world assurance of a man.' The reputation has since become national of the then capable but comparatively unknown young man whom we so esteemed and respected. He was then just beginning the practice of law, having finished his studies after his return from Mexico, where at Buena Vista, he, as Adjutant of an Illinois regiment, 'flashed his maiden sword,' and achieved distinction. Honorable to a fault, in love with his profession, faithful to his clients, and decidedly talented, he 'pursued the even tenor of his way,' and at the time the body politic had become covered with the festering sores of rebellion and the machinations of the conspirators were fully *developed* in the memorable bombardment of Fort Sumter; he was in the enjoyment of a large practice, and was the center of a host of admiring friends. Born of Southern stock, he was yet utterly loyal, and at once placed himself at the disposal of his country. Unanimously, and without solicitation on his part, he was elected to command the Illinois Eleventh, and, having good material with which to work, he soon made it one of the finest regiments in the service. As commander of the Post at Bird's Point and as Chief of Brigade at Fort Donelson, he evinced those high qualities, that aptitude for command, and that calm courage, which fully proved his right to the encomiums which were so cordially bestowed upon him, and he reflected honor upon the West, and upon the Fraternity of which he was so earnest a member. At Pittsburg Landing he commanded a division, and fell at the head of his column on the first day of the fight. When struck by the fatal bullet he dismounted as coolly as if on parade * * * supported by two of his comrades he laid down to die. In the 'hurly burly' of those 'moving accidents by flood and field' the retreat, the rally and the repulse, which rendered famous the subsequent thirty-six hours our brother was forgotten. After the battle, search was made for him and he was found on the spot where he had lain so long, exposed to the elements. He was insensible, and not long afterwards he breathed his last. Sorrowing companions in arms bore him to a place of shelter, and to his stricken wife; and thence his body was brought to Ottawa, Illinois, where he had so long lived and where it was buried with Masonic honors one day last week—the whole population mourning in unison with his bereaved family.

"Brave and capable W. H. L. Wallace! Ten thousand rebels slain cannot compensate for his loss! 'His work was unfinished, and brethren mourn. Green be the sod above him; honored be his memory! Eloquent advocate, true patriot, faithful brother, gallant soldier; he has gone to his reward in the Celestial Lodge above and 'after life's fitful fever he sleeps well.' "

CHAPTER XX.

Public Opinion of General Wallace. His Services as An Officer. His Character as a Man. Memorial Window.

A STRONG friendship existed between General Wallace and General T. E. G. Ransom—they were kindred souls. Ransom went out as Major in Colonel Wallace's regiment, rising to Lieutenant-Colonel, Colonel and Brigadier-General, the latter position before he was thirty years old. Dr. Eddy says of him: "Young, heroic and handsome, brave, enthusiastic and manly, courageous as a lion, tender as a woman. No man so completely recalls the best qualities of the days of chivalry. No braver heart was laid upon the country's altar, no clearer head was bowed before the great destroyer, no more unsullied sword has been laid upon the wall. Yielding up his life in the very flower of youth he will remain in memory ever young."

After General Wallace's death Mrs. Wallace gave his Colonel's shoulder straps to Colonel Ransom, who writes her the following letter:

"Headquarters, Eleventh Illinois Infantry,
"Camp Stanton, April 28, 1862.

"Dear Madam:

"Your present, with the accompanying beautiful letter, handed to me by your brother, are before me. I can only express my gratitude for the honor you would confer in your expressed wish for me to wear the 'pasantz' of your late lamented husband. While I appreciate your noble motive, while I feel honored with the trust, my love for your husband, my reverence for his memory, prevents me from placing the sacred emblems so lately worn by him upon my unworthy shoulders.

"But I will promise you that they shall be worn nearer to my heart through the battles that may follow. I trust they may constantly remind me of him who has gone before and may they nerve me to emulate his noble teachings and example. And then when these scenes of blood and carnage are past and Peace once more reigns over our land, I shall hope to return these precious relics to you. If it should be otherwise and I fall at the head of the 'old Eleventh' I shall but follow in the steps of the illustrious dead, our former brave commander, and still 'the eagles' can be borne to you by other hands, who will tell you whether the laurel won for them when worn by their late owner, have had their luster dimmed while entrusted to my keeping.

"As the friend of your late husband and of yourself, having received so many flattering evidences of your confidence and esteem, it perhaps, should be my mission in this hour of your deepest sorrow to offer you consolation, but, my dear Madam, I am unequal to this task. I know in expressing my own feelings I should add new pangs to your already overburdened heart. I could but tell you of long hours of sadness, of frequent lonely rides to the spot where he fell and how I bow with sorrow when I reflect that never more can I meet that noble man on earth—how *can* I who have been governed by worldly thoughts, ambition and pride, intrude upon the sacred grief and offer consolation to one whose Christian life and happy belief points to a higher, nobler sphere, where as your beloved husband said, 'We meet in Heaven.' Then let these last beautiful words of that dying hero serve as a bright light to guide you through the dark paths of this life.

"That this hope will sustain you, that a kind Providence who has promised to care for the widow will watch over and protect you amid the many trials that are before you is my earnest prayer.

"Believe me, Madam, that anything that it may be in my power to do to lighten your burden of cares thrown upon you in any way whatever I shall be happy to assist you, and trust the near ties that bound your late husband and myself together, the love I shall ever sacredly cherish for his memory, will be evidence to you of the happiness I should feel to be of the slightest service to you, his nearest friend.

With expressions of highest esteem,

"I am truly your friend,

"T. E. G. RANSOM.

"Mrs. Ann Wallace, Ottawa, Illinois."

Captain William McMichael, Assistant Adjutant-General to Major-General C. F. Smith, and acting in the same capacity for General Wallace at the battle of Shiloh, was taken prisoner on that fateful day. When he returned from captivity, he wrote the following letter to Mrs. Wallace, giving some additional facts of the battle and her husband's movements:

"CORINTH, MISS., June 29, 1862.

"MRS. W. H. L. WALLACE, MADAM:

"I have recently returned to our lines from captivity in the South and take the liberty of thus addressing you in order to communicate some facts in reference to the late General Wallace. The desire which I feel to express to you my sincere regret at General Wallace's death, and the presumption that any incidents of the action on the battlefield of Shiloh would prove of interest are my excuses for writing.

"Together with other officers of Major-General Smith's staff, as well as the General's own immediate aides, I was with him when he placed his division in position on Sunday morning. I had the honor of serving with him during the day and was riding in his company when he received the fatal wound from which he has since died.

"Our division at the time was changing front, when General Wallace, who was riding slowly immediately by the side of his men, was struck. A line of skirmishers from the enemy's forces was deployed on a ridge commanding the open space through which we were passing at the time, and my impression has always been that General Wallace received his death wound from one of these. He rose slightly in his saddle, uttered a brief exclamation of pain, and then fell apparently lifeless to the ground. I had supposed that he died immediately, but with a view of saving his body it was taken charge of by four men to be borne to the river. I afterwards ascertained they were obliged to leave the General, owing to the galling fire which was poured upon them by the enemy.

"After my capture, having heard that the General was still on the field, I succeeded in finding his body, and remained with him until removed to the rear to join the other prisoners. I found him still alive, and when I spoke to him he seemed conscious in a measure, but wholly unable to speak. Although obliged to leave him myself, yet a Southern General who was present promised that his wounds should be dressed and every attention paid him. Since my return I have learned of his recapture and subsequent death.

"Permit me, Madam, to express to you the deep regret with which I heard the last sad news, and to say that the feeling of sorrow at the General's death is universal throughout the division which he that day commanded.

You know that at Shiloh he led the troops of General Smith's division. He had been with us for only a short time previous to the battle, but possessed the perfect confidence of the division. His intrepid conduct at Donelson and the equally honorable history of his earlier life were familiar to us all, and he filled as successfully as any officer who could have been placed over the division the place vacated by the sickness of our commander, General Smith.

"You have, of course, heard how gallantly General Wallace's command behaved that day and how often the enemy were repulsed from his line. Four regiments of our division, or rather their remnants after the losses of the day's severe fighting were, it is true, captured, but it was not until some time after the General himself had fallen, and our division had become separated by the want of co-operation incident upon his loss. He was shot at a most critical juncture, just as we were changing position. Had he escaped wounds that day the advantage to our cause cannot be too highly estimated. He fell about five o'clock, having preserved his line through the entire day, and it is more than probable that had he survived, not only would the regiments of our division have been saved, but also those gallant men of General Prentiss' command, who were co-operating with us on the left, and who were captured at the same time with the men of our division.

"General Wallace communicated frequently with General Prentiss during the day, their last interview having taken place about four o'clock. General Prentiss' impression was at that time, and he is of the opinion that it was General Wallace's also, that the right wing of the army was still firm, and hence they decided to still maintain their ground from which the enemy had failed to drive them, the men being in excellent spirits.

"The capture of General Prentiss and the death of General Wallace have prevented a correct report of the actions of their respective commands from being made known, but I am sure that when the true history of Shiloh shall be written the chief glory of Sunday's fighting will rest upon them—upon General Prentiss, who, overwhelmed and outnumbered by the enemy, was driven from the first position, but rallied a portion of his command (composed though it was principally of raw troops) and taking position on our left, refused to retreat from a line he had been ordered to hold, and which he still believed tenable—and upon General Wallace who fell by the side of the men he had so gallantly led that day into action, whom he had protected by his skill, inspired by his presence and whom he had never seen falter.

"In reference to General Wallace's high qualities as a man, aside from his distinguished ability as a soldier, it is not for me to speak; but I may mention as another evidence of that generosity for which he was so well known, that on Sunday he gave regiment after regiment of his best troops to strengthen points which seemed to be more severely threatened than his own division. Into his military creed there entered no selfish principle; when he fought it was not with a view to personal aggrandizement, but with the one patriotic aim for the success of our general cause. Like the brave General whom he succeeded in command, he scorned to seek reputation by the petty means by which some men endeavor to rise, and like him, his name has become a synonym of all that is true, gallant and soldierly.

"Very respectfully yours,

"William McMichael,

"Assistant Adjutant-General to late Major-General Smith."

When General Wallace fell he was but seventy-five feet away from the enemy and his commanding figure, dignified bearing, and utter disregard of self-preservation in the midst of the hurricane of danger around him, begat the admiration of his foes, so that General Leonidas Polk sent one of his officers to ascertain who he was, as came out in the following correspondence sixteen years afterwards:

"SAVANNAH, GEORGIA, June 9th, 1878.

"TO THE GOVERNOR OF ILLINOIS, SPRINGFIELD—SIR:

"On the afternoon of the first day's fight at Shiloh (called by your side Pittsburg Landing) an officer was seen trying to stop his men from retreating, and when he found that he could not, he deliberately reined his horse and rode slowly off. He was shot, and he fell immediately from his horse.

"General Polk expressed a wish to know who 'that brave man is.' I use his words, and I galloped up to the body and took from his coat breast-pocket the enclosed papers, proving him to have been General W. H. L. Wallace of your State. These papers I sent to my home then in Sola, and I have only to-day found them among old papers. I beg to hand them to you with the request that you cause inquiry to be made for his family and return to them these papers taken from General Wallace's body for the purpose of finding out who the brave officer was who lost his life within seventy-five feet of us.

"Though an enemy at the time we could not but respect him for the brave manner in which he acted when his command was in retreat. He fell in a road, but we took his body up and moved it out of the way of cannon and caissons and I suppose that of course as the 'tide of battle' turned in your favor the next day, his body was recovered. I beg to say that if I could have found these papers before they should have been returned as they now have been.

"I will be pleased to hear from you that this package has not only been received by you, but that you have found the family of General Wallace and have had the same delivered to their hands. I am, sir, yours respectfully,

"M. R. TUNNO."

Governor Cullom to T. Lyle Dickey.

"EXECUTIVE OFFICE, SPRINGFIELD, ILLINOIS,
"June 27, 1878.

HON. T. LYLE DICKEY, DEAR SIR:

"It gives me great pleasure to hand you herewith a letter from M. R. Tunno, Esq., of Savannah, Georgia, enclosing certain papers taken from the body of General W. H. L. Wallace at the time he fell on the field of Pittsburg Landing, with a request that you will forward them to his widow.

"Mr. Tunno's account of the circumstances attending General Wallace's fall and the testimony he bears to his gallant conduct will be highly valued by his family.

"Yours respectfully,
"S. M. CULLOM."

Judge Dickey to his daughter, Mrs. Wallace:

"GRAND PACIFIC HOTEL, CHICAGO, ILLINOIS,
"June 28th, 1878.

"MY VERY DEAR DAUGHTER:

"This morning while at breakfast I read in the Chicago *Times* of this date, the article headed 'A Reminiscence of Shiloh' relating to an incident attending the fall of your noble husband at that battle. I have this moment received the papers referred to with Tunno's letter to the Governor of the State and a letter from Governor Cullom to me.

"I enclose to you herewith a slip cut from the newspaper containing the article referred to and the package sent by the Governor.

"Everything connected with that dreadful hour is of intense interest to me as well as to you.

"It seems strange to me that no other papers were found on his person, if it was in fact examined immediately after he fell. At this length of time the recollection of Mr. Tunno as to all the circumstances may not be entirely accurate. My recollection is that General Wallace, after he fell, was carried a short distance by Cyrus, assisted by some orderlies and then laid (not in the road) but by the roadside and near a tent, and that he was found by Cyrus on Monday morning at the same place, but evidently cared for in some degree by the humane hand of some of the enemy.

"I will write to Mr. Tunno at once in relation to his sword and watch. I think the probability is that Mr. Tunno's account of what he saw and heard at the moment of Wallace's fall is strictly correct, but that by reason of the excitement of the hour it is not accurate as to time when the papers were taken from his person. That probably occurred after the fierceness of the action had subsided. General Polk probably spent the night near where General Wallace lay wounded.

"Your father, With much love,

"T. LYLE DICKEY."

At the dedication of the new Supreme Court House, at Springfield, Illinois, Colonel Wood, of Effingham, made an address which was reported in the Chicago *Legal News* of February 15th, 1908, in which he refers to General W. H. L. Wallace as follows: "Wallace, a General in command of a division in the 'Hornet's Nest,' near the Shiloh Church, ended a faithful service to his country with his life. His trophies were a front line firmly maintained during a long day of bloody conflicts—a battlefield held—an army saved."

General Wallace evinced such marked military ability his friends often speculated as to what his career might have been had he survived the battle of Shiloh. Many years after the war General Grant was asked by Captain Town, a surviving member of the old Eleventh Illinois infantry, what his opinion was of W. H. L. Wallace's ability and future. General Grant's answer was, "Had he lived, I would not be where I am now."

When Mrs. Wallace went to Europe in 1869 President Grant gave her the following letter of introduction, which honors her no less than her husband.

General Lew Wallace in his Autobiography speaks of General W. H. L. Wallace "as a man gallant as one may ever hope to encounter. And here I may as well answer a question often asked. I do not know of any relationship between Colonel W. H. L. Wallace and myself. I do know, however, that I should be very proud did such exist. Had he lived high rank was just ahead of him. He possessed all the elements of a great soldier."

On Decoration Day, 1874, at Ottawa the Knights Templar had charge of the day's services, which were very impressive. In the afternoon after the other exercises were finished they proceeded to the grave of General W. H. L. Wallace on the bluff near his late residence. "At the grave the flowery tribute as well as the solemn appearance and knightly bearing of the commandery was very imposing. Wreaths and bouquets were placed around the tomb by a delegation of young ladies, while the Knights so placed their flowers as to form a cross o'er the breast of their illustrious though fallen comrade. A beautiful white cross within a triangle of evergreens rested at the foot of the grave and a cross and crown decked the head of the grave of the departed hero."

Then Hon. Washington Bushnell gave an eloquent eulogy, which did honor to the heart and intellect of the living friend no less than the dead friend eulogized:

"He is not dead but sleepeth."

"Yes, 'he sleeps the sleep that knows no waking.' Look upon his grave! Behold his tomb, but do not imagine that he is dead. A form so erect and manly may rest in the grave, but a spirit so noble cannot die. It is yet abroad working for good purposes and ends. Who remembers him but as kind and gentle, yet firm? Exalted in his manners and example, and pure in all his impulses? Look through this leafy grove. Can you not see him walking from that front door to yonder gate, with form erect, countenance beaming with kindness and flashing with thought and intelligence? Be not deceived, for looking again you see him not, for here he lies.

"And here let me say to the widowed wife, lay aside your grief, forget your mourning, for what woman has had bequeathed to her a legacy so rich as the name and fame of him of whom I speak, and who yet liveth in spirit to comfort and protect you.

"The inanimate form which this tomb confines was but a short time ago the abode of one of the purest patriotic hearts that ever honored our land. He was one of the first to volunteer in the Mexican war, and won unextinguishable honors as a brave officer in the First United States regiment. At the breaking out of the rebellion he was the first of our citizens to offer his services to the Government. I need not detail his subsequent career, for it is as familiar as a household word. Mortally wounded upon the sixth of April, 1862, he died upon the tenth. Pittsburg Landing, how hallowed the name, how glorious, yet how sad, the surroundings! Whether making friends in the social circle, or gathering laurels in legal contests; whether carrying materials upon his shoulder up the bluff to beautify an early home, or wearing upon the same shoulder the glittering epaulets upon the field of strife and carnage to victory and ultimate death, yet he was Wallace ever, he was Wallace still. Oh! how the hopes of true-hearted friends drooped, like these fading flowers upon his grave as they heard the mournful news! Around his tomb to-day are thousands of those who knew him best and love him longest. To them and his country his death was a calamity, but to him it was a glorious fading into immortality.

"Fearless and self reliant, open in dislikes, warm in friendship, he ever marched straightforward in the line of duty and truth. As a man to be judged in private life few were his equals. Never was *he* charged with broken faith or violated trust.

"And now at eventide as the shadows lengthen toward the East, where he loved to sit so well and from whence we have often obeyed his gavel call, let us turn again to the West and behold his sepulchre, fully realizing that the Grand Supreme Commander of the Universe has by His gavel called our comrade to his final and peaceful rest. Gentle neighbor, good friend, true patriot and noble hero, hail! and again farewell."

As the concluding sentences of the eulogy were uttered the knights presented arms and with heads uncovered showed their appreciation of the dead hero. As the last word, "farewell" fell from the eloquent speaker the trickling tear and moistened eyes of the vast concourse of people told plainly of the love and respect which was gathered there to pay tribute to the memory of the fallen patriot.

After the ceremony at the grave the knights visited Mrs. Wallace at her residence and by words of comfort renewed the assurances of their sympathy.

Some years before the Knights Templar had presented Mrs. Wallace with a beautiful oil painting of her husband —thus showing their respect and esteem for her no less than the loving memory held of her husband.

For many years Mrs. Wallace had a desire to place a memorial window in the church at Ottawa in memory of her husband. She gave much thought to the subject, visiting many churches in her own country and in Europe. In the Glasgow cathedral she especially admired the stained glass where the windows are exceptionally fine. They are all memorials given in the years 1861-1863. A committee selected of Glasgow citizens recommended a uniform plan of illustration and harmonious treatment of the entire series of windows. The Royal Establishment of Glass Painting at Munich was selected to carry on the work, and many of the most eminent artists in Germany were the designers of the windows. One window especially interested Mrs. Wallace. It was the subject of the Resurrection, designed by Professor Julius Hubner of Dresden, director of the Royal Gallery and one of the finest artists in Germany. She made a note of the name, and when two years later she visited Dresden, called upon him, asking if he could suggest some artist to design a window for her. She told him she would like the subject of the Resurrection, but as her means were limited she feared she could not have a design so elaborate.

Professor Hubner became very much interested in her and her project and offered to undertake the work himself. As he would like to have some of his work in America, he would charge nothing for it, only for the mechanical part of the glass worker. His work consisted principally of large canvasses on historical and biblical subjects which hang on the walls of many public and private European galleries. Occasionally he made designs for memorial windows, some of which were placed in the chapels of the royal palaces near Dresden, to which he gave Mrs. Wallace and her friends the entree to see his work and visit these interesting places.

He made a most beautiful design of the Resurrection for Mrs. Wallace's window. There is the figure of the Christ with the angel holding open the tomb. On the halo around the Christ head is the text: "Grave, where is thy victory?" After the window was completed Professor Hubner made Mrs. Wallace a present of the drawing of the window, which she had incorporated into the book cases in the library at her home in Ottawa.

The window was placed in Christ Episcopal Church in 1872. The lower section of the window represents the life of General Wallace in pictured scenes. It was executed under Mrs. Wallace's direction by a less renowned artist than Professor Hubner. The first scene is a log cabin representing the childhood home with the date 1834 and the text: "That our garners may be full." The next scene, 1840, represents the student's life with table and books and the text: "Take fast hold of instruction." The third and central figure represents his profession, Justice with her scales and the text: "Teach me thy statutes." On a pillar to the right in this scene is a Masonic emblem showing his connection with that order. The next scene is the Mexican War in 1846, with the text: "Thou hast covered my head in the day of battle." The lower picture and last one is the river at Pittsburg Landing with boats and the smoke of the battle in the distance, and the riderless horse, with the text: "In the Lord I have put my trust. I will not fear what flesh can do unto me." In the right corner of this same picture is a beautiful oak tree in full vigor riven by lightning and broken in twain; clinging to it is a vine with the text: "Thy will, not mine, be done." The oak tree representing the vigorous manhood cut down in his prime; the vine, the woman's love remaining the same both in life and in death.

Thus in beautiful stained glass is pictured the blessed truth of a risen life beyond the sorrows and disappointments of this earthly life, where the noble deed of heroes and patriots find a reward more exalted than the plaudits of their fellow men, for a country saved in its entirety by noble self sacrifice and exalted patriotism.

CHAPTER XXI.

Mrs. Wallace.

A FEW sketches are here added of Mrs. Wallace's life after the death of her husband, whose memory she cherished with devoted love. She did not retire from the world in selfish sorrow, but lived a brave, heroic and unselfish life, lightening the burden of others, thereby bringing joy into her own saddened life.

During the war she made several visits to her relatives in the army and the following incident of one of these trips shows her quick presence of mind in an emergency. She, with her little daughter, had been spending the winter in Natchez, Mississippi, with the family of General Wallace's brother, Colonel M. R. M. Wallace, commandant of the post there, and were returning in the spring to their northern home.

The steamer Luminary, on which they were passengers, tied up one day at a lonely place on the Mississippi river to take on wood; and while they were engaged in loading, a band of Guerrillas rode out from the thick wood and opened a heavy fire on the boat. The rope that held the steamer to the landing was quickly cut and for greater safety the boat made for the middle of the river.

Mrs. Wallace's stateroom, with glass doors leading onto the deck, was on the side of the firing, so was in a very exposed position. Her first thought was for the little girl running about the deck, who, when told she must come in or the "rebels would shoot her," was very reluctant to do so, as she could not understand why the rebels wanted to shoot her, for she had been playing with them all winter and had encountered no harm. Her mother persuaded her with some force, placing her behind a trunk, then she hastily took the mattresses from her bed and placed them against the glass doors making a protection that was perfectly bullet proof.

In the saloon tables were overturned and fine ladies

crouched tremblingly behind them. The boat soon steamed out of harm's way and went gallantly northward with no damage but many bullets imbedded in her wooden sides.

In 1868 Mrs. Wallace with her daughter spent much time in Washington City at the home of her father, then Assistant Attorney General. While there she renewed the friendship made in war times with the families of General Grant and General Sherman. Mrs. Wallace was very unassuming, but had the faculty of making and retaining friends.

A long cherished wish of going to Europe was accomplished the following year, President Grant and General Sherman both giving her letters of introduction. General Sherman's letter is here given, President Grant's having already been given earlier in this volume.

"Headquarters Army of the United States,
"WASHINGTON, D. C., August 3, 1869.

"MRS. GENERAL W. H. L. WALLACE,
"WASHINGTON, D. C.

"DEAR MADAM:—I learn that you propose soon to sail for France to spend a year or more, partly for the purpose of educating your child. I feel assured all you need there will be to have it known that you are the widow of one of our War Generals who fell in battle in the early part of the war.

"Should you take up your residence in France you should see the Hon. E. B. Washburne, who would gladly provide you the necessary credentials. Or if you go to Germany I commend you to the special care of our Minister at Brussels, Mr. Jones, or to our Minister at The Hague, Holland, General Ewing, my brother-in-law. I know that either of these gentlemen will take pleasure in giving you the benefit of their official stations.

"Wishing you health, happiness and a safe return to your family and friends. I am truly yours,

"W. T. SHERMAN, General."

Mrs. Wallace encountered friends wherever she went. In Paris was the Hon. E. B. Washburne of Illinois, who was kindness itself to Mrs. Wallace, and many other American ladies in the trying times of the Franco-Prussian war and the siege of Paris. Mr. Washburne won renown, honor and respect both from Germany and France, no less than from his own country, in the wonderful manner in which he conducted diplomatic affairs at this time. As the German Ambassador could not remain in Paris during this war, Mr. Washburne acted for the German Government along with his duties to his own country. He aided many a poor German to return to the Fatherland.

It was Mr. Washburne who notified Mrs. Wallace of the near approach of the Prussian Army and that a quick exit from Paris was wise. On a day's notice she and her little girl left Paris for Brussels, the city of refuge for so many Parisian refugees. They left Paris none too soon to escape the horrors of that dreadful siege. They spent a year and a half in Germany, returning to their own country in 1872. Ten years later they crossed the Pacific ocean, spending two years in the sunny isles of the mid Pacific, Hawaii, where Mrs. Wallace's brother, C. H. Dickey, and sister, Mrs. C. H. Wallace, were residing. It was then foreign soil, but is now loyal American territory with a people to be proud of, with scenery and climate scarcely to be equaled on the globe's surface.

Mrs. Wallace's life was one of great activity and variety, travel and change, but no one was more devoted to her home, her town or her friends. She loved to fill her house with guests, especially the young, and entertained with true Southern hospitality which had been born and bred in her.

Ill health came to her in her later years, but her cheerfulness and interest in everything around her never flagged. Even in the months of her last illness, helpless from a stroke of paralysis, her sweetness, amiability and cheeriness never forsook her, and when the end came in April, 1889, she passed to her merited reward, to be reunited to the beloved gone on before.

Hers was a rounded, beautiful life, a life of good deeds given from the overflow of a loving nature, not deeds that merited to be trumpeted abroad, but every-day kindnesses that sweeten daily life—a Samaritan to any who required her aid on life's highway.

* * * * * * * * *

Members of the Grand Army Post and Sons of Veterans assisted in the burial of Mrs. Wallace. "After the services at the house the pall bearers raised the casket and preceded by the officiating clergyman walked to the beautiful private cemetery * * * * where the last sad rites were performed and Martha Ann Wallace was laid with sadness to rest with those to whom in life she was so sincerely devoted, and whose memory she so ardently cherished. Just as the last service was performed the setting sun shone brightly through the clouds, and the quiet of the evening seemed as a benediction to a pure and holy life."

INDEX

Shawnee Classics: A Series of Classic Regional Reprints for the Midwest

Prairie Albion
An English Settlement in Pioneer Illinois
Charles Boewe

Personal Memoirs of John H. Brinton
Civil War Surgeon, 1861–1865
John H. Brinton

Behind the Guns
The History of Battery I, 2nd Regiment, Illinois Light Artillery
Thaddeus C. S. Brown, Samuel J. Murphy, and William G. Putney

Stagecoach and Tavern Tales of the Old Northwest
Harry Ellsworth Cole
Edited by Louise Phelps Kellogg

The Great Cyclone at St. Louis and East St. Louis, May 27, 1896
Compiled and Edited by Julian Curzon

A Knight of Another Sort
Prohibition Days and Charlie Birger
Gary DeNeal

"Black Jack"
John A. Logan and Southern Illinois in the Civil War Era
James Pickett Jones

Reminiscences of a Soldier's Wife
An Autobiography
Mrs. John A. Logan

Before Mark Twain
A Sampler of Old, Old Times on the Mississippi
Edited by John Francis McDermott

History 31st Regiment Illinois Volunteers
Organized by John A. Logan
W. S. Morris, L. D. Hartwell, and J. B. Kuykendall

A History of the Ninth Regiment Illinois Volunteer Infantry, with the Regimental Roster
Marion Morrison

Tales and Songs of Southern Illinois
Collected by Charles Neely
Edited with a Foreword by John Webster Spargo

The Outlaws of Cave-in-Rock
Otto A. Rothert

Afloat on the Ohio
An Historical Pilgrimage of a Thousand Miles in a Skiff, From Redstone to Cairo
Reuben Gold Thwaites

A Woman's Story of Pioneer Illinois
Christiana Holmes Tillson
Edited by Milo Milton Quaife

Army Life of an Illinois Soldier
Including a Day-by-Day Record of Sherman's March to the Sea
Charles W. Wills